THE SECRET SEDUCTION
and the Enigma of Attraction

VICTORIA THOMPSON

ARCADIA

This is a work of fiction. Names, characters, places and incidents are the products of the author's imagination or are used fictitiously. Any resemblance to actual events, locales or persons, living or dead, is entirely coincidental.

First published in 2015 by
Australian Scholarly Publishing Pty Ltd
under its Arcadia imprint and in its Press On Series (No. 22 City of Longing)
7 Lt Lothian St North, North Melbourne, Vic 3051
tel 06+3+93296963 / fax 06+3+93295452
aspic@ozemail.com.au / www.scholarly.info

ISBN 978-1-925003-99-4

Cover design Paula Garrod, graphic designer

Of Victoria Thompson's Losing Alexandria _and_ City of Longing

Losing Alexandria is a delicious memoir—a judicious mixture of sights, sounds, tastes and experience.—Dr Ann Skea, *Australian Book Review*

Losing Alexandria, Victoria Thompson's memoir, is a superb piece of literature, and I salute her for what she has achieved. So much nuance, so much pain, so much longing. All qualities that the Levant exudes in abundance. Her book has sent me back to Cavafy whom I have admired for centuries. She has enlivened my life and brought back fond memories. I am entranced. She has captured a world so perfectly. And her style—well, it is airy, elegant and utterly honest. This is a major work. I absolutely loved her dialogues in the chapter 'City of Plague'. She captured Cleopatra, Cavafy and Lawrence Durrell so well. An original touch, I thought. Once again, I reiterate: this book is a major work.—
James Cowan, internationally acclaimed author, awarded the Australian Literary Society Gold Medal for Literature.

Pain is a constant thread in *Losing Alexandria,* although the book is also lusciously sensuous and has its moments of gossip and fun.—Jane Sullivan, *The Age*

Losing Alexandria seems destined to take its place among the classics of writing about Egypt. Her recollections are so precise, so poignant, and so evocative they bear comparison with Lawrence Durrell or Naguib Mahfouz. As a memoir I found it both moving and informative.—Peter Cowie, *Variety*

What a triumph! To the words charmed, surprised, intrigued, I have to add wonderful, fascinating, courageous. It was an absorbing read and I could not put it down.—David Zweck, film producer

Losing Alexandria is a joy to read—a rich, evocative autobiography which moves back and forth through time, with a colourful casts of characters, real and historical. This is a wonderful story of exotic places, famous people and extravagant experiences. Must read.—Sue Wannan, *Bookshelf*

City of Longing is a deeply romantic love story, but it's also much more—a meditation on literature, history, animal rights, human kindness, the politics of modern medicine, the world of Art, bankers, globalisation—and the ramifications of the personal choices we make. —Tracey Mair

I love the *City of Longing*: it's gorgeous. Lyrical, haunting, elegant, spare.—
Jenni Caffin, *Director Byron Bay Writers Festival*

In the final count, every city is a city of longing. The reader is confronted with Victoria Thompson's revelation: *We hide certain traumatic events in our lives and unless we resolve them, they resurface, perhaps years later, like toxic waste, either in disease or sabotaging our chances of happiness*—Patricia Anderson, *Australian Art Review*

Of The Secret Seduction and the Enigma of Attraction

This remarkable author has taken her reader to a place where few writers have been before. The professional bond between therapist and patient has at last been broken; now we are able to explore its tragic consequences. *The Secret Seduction* glows like cobalt: its colours are often passionate, moving, and sad. —James Cowan

The sexual scenes are indeed very erotic and it will appeal to many. The story is hypnotic.—Jeffrey Moussaieff Masson, psychoanalyst, best-selling author

An immensely talented writer. This is a very beautiful and compelling story for readers of those who want to lose themselves in a tangled story of love, lust and betrayal, as well as those who are interested in psychology, and also drawn to literary fiction. —Anouska Jones, editor, publishing consultant

Victoria Thompson writes erotica so well and so bravely. The sensuality of this book is outstanding. But of course this isn't its main theme. I read this as a haunting tale of two complicated, wounded, intelligent people trying to redeem themselves through each other, looking for salvation and almost finding it. This is a heartbreaking book. I don't know if it's based on her life, but I was really affected by how powerful it is.—Lee Kofman, author

To

the memory of scent

Contents

I discovered there was an endless source of robust enjoyment in trifling with psychiatrists, cunningly leading them on; never letting them see that you know all the tricks of the trade; inventing for them elaborate dreams, pure classics in style, which make them the dream-extortionists, dream and wake up screaming …

Lolita, Vladimir Nabokov

Perhaps people who have really found love can't always be together. Perhaps real love belongs to some greater pattern which we can't see, but which makes sense in the long run. It may be that what we created together is necessary for something else, to help us give to, or do, something which is important.

Bond of Perfection, Stella Zilliacus

1 The Psychiatrist

Geneva 1930

Andreas wakes and rushes to the window to pull back the curtains. The lake is blue and calm. Those dark clouds which scare him are nowhere to be seen. He collects his pants, shirt, pullover, socks—even wraps a scarf around his neck—and sits on the edge of his bed and waits.

What joy! Soon Nanny and he will be running through the garden to sit on the old stone wall and feed the swans. Afterwards, Nanny promised, they would promenade to the terrace of the Beau Rivage for a strawberry *frappé*. Andreas squeezes his teddy bear to his chest. He can barely contain himself.

And so he waits in the silence, his eyes fixed on the door.

Nanny is late. Again!

Now the boy worries that his Nanny does not love him anymore—will not play with him like she used to. She is sick a lot—goes to the bathroom and makes funny noises and then flops down on his bed. But he can play doctor. Nanny lets him lift her skirt, uncovering her thigh. He gives her injections with his pencils—bandages her head. It is a consolation.

The boy can see those clouds hovering. Soon they will overshadow the lake—the water will be dark and the swans will hide. It will be too late. And Mamma and Pappa will be back, without Irina. They have taken her to Bedales, her school in England. Andreas will not see his sister for a long time.

He worries too about Mamma—she has been fighting with Pappa over Nanny. Mamma wants to send Nanny away.

'He doesn't need a nanny! He needs a governess now!' Mamma

shouts.

What's a governess? Andreas does not like the sound of the word. It does not feel as nice as *Nanny*.

He hears something. Footsteps? Andreas recognises the sound of heels. Nanny does not wear heels. And Mamma's make a loud clatter.

'Nanny!' he cries.

He is about to rush to her as he does every morning, to wrap his arms around her skirt, but he stops. He has never seen Nanny look like a princess from one of his books before. She is wearing a white dress and her hair is loose and long. Is her dress made of lace? It has white butterflies embroidered all over the skirt so that when she moves they look as though they flutter, and she has a pink sash tied around her waist. He loves how she looks, but what will Mamma say? Will she be cross because Nanny is not wearing her grey uniform? Or hiding her hair under her cap?

He throws himself at her anyway. Nanny holds him. He sighs. He breathes in her scent. He can smell perfume. Why is she wearing perfume? He loves it. She kisses his face, looks into his eyes, holds him closer. The boy clasps his arms around her neck. Holds on tight. But she is crying. He can feel her sobs beating against his chest. She pushes him away and runs to the bathroom. He can hear those sounds she makes—as if she is in pain.

Nanny does not want to come out. He has knocked on the bathroom door but she ignores him. It is getting dark. The boy panics. Bangs on the glass of the door—kicks the frame, screams and shouts: 'You promised! You promised! You promised!' But still Nanny will not come out. Andreas is broken hearted, beyond consolation. He hates her. He chokes, splutters and coughs. He wants to die.

Suddenly he is pulled away from the door. It is Pappa. He has come home.

'Anna!' His father rattles the door handle. He can smell gas. He runs to the French doors and throws them open. He is like a wild man now. The boy has never seen his Pappa like this before.

The glass splinters under the man's fist. He disappears into the bathroom and comes out carrying the girl's body. He lays her on the bed. And weeps. He bleeds. The boy watches his Pappa bleeding and his Nanny lying lifeless on his bed. There is blood all over Nanny's skirt.

His father takes his trembling son in his arms and rocks him.

'What have I done!'

* * *

Sydney 1977

The first time they saw each other was at a fund-raising event for a new wing of the Prince of Wales Hospital, in the ballroom of the Regent Hotel in Sydney. He watched her being swept around the dance floor much too fast by a rather foolish young man. He could not remember ever having waltzed a beautiful woman.

He went on glancing her way, not realising she was the wife of the man who was talking to him. There was something about her that captivated him. Her bearing and gestures conveyed an air of delicate romanticism, as though she belonged to some other time, a tragic episode of history. And when she looked in his direction, it left him shaken, despite her expression of cool disinterest.

Annabelle Eichler was actually seeking out her husband, hoping he would rescue her from his young colleague who was trying so hard to ingratiate himself with the professor's wife. She was being used by the young man to show off his charm, for others to notice—and because she remained aloof, he tried even harder to be entertaining.

It would be unfair not to mention that sensing his discomfort, Annabelle did attempt to be reassuring. She smiled, tilted her head to one side, a much practised gesture, to give the impression of attentiveness. But she could feel the tension rising towards her neck and knew she would be spending the next three days in bed with migraine.

The man Annabelle saw with her husband was tall and appealing, with greying hair and a distinguished countenance—the patina of the privileged. There was something of the Tartar in the broad face with the high cheek bones. She was soon to discover he was an educated man, who spoke the English of Oxford and Cambridge, a man of intellect and culture, superb manners and great charm.

He kept his gaze on her. Soon Annabelle's air of detachment was replaced by indignation as she felt that her husband was abandoning her to the mercy of an exceedingly irritating young man and the lecherous stare of an ageing one.

* * *

'Come here, Annabelle,' David placed a proprietorial hand on his wife's arm. 'I see Jason had you cornered again, but I knew you'd manage,' he said. Then trying to smooth the frown on her face, David swept a glass of champagne off a passing tray and planted it in his wife's hand. 'I'd like you to meet Andreas Zill. Andreas is the psychiatrist at the Bollingen Clinic.'

The man bowed his head in the European way as he took Annabelle's hand. When her eyes met the stranger's gaze she suddenly thought of snow. His eyes were a cool blue-grey, the colour of the sky where the air is pure and rarefied, near the very peaks of mountains. And almond-shaped, like those of an Oriental. The heavy lids and thick brows, gave his Buddha-like face an ambiguous expression—of wisdom and melancholy.

'Can I leave my wife with you, Andreas?' David asked the psychiatrist. 'I need to work the room. The auction will soon be taking place. She too speaks French,' he added, hastening to greet the guests.

'Your husband is very good at what he does,' the man said, when David left.

The refinement and subtlety of his voice did not escape her. At the same time, it had a profound unsettling effect on her. She waited for an opportunity when she could take her leave.

Annabelle nodded. She wanted to tell him there was nothing her husband could not do. He was always moving, committing, exploring. And networking—a word she disliked for some reason—his favourite pastime.

Doctor David Eichler had the abundant energy and courage of the short man, and a muscular body he maintained with gym sessions, squash and tennis. He had lost all of his hair at an early age from too much testosterone, an irony not lost on Annabelle given her repressed sexuality. She knew he was attracted to her beauty because he constantly mentioned it, but did not realise it was also the sadness in her eyes that drew him to her, reminding him of his mother. David's mother had survived the concentration camp where her family had been murdered because she had been a child virtuoso, and the camp commandant liked to hear her play the violin at night.

David and Annabelle had met when he was auditioning actresses for a production of *Don Juan* that he was staging for SUDS, the dramatic society at Sydney University. He cast her in the role of Inés, Don Juan's great love, because he had wanted a beautiful actress for the part. Appearances mattered to David. For several years, he had wanted Annabelle to consider seeing a therapist but she had resisted him. He saw her as anxious, insecure, neurotic—he never stopped telling her—yet he knew that she was also strong-willed, complicated and intuitive, with an exceptional ability to analyse people. And she mystified him, too, which he found irresistible.

* * *

Something strange was happening between Annabelle and the psychiatrist from the Bollingen Clinic. As soon as they began conversing, everything else seemed to fall away. It was simply uncanny the way they connected. They shared all kinds of thoughts and feelings about writers, music and places they loved.

After a while, they even began to hum and recite the same nursery rhymes, which perplexed Annabelle because there was a considerable age difference between them, he was in his fifties while she was only in her thirties. Their origins too, he came from the cold countries—his ancestry went back to the wild plains of Russia, Finland and Sweden—whereas Annabelle was from the romance lands, Spain, France and Ireland.

The auction was beginning. David made a speech meant to appeal to the vanity and fears of the patrons. A celebrity, also, had been enlisted to entertain and excite them. Her loud voice, jokes and background music, became unbearable to some. Especially for the two people standing apart from the crowd.

The night before, Annabelle had argued with David over an article she had read about philanthropists donating to medicine. It had confirmed her beliefs, that their generosity was usually generated by self-interest, to increase their status and minimise their taxes. Also fear.

'When they give to medical research they do so because of fear—fear of death and disease from which money cannot protect them. It's an illusion that the medical industry can save them from death!'

'You don't know what you're talking about,' he had told her.

But Annabelle had been defiant. It was a subject she felt passionate about.

'The rich are exploited too, David! Medical research and experiments on animals have very little to do with the wellbeing of humans. It's all about careers, status, peer approval, grandiosity and greed! But you won't admit it!'

'You don't know what you're talking about,' David had repeated.

* * *

'Excuse me, I need to get away from this noise,' Annabelle told the psychiatrist.

She escaped from the ballroom and found an alcove with a picture window overlooking the harbour. There was a white leather seat, but Annabelle chose to sit on a couple of marble steps so she could look out across the water to the sails of the Opera House. It looked different at night. Magical and mysterious.

A few minutes later, she heard his voice.

'Would you like a drink?'

He had a glass of champagne for her.

'Thank you,' she said, taking it from him.

'May I?'

She nodded.

Andreas settled down beside Annabelle on the steps.

They sat in silence, watching the harbour city below, their eyes following tiny coloured lights—boats scampering along the surface of the dark water. But it was the night sky with the stars and the moon, and the seagulls chasing insects caught in the upward lights, that held their fascination.

Finally, they turned their gaze upon each other.

'We seem to have a profound affinity. Goethe wrote about the enigma of attraction and the atoms which link people to each other.'

Annabelle's eyes brightened. She was drawn to his mysterious intelligence.

'It's the title of one of his works, *Elective Affinities,*' he continued, 'the deep affinities between two people—that they choose each other. It's very powerful. Have you read it?'

Annabelle felt a shiver of recognition skimming along her skin. She shook her head.

'Goethe harvested his diaries when he wrote his novels. He said he lived every word of his *Elective Affinities*. It is full of insights into love, conflict, philosophical thought and the inescapable force of fate.'

Annabelle had a strong desire to know more about Andreas. She asked questions, and he was happy to talk about his past.

'We lived in Geneva. My father worked for the League of Nations—an idealist, a left-wing intellectual, American of Swedish-Finnish extraction, born in Japan, educated in England and Yale.'

'How fascinating!' Annabelle said.

Andreas smiled.

'When he was a boy he was sent to Bedales in the English countryside, just as I was. It's a co-ed independent school, known for its liberal ethos and relaxed attitudes, *a bohemian idyll with bite.* Pretty scandalous for those days,' he laughed. 'My father, studied social science and history at Yale and was the first to graduate in his class. He loved to boast that he spoke thirteen languages but it was actually nine. My father served in the war but was so shocked and angered at what he saw, that he worked assiduously with the League of Nations to stop people killing each other. But when the Nazis invaded Czechoslovakia he was heartbroken that he could not stop the war. He died of leukaemia. In the obituary which appeared in the press he was described as exotic, ebullient and cosmopolitan with a magnetic personality. He was very attractive to women, much to my Russian mother's chagrin. They met on a tennis court in Vladivostok but they were spectacularly ill-matched.'

'I would have loved to have known him.'

'Yes, he would have taken to you,' Andreas said, looking deeply into Annabelle's eyes.

At that moment, fireworks from the Opera House erupted into the sky, frightening and scattering the seagulls.

* * *

When the Eichlers were leaving the hotel Annabelle saw the clown for the second time. She had noticed it before on the way in, a clown standing on the pavement in a patchy multi-coloured garment. But it was the tune, and the mournful sound of the flute which drew her now to it. She moved towards the weird apparition with the tragic white-painted face, like a character from a Fellini film. Its sex was androgynous. The wilted flowers scattered in the wild woolly hair could have been a clue that perhaps this creature was a Flower Child making some form of protest.

David came and stood beside Annabelle. He took some loose change from his pocket and tossed it into a basket near the clown. Then putting his arm around his wife, almost carried her away to where the chauffeur was waiting in the black limousine. Hippies made him uneasy, indeed, anyone did who threatened his beliefs and aspirations, and the ordered world he inhabited.

It was the second time in the same night that Annabelle had been moved by an encounter. The clown had smiled a strange conspiratorial smile at her.

* * *

Something else occurred that night unsettling her further, leaving her wondering, dreaming and desiring. It happened when Annabelle collected her coat from the cloak- room and suddenly felt his presence behind her. Andreas was helping her with her coat and as he did so, his fingers brushed ever so lightly across the back of her neck—and made her gasp.

When David and Annabelle arrived home she immediately went to the book containing her favourite poem. There in the lines of *Eugene Onegin*, she read:

I saw you in my dreams; I'd waken
To know I loved you; long ago
I languished in your glance, and oh!
My soul hearing your voice, was shaken.
The moment that I saw you coming,
I thrilled, my pulses started drumming,
And my heart whispered: It is he!

As she lay in bed Annabelle remembered the inscription on a tomb in Ancient Egypt: *I have known you before, today and forever,* and had a strong premonition she and Andreas were destined to meet again.

2 The First Consultation

And so Annabelle became Doctor Andreas Zill's patient.

When she walked into the consultation room at the Bollingen Clinic, there was no mistaking the expression of pleasant shock on his face. From then on, he concealed his excitement with an air of serious professionalism.

It had taken her three months to raise the courage to telephone his office and make an appointment. Annabelle had to keep reminding herself of his words on the night of the fund raiser when Andreas had suggested she call him—she was inquisitive about psychoanalysis—and suffered from migraine. One day she hoped to become a writer, and a writer had to know herself before she could write about others. Annabelle had also been engrossed in mysteries, even dreamed of becoming a detective when she grew up. Freud and Sherlock Holmes were her heroes. But with the years Holmes lost his appeal, and she was drawn to Freud and the regions of the mind offering promises of deeper mysteries and darker secrets.

The sky was bathed in the glow of late afternoon giving the room a warm, intimate feeling. Sitting on the green velvet settee beside the window, overlooking Sydney Harbour, Annabelle slipped easily into the role of patient having trained as an actress, and succumbed to the psychodrama of *a dangerous method*. She told the psychiatrist about the headaches which had tormented her since childhood. He sat opposite her in a big leather armchair concentrating, observing, waiting for his patient to reveal fragments of herself.

Annabelle had waited a long time for this very special moment and was elated to have finally arrived at her destination. She looked around and liked what she saw. It was a sheltering room with wood-panelled walls, comfortable seating and *chachkas,* as David would call them, craft work from the doctor's patients.

Annabelle glanced at the impressive antique desk with the green leather top and gold inlay around the edges. There was a silver-framed photograph of a gentleman in an elegant uniform, whose country Annabelle could not identify. It seemed to belong to the late 19th century. She guessed it must have been a relative because there was a strong resemblance to the doctor.

'It's your grandfather?'

'You remembered,' he said, both pleased and surprised. He rose and retrieved the photograph from the desk.

The night they met Andreas had spoken about his grandfather, a hero and activist of Finnish independence who fought to free Finland from Imperialist Russia by organizing the smuggling of weapons. He was also involved in the Russian Revolution.

Did his grandfather's actions lead to the death of the Czar and his children, the young princesses murdered in the cellar? She had seen a photograph of the beautiful innocent girls and found it deeply moving when thinking of their deaths.

'My grandfather ended up living in exile in Japan. He helped the Japanese who were fighting against Imperialist Russia. The Russo-Japanese war was the first great war of the 20th Century.'

There was pride and deep affection in his eyes as he spoke.

'You look so much like him,' Annabelle said, examining the perfect features of the man in the photograph—the pale exotic eyes; heavy lids; straight fine nose; generous oval face; hair smoothed back, straight and lustrous. The full sensuous lips with the turned-down corners reminded her of a disappointed child. Annabelle loved the small round metal-rimmed glasses he wore, and the way the collar of his shirt was turned up with the silk cravat fashioned at the throat. The uniform was understated but superbly realised. Annabelle sighed.

There were no other photographs of family, no other intrusions of the personal in this professional space.

A lacquered Chinese screen with birds in flight caught her attention. It seemed rather lavish for a doctor's room. Was it for patients to undress behind or to hide his personal belongings? Her eyes wandered around the room to a fading water-colour on the wall, then a bookcase and an examination couch—a rather elegant one, covered in brown leather.

'I like the painting,' she said, referring to the water-colour.

'It's the *John Grafton*. One of the three English ships my grandfather tried to land on the Finnish Coast. They were full of guns and ammunition which he bought for the groups fighting against the Czar. He guided them all the way from Britain to the Finnish Coast. In the end, it was a disaster. He had to blow them up.'

Andreas liked telling Annabelle about his past, but it was time to change the subject.

'We should be talking about you,' he said. 'That's why you're here, isn't it? What would you like to talk to me about, Annabelle?'

'I don't know,' she said.

The fifty-minute hour would soon come to an end.

'Would you like to tell me about your father?'

Annabelle inclined her head to one side.

'Perhaps I will tell you about my bogeys,' she said, at once playful, wanting to engage him.

'Your bogeys?' Andreas made a quick mental note about the childish choice of words.

'My fears. Do you want to know about them?'

He nodded, unable to take his eyes off his patient.

Annabelle succumbed to his gaze and was, for a while, reluctant to relinquish it.

'I hate hospitals,' she said, finally. 'I think that's one of my greatest fears to be in a hospital feeling helpless.'

'You mistrust people …'

'The loss of freedom is the most terrible thing. I would rather die a violent death, in an exploding aeroplane, or shot like a bird. A seagull. *I am a seagull,*' she said, remembering, then laughing at the connection. 'Sorry, Chekhov. I played Nina in *The Seagull.*'

'Yes, you're an actress.'

'Was. Gave it up. I was a lousy actress. Couldn't show any emotions. Can't cry.'

'Are you attracted to violence? Does that make you feel excitement?'

'On the contrary. I can't bear it. When I used to walk with my father, if we

passed an accident or an animal being killed, he was always drawn to it. Wanted to watch people and animals bleeding. I would pull and beg him to take me away. He just laughed.'

'Is that where you came to believe people are cruel?'

Annabelle was silent.

'But people are cruel, aren't they?' she said after a while. Her question came out in a soft whisper as though she was frightened of being overheard.

Andreas gave her a sad gentle smile.

'No, not at all. Or rather, not all are.'

His voice was kind, encouraging.

A sigh of relief escaped from her lips.

'The men in our family were very spoilt, arrogant, deceitful. It was very much a patriarchal family. They had mistresses and treated their wives very badly.'

'Did your father have mistresses?'

'Yes, beautiful women. I hated them.'

'Why, because they took your father away from you?'

'Yes.'

'And your mother?'

'She was left at home alone with me and cried a lot. I had to comfort her, distract her. She was going to be a ballet dancer but gave it up when she met my father. He took out other women. He loved actresses. He loved gambling too. He gambled all the money away, never left the table if he was winning. He stayed until he lost everything.'

'Gambling is about seeking love. People who aren't able to find love, test their luck,' Andreas said, watching her now with intense interest. 'Are you similar? I suspect you test people, don't you?'

'Poor Daddy,' Annabelle said, ignoring his analysis.

'You must have loved him very much.'

'Yes, I would have died for him.' There was a pathetic wistfulness in her expression—it touched him, and surprised him. 'He was very good looking, and dressed beautifully. Like you,' she added.

'Tell me about the rest of your bogeys, Annabelle.'

Annabelle looked across to the door to see if anyone was listening, then said: 'They're innumerable. I close my eyes and see every sin perpetrated by man upon man, by man upon animals.'

'By man upon child,' Andreas said.

'So many horrible images. I cannot change the world so I become dreadfully depressed and want to die.'

Annabelle was silent again, quietly collected with her thoughts. The minutes ticked by—the session would soon be over.

'Were you ever encouraged to express an opinion as a child?'

'Children should be seen and not heard,' Annabelle said. It was something well understood.

'Is that what you were told?'

She nodded.

'Who told you?'

'Mother. Father. Grandfather, too. He hated me because I wasn't a boy. But I paid him back.'

'How did you do that?'

Annabelle hesitated for a moment. Would Andreas think she was *bad* if she told him? After all, it was pretty heartless what she did.

'When I was twelve and he was dying from cancer, I stood outside his bedroom door and watched him. He saw me and beckoned to me. It was a shock because he had always treated me with contempt, ignored me, criticized me to my parents. I stood there, looking at him, then shook my head slowly, like this, and walked away.'

'Is that how you express your anger, Annabelle?'

'I find it easy to show anger to people I don't know. I'm quite fearless in fact with anyone bullying other people or intimidating children or animals. I felt angry with a red-neck cop during an Anti-Vietnam-War demonstration and had no difficulty in telling him off when he started harassing the students. He was dumbfounded but didn't arrest me. In fact, he came over afterwards and wanted to know, What's-a-nicely-dressed-girl-like-you-doing-here? Which was great because I was able to tell him how wrong the war was.'

'But you're not capable of showing anger to someone close who is hurting you.'

'I do it in other ways. I become cold. Freeze them out. I'm quite good at that. I sometimes use words—cruel, sarcastic words.' Annabelle sounded proud of her ability to punish or keep others from hurting her.

'Sarcasm and aloofness are different to actually expressing anger.'

'But they're safer, more acceptable.'

'What do you assume should happen if you show your anger, Annabelle?'

Annabelle frowned. She disliked being interrogated.

'I hope I'm not frightening you with questions so soon into therapy. But I have faith in your intelligence.'

'They should stop hurting me?' she said, brightening up, hoping her question pleased him.

'Yet your early experience must have shown you that if you show your anger, they'll stop loving you,' Andreas said. He was looking at Annabelle, his fingers tapping the armrest of his seat, deep in thought. Then he stood up and took a cushion from the settee.

'I want to show you how you sabotage yourself. Lie back. You can kick your shoes off if you like. Let me put this cushion under your head. Close your eyes and relax. I want you to listen to what I'm saying, make pictures of the words.'

Annabelle's eyes expressed the amusement she felt at the attention Andreas was bestowing on her.

'Are you going to hypnotise me?'

'I'm trying to help you,' he said.

'All right,' she said, stretching out, playing to please. She detected his nervousness.

'Annabelle, please listen.' Andreas began speaking slowly, soothingly: 'I think my problem is my anger, whereas it's that someone is hurting me. But as I learned that it wasn't safe for me to show my anger, I turn it into fright so that they'll keep looking after me and loving me, because as a little girl, if I'm angry they won't love me. I allow myself to become scared, instead of angry, by going off to places like wars and hospitals, and other really frightening situations. I do this, so that I can remain frightened, believing as long as I stay frightened I can't be angry. And so, I can keep on being loved.' Andreas paused. Annabelle's eyes were closed. 'When you escalate your fear, Annabelle, you incapacitate yourself with depression and headaches.'

After a while, Annabelle opened her eyes. There was a long silence while she tried to make sense of what he had told her.

'Interesting, isn't it, Annabelle?'

She nodded.

'I'm going to give you an anti-depressant, it will help with your depression and headaches.'

'I don't want drugs. I don't want to become dependent on pharmaceutical drugs,' she said.

'These don't affect you like that. They make you feel more alert by alleviating some of the effects of depression,' Andreas said. 'There are a few things to remember, however. A list of things you're not allowed to have while taking these tablets. Cheese, liver, sour cream, avocadoes, chocolate and bananas, for example.'

'What happens if I do?'

'You could get the worst headache of your life.'

'Why?'

'Because the interaction of these foods with the drug can create a dangerous elevation in blood pressure. You could get a leakage, at the back of the head,' he said. Now it was she who was making him uncomfortable with her questioning.

'What sort of leakage?'

'A blood vessel …'

'Oh, you mean a brain haemorrhage, doctor?'

She could make him feel stupid.

'Yes …' he said.

'I wonder what it's like to die like that?' Annabelle brightened up, her eyes gleaming at the possibilities.

'It's the mother of all headaches, believe me. I have to stop here now. I'll write you a prescription,' he said, rising and walking to his desk. He turned and looked at her with concern. He had wished the session had taken a different course.

Annabelle met his look, questioning, engaging while playing with a strand of her long hair.

'David thinks you're a brilliant shrink.'

'I don't know where he got that impression,' Andreas said.

'I don't know, either,' she teased.

Andreas was entranced.

'Goodbye, doctor,' Annabelle whispered, as she collected her things and walked away from him.

3 Frankenstein

Doctor Andreas Zill was relieved when one of his patients cancelled his appointment. It gave him time to think about his next one with Annabelle Eichler, and he wanted to sit quietly for a while to gather his thoughts. He was completely bathed in the sensation of being with her for the next hour. It was foolish, he knew, but for his part, he neither could nor wanted to check his emotion for the moment.

When she had walked into his room at the clinic three weeks before, it had provoked unimaginable happiness, although he had managed to not let it show. It occurred to him that he had been waiting all his life for someone like Annabelle, who could respond, and look and think *exactly* like she did. He had been waiting, without knowing it. He could not stop thinking of Annabelle. And it frightened him.

Andreas was suddenly struck by the reality of his woeful existence. It was hopeless. Was he insane? How could he possibly have contemplated such thoughts? *Madness,* he told himself. Was he really mad? Sometimes he wondered. Ever since that incidence. He saw it all the time, the wrecked lives of his patients, ruined by cancerous guilt. All this, he would reveal to her in time, as lovers do.

He heard her voice with the slight accent he had not been able to place until now. It was familiar, and familial, like his own, over enunciated, perfect diction, known as an international accent. She was talking to Jess, one of his secretaries, paying her bill, making another appointment.

Andreas rose from his seat to greet Annabelle.

They shook hands.

He looked at her appreciatively, yet careful not to let her see how she affected him.

What he failed to notice was that she had the same reaction—overjoyed, excited and ecstatic to be in his presence. She too, was a good dissembler. They were practised people.

Annabelle sat in her usual place, at the end of the settee, facing Andreas in his leather armchair. Her long, untamed hair reminded him of the mermaid from a favourite fable from his childhood. For a moment nothing was said. There was no need to speak. It was enough to gaze.

The spell was broken by a knock on the door. Andreas rose to answer it. It was his wife. They exchanged a few clipped words.

'I'm sorry for the interruption,' Andreas said, returning to his seat. 'Have you had any dreams?'

Annabelle smiled, wanting to reassure him. His wife's visit had unsettled him. He kept glancing at his watch, counting how many minutes were lost, what remained.

'Yes. I dreamed I was travelling on a train, across a barren landscape,' she began, eager to tell him about her dream because he was in it. 'The train stopped at a railway station. Inside the waiting room on a wall, was a drawing of a family tree. Your name was the last addition!'

'Is that the dream?'

'Yes.'

He relaxed and delighted in his patient's intelligence because psychotherapy was indeed like a train journeying through the past. He shook his head at his luck.

'Why are you shaking your head?' Annabelle's ability to read people was something she developed early in childhood from a need to understand why things happened the way they did. It had become a major part of her survival strategy.

'I was releasing some stiffness in my neck. Tell me about your childhood, Annabelle,' Andreas said, quickly deflecting the attention from himself.

'I was born in France, grew up in Spain—where evil flourishes—a country which has made animal torture a *tradition*. When I was seven, I was sent to a convent, the Sacred Heart in Ireland, by the sea, a cold place. My mother was Irish. The nuns were very punishing.'

Andreas noticed Annabelle had wrapped her arms around her body as if to keep the imaginary cold away. He stood up, took the blanket which was folded over the back of the settee, and placed it gently over her shoulders.

She looked up at him with a mixture of surprise and adoration. Annabelle was deeply moved by kindness.

'Thank you,' she said.

Andreas averted his eyes.

For a moment she felt his nervousness, or maybe it was his shyness. It was tantalising for Annabelle to glimpse Andreas's emotions. She kept looking at him, studying him, wanting more of what lay beneath.

'Tell me, Annabelle, what do you remember of the convent?'

'A seagull, tangled in a fishing line, dying on the beach. I felt helpless. There was nothing I could do.'

'It must have been very distressing for you,' Andreas said.

'One girl killed herself. The nuns said she drowned, but it was suicide, we all knew. She had walked into the sea in the middle of a storm for a swim.' Annabelle paused, lost in a thought. 'I liked the church. I could dream there. It was dark and peaceful and always smelt of perfume.'

'Incense, you mean?'

'Yes,' she said.

'What kind of incense do they use in the Catholic Church?'

'Frankenstein.'

'Frankenstein? Is that so?' Andreas could feel a smile breaking out on his face. He quickly suppressed it.

'I meant *frankincense.*' Annabelle smiled too, realising her Freudian slip.

'How do you feel about the Catholic Church now?'

'Frankenstein,' she said.

'I get it,' Andreas laughed. Then he asked Annabelle: 'What is the perfume you're wearing? Is it jasmine?'

'Yes, *Je Reviens.*'

There was a moment of mutual contemplation. Had he brooked boundaries, revealed too much of his feelings, his enjoyment of her scent? What was she feeling? There was an enigmatic smile on her face. She was calm, self-assured, daring and dauntless, insuperable.

'We have to stop here, I'm afraid.'

Andreas had not meant to sound regretful.

'We'll continue next week,' he said.

'Goodbye Doctor,' she said.

Annabelle was deliriously happy that Andreas had noticed her perfume.

4 The Red Dress

The last time Doctor Zill's patient had walked out of his consultation room, she had left behind the scent of wild narcissus and the heady notes of jasmine, orange blossom, violet, neroli and ylang-ylang, all ingredients in her perfume. It had lifted the gloom for him and he was looking forward to her return. That was precisely the hopeful message of *Je Reviens* when American soldiers gave the perfume to the girls they were leaving behind. How fitting, how perfect, he told himself as he waited for her return.

Andreas heard the sound of her heels on the stairs. He listened, and when her footsteps became muffled as she walked on carpeted floors, he became tense with expectation. He rose to greet her, but she walked past him, avoiding his eyes. It was not how he had expected her to be and he knew she was angry. She was wearing a red dress.

Annabelle used clothes in a creative way to express her emotions at certain times. She had come to him dressed in sheer white cotton and lace, in pale pastel handkerchief linen, clinging crepe and sometimes silky black velvet—all from the nostalgic Vintage shops she frequented. He loved the white best of all. But the red made his heart beat faster. With the back of his middle finger, he surreptitiously brushed away the beads of perspiration which had formed over his lip since she had arrived.

Red was for anger. And also the colour of love.

It was a dress with sleeves caught tightly at the wrists with small covered buttons. Three more buttons narrowed the dress at the waist. He pictured for a moment the naked roundness of breasts and buttocks beneath the garment. The longing to touch, hold and take possession stole over him again but he pushed desire aside.

Annabelle sat with her black-stockinged legs crossed, coldly observing the doctor and his thoughts. The heels of her shoes reminded him of a pair of lethal Venetian stilettos he had inherited. What had happened to them? So much had been lost, so many things had gone forever from his life.

Andreas waited anxiously for Annabelle to speak.

'It's really terribly self-indulgent of me to be seeing you. I'm here under false pretence. There's not very much wrong with me. I'm wasting your time and mine. Here I am and here you are seeming to be interested in my pathetic problems when half the human race is in agony, living in fear, pain and deprivation …'

'Deprivation?'

'Yes, lacking food, shelter, love!'

Andreas gave a sigh of relief.

'Annabelle, you're feeling vulnerable. You're compensating by wanting to appear dangerous. I mean, angry,' he quickly corrected himself.

'I'm angry at how unjust it all is, and I'm angry at being part of the masquerade, a pawn in someone else's dreadful joke,' she said, flicking her hair back with her hand.

'Who is this someone?' Andreas asked.

Annabelle sighed.

'I don't know. God, I suppose.'

'I see,' he said. 'Do you believe in God, Annabelle?'

'No,' she replied, shaking her head, looking as though the thought pained her.

'Who, then?' he asked.

'I don't know. People I guess,' she said, shrugging her shoulders.

'Annabelle, when one talks of *people* one really means one's parents.' Andreas was leaning forward in his seat, as if he wished to reach her, or at least take her hands into his.

It softened her stance. She looked at him with renewed interest.

'Oh?'

'Tell me about them,' Andreas said.

Annabelle sighed and curled her legs beneath her on the settee.

'What do you want to know? I loved my father and hated my mother.' Annabelle was looking at Andreas with an expression of sultry resignation. Then she brightened up at the memories. 'My father loved me. We were, you could say, close, really close. At Christmas or on my birthday he would plan surprises. The games he played with me! Boxes arrived with dolls. Sometimes he gave me little boxes with bracelets, a fine gold chain, earrings or a ring. And he would tease me beforehand, telling me that they were presents for another little girl, someone prettier than me. He was marvellous at generating all this excitement and mystery.'

'And your mother?'

'She didn't fit in at all. I used to have these horrible dreams about her. I still do. They're awful, really.' She pressed her hand against her mouth, trying to suppress laughter—laughter, as the defence to the fear she was experiencing. 'She never listened to me, or even saw me. Sometimes, I've got her by the throat and I'm shaking her and trying to choke her like a rubber toy …' She broke off laughing but there was something reckless and desperate about her laughter.

'Tell me more,' Andreas said, relieved when she settled and grew serious.

'She threw a knife at me once.' But Annabelle wanted to change the subject. 'What time is it, please?'

'You've got plenty of time, Annabelle.'

'You haven't answered my question,' she said, looking around for the clock. She had forgotten to wear her watch.

'It's five-thirty,' Andreas said with a sigh.

'Why do you sigh, doctor?'

'Did I sigh?' he said. Where was she leading him now?

'Yes, you did,' she whispered.

'For breath, I suppose,' Andreas said, enjoying the rapport.

'People sigh when they've been holding their breath, and they hold their breath when they're too tense to breathe. Why are you tense, doctor? Do I make you nervous?'

Andreas noticed she was playing with her hair again, provocatively twisting a fine long strand around her finger.

'No,' he said.

'Liar,' she whispered again, under her breath. 'Are you afraid of me, then?'

Andreas gave a funny nervous laugh.

'No.'

'Then why do you laugh?'

'*Touché!* You amaze me,' Andreas said. 'You're pleased with yourself now, aren't you? Look at you, bouncing with delight, like an excited little girl.'

'I'm a *wicked* girl. I'll tell you a secret,' she confided. 'I'm here under false pretence. I tried to tell you…'

'Oh?' Andreas said, feigning ignorance.

'Yes, I'm not what I seem. I came as a huntress, a seductress,' she said, continuing in her breathless voice.

Andreas nodded slowly.

'I know.'

Annabelle straightened up suddenly. On guard. She was a good fencer.

'You know?' she said, surprised. 'How?'

'You loved your father very much and as a child you wanted to seduce him. In psychotherapy the therapist becomes the loved one, the parent. It's called the *transference.* But there's a taboo, against physical and sexual expression which must be observed.' He rubbed his temple with his knuckle conscious of the difficult times ahead. 'Let's stop here. I'll see you next week,' he said, with a weary smile as he led her towards the door.

Annabelle stopped and turned to look at Andreas. It took great control and strength for him not to sweep her in his arms, take her to the couch and make love to her. She saw it all in his eyes and understood the struggle he was facing.

She was prepared to wait.

5 The Transference

All week, Annabelle had been thinking of the next session with her analyst.

Suddenly there was excitement in her life, something to look forward to, dress up and look lovely. Most of all, to see it reflected in his eyes. The transference, now, was complete. Yes, she knew the effect she was having on Andreas. And he on her.

Driving over the Harbour Bridge, across to the North Shore, Annabelle felt she was leaving her other life behind. She was euphoric at the thought of seeing Andreas again as she pressed her foot down on the accelerator, and flew off the exit towards the Bollingen Clinic. Only to be stopped by the sound of a police siren. The officer stepped off his motorbike and ordered her out of the car. He asked Annabelle some questions and obliged her to walk a few steps to see whether she had been drinking. All this made her impatient and eager to escape, but she was careful not to insult him because she did not want to be held up any longer.

When she came to the Bollingen Clinic, Annabelle ran from the car park, stopping for a second to break off a sprig of jasmine growing on a wall. She rushed up the stairs arriving breathless on the first floor.

'Doctor Zill is waiting for you,' Jess, the secretary announced, while Annabelle paused to compose herself. She did not want Andreas to see her flustered.

'Hello,' she said, hesitating at the entrance to the consulting room.

'Come in,' he said, rising and then waiting for her to settle down. 'Make yourself comfortable.'

'Thank you.'

Andreas appeared cool and detached. Immediately Annabelle's enthusiasm dissipated. She collected herself and sat with her back straight, then looking around the room and at the scenery outside. The harbour view did not impress or soothe her now.

The minutes ticked by but she did not care about that either. She was only conscious of his mood, agonising over whether he had stopped liking her.

Andreas waited.

Annabelle sighed and said: 'It must be very boring for you to get so much love from your patients.'

'I also get a lot of hate.' Was she hating him already?

'I thought you said the other day that the doctor becomes the loved one,' Annabelle said.

'The loved one also becomes the hated one. Hate is the frustration aspect of love. We can only hate a person whose love we desire. A demand for love turns to hatred if that love is not forthcoming. Hence, the greater the love, the greater the hate.'

'I had a dream about you last night. It wasn't very nice,' Annabelle said.

'Tell me about it.'

'It was night time. I was waiting for you in a dark street. Suddenly you appeared with your wife and friends. They were all old. You were walking very slowly, shuffling your feet. I turned and almost stumbled over something lying in the gutter. It was a newly born creature, albino, and even though it was a female, it had a tiny penis. A hermaphrodite. It was repulsive. There was a streak of faeces across its chest. It was horrible. But I couldn't leave. I felt responsible for it.'

Annabelle looked up and was alarmed to see how pale Andreas had become.

'I think you have very ambivalent feelings about me,' he said. 'I think part of you finds me repulsive.' He looked at his watch. 'I have to do an errand,' he said, standing up suddenly. 'I'm sorry. I'll see you next week, same time.'

Andreas was dismissing her. Annabelle hesitated for a moment, perturbed by his troubled reaction. She felt a strong desire to put her arms around his neck, kiss his cheek and tell him that she really thought he was a very beautiful man. She was afraid he might not like it and reject her. Instead, she gathered the jasmine she had picked on her way in and nursed in her lap. 'Do you like jasmine?' Annabelle said, handing Andreas her peace offering.

'Yes.' Andreas took the flowers and brought them to his face, inhaling the fragrance, but also to hide the shock he felt when their hands touched. He knew she felt it too, saw it in her eyes. It was a consolation.

When he tried to hold her gaze, she turned away, unprepared for the sudden intimacy.

Annabelle would disturb his sleep, forever.

6 Beauty and the Beast

Doctor Zill was somewhat relieved to notice that Annabelle was wearing a white embroidered dress.

'Vintage', she said, reading his mind. 'From an op-shop.'

He liked that. How original. His wife would never have dreamed of stepping inside one of those second-hand shops.

They were sitting opposite each other, she on the settee, while he occupied the leather armchair. The light from the window played on the golden hues in her long hair. He shifted his weight, becoming suddenly conscious of his unwelcome bulk. He had started a diet. All he had had for a week, was some unpalatable pink liquid out of a can. He was supposed to drink three cans a day to help him lose weight. It left an odd taste in his mouth, like strawberry-flavoured disinfectant.

'My father brought me lots of books—fairy tales and adventures,' Annabelle was telling him.

'He encouraged you to live in fairy tales, where the prince is set an impossible task. It's one way of never getting close to anyone, because they're bound to fail, to meet with your displeasure. He has to slay the dragon or survive an ordeal before he can win the princess,' Andreas said.

Annabelle heard sarcasm in his voice. Disapproval. It made her apprehensive. 'Yes, I think it's an act of love I expect. I need proof.' She suddenly became arrested by an idea. 'It's usually the most difficult thing,' she said finally. 'Oh, I'm not unreasonable or heartless. I wouldn't dream of asking a man to do anything to endanger his life—climb a mountain or fight a battle. No, what I would expect from him...' Annabelle paused for a second until she felt she engaged Andreas completely. 'Take yourself, for instance. The greatest act I would expect from you would be to break the *taboo*!'

'That would be impossible, Annabelle.'

'Sometimes the impossible can be brooked.'

Andreas fought to match her gaze. Her fragile appearance belied an unsettling invisible strength.

'Which was your favourite fairy tale?' he asked.

Annabelle's eyes were luminous as she remembered days of dark enchantment with the Brothers Grimm, Hans Christian Andersen and La Fontaine. They were lived in charmed forests and magic kingdoms. She had been the sleeping, the lost, the unhappy, the difficult and the beloved princess. There was a favourite one.

'La Belle et la Béte!'

'Tell me what you recall of the story.'

'I may have forgotten it.'

'Won't you try?'

Images from the fairy tale began to materialize—a story about transformation and the power of love. Suddenly Annabelle was looking at Andreas as if under a spell. She felt herself melting, warm honey coursing through her body, between her legs. No one, had ever had such an effect on her.

'Once upon a time,' she began, hesitatingly, enraptured by what was happening to her, 'there lived a good man who had three daughters. The youngest was called Beauty. Besides being very beautiful, Beauty was also gentle and kind and loved her father very much, unlike her sisters who were wicked and thought only of themselves.

'When her father has to go on a journey, he asks his daughters what they would like him to bring them on his return. The greedy ones want expensive gifts but Beauty asks her father for a single rose. Little does she know that she has set him a very difficult task indeed.

'On his way home, the father stops by an enchanted castle and cuts a rose from the garden for his daughter. Suddenly the Beast appears. He is very angry. He tells the old man that his punishment for taking the rose is death, but he can go home to say goodbye to his daughters if he promises to return. When Beauty learns about her father's predicament, she insists on taking his place and returns alone to the Beast and his castle.

'The Beast, on seeing Beauty, falls in love with her and spares her life. He makes her mistress of the castle, lavishes riches, clothes and nourishment on her. He likes to sit by her side and have lengthy conversations. The Beast asks Beauty to marry him. But Beauty finds him ugly and repulsive. One day, while she's in the enchanted garden, a little bird tells her that her father is ailing. She begs the Beast to allow her to see him. He permits it only if she promises to return within three days.

'At home, her dear father is so glad to see her, he recovers. Beauty is happy to be home and forgets the promise she made. One night, she dreams the Beast is dying—heartbroken, longing for Beauty. She hurries back, full of guilt, promising the Beast she will be his wife forever if only he will live. Because Beauty gives the Beast her love, he is at once transformed into a handsome prince. And so, they live happily ever after.'

'You seem to have remembered it all, rather well,' Andreas said.

'Yes I have, haven't I?' Annabelle was pleased with the effort she had made for him.

'The implication is,' Andreas said, 'that only after much suffering, a difficult quest and through her unconditional acceptance and love for the Beast, can she make him able to redeem himself.'

He too, liked the tale. There was hope.

'How are you feeling now? You're stroking your neck.'

Annabelle paused, selecting her words for effect.

'Wanton,' she said.

Andreas was taken aback by her reply. At the same time he found it deeply arousing.

'Who else used to stroke you like that?'

'My father, of course. But how did *you* know to touch me so, in the first place? The night of the ball, when we first met, when you helped me with my coat, your fingers brushed my neck. How did you know where to touch me?'

'But I didn't,' he said.

For a moment Andreas was overcome with a feeling of defeat. Then his countenance brightened as he caught her rapture.

7 The Countertransference

Andreas pulled on his belt to reassure himself one more time, feeling it loose around his stomach. He had lost a few inches. The diet was working and he was exercising. He had ordered a stationary bicycle he had seen advertised on television, and taken to cycling every morning and evening on the veranda. He could look at the water and the boats on the harbour, and when the sweat and effort became too much, her image would spur him on to improve himself.

Annabelle was not in the waiting room when he looked in. He turned and went back sinking in his leather chair, slowly deflating. Andreas tried to prepare himself for the time when he would not see her again but found it difficult to contemplate. In fact, the thought filled him with dread. 'It's too soon, too soon,' he repeated, reaching for a tissue from the box on the table. Perhaps he could have a quick drink before she arrived. If she came at all. There was a bottle of gin in the cupboard but before he could rise to his feet, he heard her footsteps.

Annabelle was standing in the doorway, dressed in black, like the Angel of Death. She came and sat opposite him on the settee.

'How are you?' Andreas said, feeling overpowered by her presence.

'You always ask that. 'How are you, what have you been doing, how's your relationship with your husband, have you had sex with him ..."

A pained look came over his face

'What would you like me to say?'

'Oh, I don't know,' Annabelle's voice was tinged with feigned boredom. She carefully peeled off her gloves. 'How are *you*? You don't look too good. Have you had a nice weekend?'

Andreas wrinkled his nose.

'I attended a seminar on grief and bereavement,' he said.

'How depressing.'

'What did you do?' Andreas was interested, yet fearful of her reply.

He always imagined her life to be exciting.

'I can't remember,' she said, brushing a speck of dust off her skirt with her gloves. 'Oh, yes. I picked up David from the airport on Friday night. He had a lovely gift for me—a tiny bouquet of exquisite flowers in a small box. So sweet. I was very touched. It's funny how sometimes a small gesture can make you feel on top of the world. I guess I'm sentimental.'

'Perhaps you always were,' he said.

'Pardon?' Had she misheard him? Then, as she realised it was jealousy that had prompted Andreas's odd remark, she began to feel deliriously happy. She wanted to clap with glee.

Andreas, on the other hand, was mortified at his sudden unexpected show of hostility but it did not stop him making the situation more uncomfortable. Indeed, he plunged headlong into more grief.

'Why are you dressed in black? Who are you burying?' he blurted out.

Annabelle could feel the corners of her mouth lifting, but she quickly suppressed the smile. 'You,' she said and waited for the result.

It came immediately. His face went ashen, a look of dread in his eyes.

'Why?' he asked, his voice cracking.

Annabelle again delighted in her victory.

Andreas stared hard at her for a moment, then his eyes seemed to moisten.

'So you wanted to find out if I was human? Well, I am,' he said, with deep emotion.

An uneasy silence followed. Although Annabelle was thrilled at her success it had made her uneasy. She was not prepared for his naked vulnerability and need, which she could now see was greater than hers. At the same time, she found herself overwhelmed with desire.

'Why don't you make love to me then?' she said.

Andreas looked dazed.

It stunned Annabelle as well.

He closed his eyes for a moment, as though he was in pain. Or maybe he did not want to look at her.

'Because Annabelle, it is forbidden. There are ethics in my profession. If we were to dispense with them, it would be disastrous.'

'It was forbidden for Romeo and Juliet, Héloise and Abelard, Tristan and Isolde,' she enticed. 'Yet still they loved.'

A new force was awakening and taking possession of her. Annabelle wanted the exaltation she could sense within her grasp—and nothing was going to stop her.

'I love you, Andreas,' she announced.

Andreas closed his eyes again but when he reopened them she was still there. No, it was not a dream. And yes, it was better than a dream.

'I'm overawed, Annabelle,' he stumbled. 'Such tenderness and honesty fills me with awe. But I have to be strong in this situation.' He tried to reason with her. 'Look at what happened to Romeo and Juliet, Héloise and Abelard and the others. All damned and doomed. Annabelle, I want you to grow up. To live your life. Please believe me when I tell you that there are strict moral ethics to protect you. I have never seduced a patient.'

'I don't believe you,' she said.

'*Please,*' he begged. 'This is very difficult for me.'

His mouth was dry. Andreas tried to rise from the cumbersome armchair but the damp leather stuck to him, holding him back. 'Would you like a drink of water?'

'No, thank you. But you have one,' Annabelle entreated graciously.

Andreas disappeared behind the screen and returned with a tumbler of water in his hand. He sat down and watched Annabelle with apprehension.

'What are you feeling?' he asked.

'What are *you* feeling?'

'What's your hand doing behind your ear?'

'I'm playing with my hair,' Annabelle said.

'You're doing more than that. You're stroking yourself,' Andreas told her.

'Yes, with my fingers, here behind the ear, the way you touched me when we first met. I told you before, you secretly seduced me the night we met at the ball. I fell in love with you *before* I became your patient and you with me. I remember how you looked at me. How could I ever forget?' Annabelle shook her head in disbelief—the memory had so much power still. 'And when we were leaving, you followed me to where I had left my coat and helped me with it. As you lifted my hair off the collar, you touched my neck, here, just behind the ear, and I was immediately seduced. So you see, we're really lovers.'

'No, Annabelle, we can't be. You're my patient.'

'Then I'll stop being your patient and be your lover!'

Andreas looked into her eyes. He was deeply moved by her willingness to sacrifice her therapy for him. It seemed her love for him was paramount.

He shook his head.

'You need help, Annabelle. You have some profound unresolved problems, mistrust …'

'I'll find another shrink,' she said.

'It's too late. Transference has already taken place. The emotional bond is very strong between us. Freud maintained this was an important part of the process of psychotherapy—for the patient to develop a transference onto the psychiatrist. You see me as your father, someone you loved very much, who was loved by many.'

'Don't you think you attach too much importance to my father?'

'He is very important to you,' Andreas said.

'Yes, I know but I don't mean it like that. I think you want to be him,' Annabelle said.

'I am *him* to you. I told you, because of the transference.'

'But I don't want you to be him! I want you to be yourself, Andreas,' Annabelle said, her impatience growing.

'That's not possible, Annabelle.'

'Why?'

'Because I told you, I *am* him to you.'

'This is absurd!' she cried.

'Let's do some work then, Annabelle.'

'I can't think of anything to say to you. I think you're trying to confuse me. You're playing some kind of game I don't understand. I feel worse now than I did five months ago when I first came here.' She stopped, brooded for a moment, then spoke what was on her mind. 'You've never done anything nice for me, like asking me to stay half an hour longer or offered me a drink. You have drinks with Shirley, your receptionist. I've seen her sitting here having a gin and tonic when I've arrived.'

'Freud introduced some strict rituals for psychotherapy. Alongside the *taboo* against physical and sexual expression, he also laid down rules about the duration of the session with a definite specified length of time, and also money. The patient has to assume responsibility for making his payment to the doctor.'

'How can you cure me if you are to remain so detached, if you don't care about me?'

'Oh, but I *do*, I *do*!' Andreas said, almost choking.

Once outside the clinic, Annabelle collected flowers from the garden. She had seen the doctor's car parked in a bay with his name. She spread the flowers all across his windscreen.

8 Desire

Annabelle had been waiting anxiously for the dawn to break, and release her from the dark she feared.

The light spirited into the bedroom, through the fine curtains on the French windows and she could just make out the delicate pattern of the iron lace on the balcony.

As the morning sun grew stronger, she watched the silhouetted birds dance on the branches of the old olive tree next to the house. For a few exalted moments, they could sing their little hearts out. All this was happening a short distance from the city, in Paddington. Its Victorian terraces with the elaborate iron balconies, art galleries, restaurants, boutiques and tree lined streets reaching down to the harbour, attracted bohemians, artists and professionals.

Annabelle lay very still in the large bed, keeping herself tightly collected, not wanting to arouse her husband sleeping beside her. She knew that, were he to feel her warm body next to his, he would pull her close and have sex with her. The very thought of David touching her body made her panic. She had always felt tense with him, ever since the first time.

Lately, there were new feelings. Feelings related to her analysis.

Annabelle tried to control the beating of her heart with her breath and when that did not work, she distracted herself with her surroundings. The large room had walls patterned in a William Morris lavender wallpaper, high white ceilings decorated with mouldings of flowers and fruit, and a carved marble fireplace laid with tiles Annabelle had painted rosebuds on. There was the rocking chair with the needle point cushion that had come all the way from Austria, when David's mother had died, together with some of his family possessions. David loved the old cushion embroidered with edelweiss from his childhood and he could look at it when lying in bed.

Annabelle had inadvertently turned the cedar chest of drawers into an altar by hanging a small Renaissance painting of cherubs gazing in adoration at the edge of the painting. It should have been the child, Jesus. They had bought the art work on a trip in Florence one summer and been so dazzled by the rich reds and gold, that they did not realise until they left Italy, that it was only a small portion of a larger canvas.

Annabelle had pinned to the wall a sapphire necklace David had given her, folding the necklace to form a cross so that the golden angels had an object to worship. Completing the scene was a candle in a glass holder which she sometimes lit when she was alone.

Next to the improvised shrine were three postcards of a Botticelli painting Annabelle had bought at the Uffizi Galleries. She loved Botticelli because of his depiction of nature and women, soft colours and beautiful clothes. The postcards were of a serene landscape, a forest and a lake in the distance. In the forest rode three young men on white stallions. They were dressed in golden armour, with pink silk cloaks billowing behind them. The men held their swords erect as they pursued three naked young women—the same maidens from another painting—the one where they had accompanied Venus, rising from the sea, in beautiful diaphanous gowns. The maidens' long tresses were braided with ribbons and flowers but their nakedness added a poignancy and vulnerability to what was being done to them.

In the second postcard, the men's hounds had caught up with the fleeing women, tearing at the flesh of their thighs and buttocks.

The third painting was of a maiden lying on the ground, mortally wounded. One of the golden knights, had dismounted from his horse and was bent over her body disembowelling her, throwing her entrails to the hounds.

Annabelle was shocked when she realised what the painting was about. Why had she not seen it before? She had only ever associated Botticelli with beauty, not violence. His graceful style, the pure visual poetry, the epitome of feminine beauty, were all deception. Now she knew, and it no longer surprised her. Annabelle had always suspected and feared the big human beast, the animal inside the man, no matter how beautiful his white horse or how golden his armour.

Her husband stirred beside her. His hands reached for her breasts and he began to pull her nightgown above her waist. Annabelle pretended to be asleep and rolled away from his grasp, curling into a ball, like a creature trying to protect its soft underbelly.

Annabelle waited, hoping the alarm clock would ring so David would have to leave the bed. But he rose soon after his attempt to have sex with her and went into the bathroom. After some time, she heard the sound of the shower. Annabelle slipped downstairs to the kitchen and prepared David's breakfast. When he left for work, she returned to the empty but now safe bed, and was overcome by sleep that had eluded her for most of the night.

* * *

It was Tuesday, her favourite day of the week and Annabelle had slept all morning. She began her ritual, showering, shampooing, waxing—wanting to be beautiful for him. But there were obstacles to her dream—her insecurity, problems with intimacy and trust. Deep down Annabelle believed she was not beautiful nor brave. She had walked away from every challenge—academic, acting, a career, being a mother and a wife. So how could she imagine that Andreas could love her?

* * *

Now at the clinic, Annabelle's session with Doctor Andreas Zill was not proceeding as she had hoped.

'I don't believe that tale of yours, about your agony, your strict moral ethics and the betrayal of trust. I think you're really afraid of me. I don't know why you should fear me. I wouldn't hurt you. I understand the taboo, to touch something that is forbidden can destroy you, so you keep away to protect yourself, for your own survival. I'm really sorry if I make things difficult for you,' she said.

Andreas nodded the acceptance she required.

'Freud was convinced that society is organised in such a way so as to control and censor its members' powerful sexual desires. Our society is built on the denial of what we really want. So, he said, we have three choices: 'We can repress our desire and sexuality; we can take refuge in fantasy; or build a particular reality to fit in with the civilisation we have chosen.' Then Andreas added: 'I believe we get what we need, not what we want.'

Annabelle sighed. She felt defeated.

'How depressing. I don't think I'm ever going to be better.'

'It would mean you would have to change. Change your relationship with David. You may have to leave him.'

She looked at him surprised. She had never contemplated leaving David. Why was he saying those things? Did Andreas want her to leave David? Why did he not say so instead of couching his hopes using her psychological situation? Perhaps she was imagining this. Even so, Annabelle would have loved to go away with Andreas. But how? And where would they go?

'I couldn't leave David. I couldn't hurt him. He's been good to me. He loves me,' she said, wanting to convince Andreas, and herself.

Andreas nodded a few times in agreement. Then he pressed a finger to his lips, as if he was trying to suppress his rising amusement.

'What?' she asked, her eyes narrowing. He was playing a game with her, she could tell.

'Oh, nothing, just a joke,' he said.

'Tell me! Please. Won't you share it with me?'

'It's just a joke, about gastroenterologists,' he said.

'I'd love to hear it. *Please.*'

'Well, here goes. What's the definition of an endoscope?'

Annabelle shook her head, animated now that Andreas was sharing his merriment with her.

'A rubber tube with an arsehole at each end,' he said quickly, but with a rather satisfied expression.

Annabelle's face went blank for a moment—shock, confusion. She tried to force a smile.

'I'm sorry, that was very coarse of me,' Andreas said, feigning abashment. 'What made David choose gastroenterology?'

'He comes from a medical background.'

'It's an area that attracts repressed homosexuals.'

Was Andreas bluffing?

'I think that's a most extraordinary remark. I just can't believe it. It's so stupid! You're trying to discredit David. And even if he were homosexual, I would still love him. I think you're jealous of him.'

'I'm sorry. I'm having trouble with my countertransference. I will have to sort this out.' He added meekly: 'How was your week?'

'My migraine was terrible. I was thrown into the depths of depression. That dreaded feeling when I wake up, the emptiness, something missing, here in my centre,' Annabelle pressed her hand near her heart.

'Tell me more. What were you angry about?' Andreas asked.

'Why is it whenever I tell you that I'm depressed, you tell me that I'm angry?' She was exasperated.

'Depression is suppressed anger, a way of not facing what we really feel. You incapacitate yourself with depression rather than feel your anger. Who were you angry with?'

'You. I wake up every day with disturbing strong feelings about you. An unbearable desire for you.'

'And that made you angry?'

'Yes!'

'Why?'

'Because you weren't there. Because I can't have you. And because I don't want to feel like this about anyone.'

'Is that what you believe, Annabelle?'

'Yes.'

'You need to go deeper,' Andreas said.

'I'm beginning to feel like a time bomb, awakening to disaster, my own destruction. I came as a huntress, a seductress but I have fallen into a snake pit.'

'You're angry and frightened, Annabelle,' Andreas said, wanting to reach out to her, but reason made him pull back.

'I won't let anything affect me. I'll withdraw, become a ghost, then nothing will touch me,' she announced dramatically.

'*Everything,* touches you. You have extraordinary awareness, Annabelle.'

'Knowing changes nothing. It doesn't make it any easier to bear. It still hurts. I envy those who walk around in blissful ignorance. I'm no longer naïve.'

'You never were, you've known all your life. There are those who are born knowing. It's as if they wear a mantle covered in receptor cells sensitive to all the pain, treachery and dissembling that goes on around them. Christ knew that. And many others. Drugs are another way of knowing. Huxley gave it a name, *The Doors of Perception*. Have you ever had LSD?'

'No, but I have friends who take it socially. I'd like to try it. I've smoked marijuana and had hash-oil baked in a cake. I ate a slice before going to the Rolling Stones concert. I don't remember the concert because when I got there, I passed out. I was high, or rather, suicidal for days after. I couldn't get it out of my system. But no, I haven't used LSD. It sounds amazing—and dangerous.'

'Why dangerous?'

'Because it unleashes all these terrible things from within you,' Annabelle said.

'You feel you have terrible things within you?'

'Don't we all? Aren't we mysterious, dark, fathomless pits of misery and mischief? Isn't man a secretive and unpredictable destructive creature revealing only a tiny fraction of himself, like an iceberg?'

'Are you a secretive and unpredictable creature, Annabelle?' Andreas said, amused at her high sense of drama.

'What do you think?' Annabelle's voice was now a low whisper. She was playing at being seductive.

'I think you are. By God, you are. You're the most unusual woman I have ever met. You're enchanting.' Andreas stopped. It was all too fast, too far. How had he arrived at such a dangerous place? Strange how Annabelle remained cool and collected, as though she had not heard any of his impassioned words.

'About the subject of LSD, doctor, please tell me more,' she said with a calm voice.

Andreas sighed.

'I think it would help you to examine some things, take a closer look at your relationships, for example. Go back into your childhood, perhaps.'

'Why not use hypnosis, like Freud did?'

'Freud was not satisfied with hypnosis. He stopped using it eventually. I don't think you'd be a good subject to hypnotise anyway. You don't trust. Besides, hypnosis is like getting there with a horse and cart. LSD gets you there on a rocket.'

'It's illegal,' she said.

'I'm permitted to use it. There's only one other doctor in this country qualified to do so. I did some work with LSD in London at the Tavistock Clinic.'

'Have you ever taken it?'

'I had several trips under medical supervision when I was there,' Andreas said.

'What happened on your trips?'

'Oh ...' Andreas smiled, then added, 'I cried a lot of tears.' He laughed as though to minimise his painful memories lest he sound foolish to her. 'The bed was soaked with tears. In the end, I'd always find myself standing all alone outside a closed door, longing to be let in.'

'Poor darling,' Annabelle said.

It took Andreas a few moments to recover from the *darling* word she had used for him. He tried to cover up his emotions by becoming absorbed in his diary.

'How about the 30th then?' he said, flicking through the pages.

'So soon?' she asked.

'I think you need to go deeper, Annabelle. Your defences are daunting.'

'What happens? How long do I take LSD for?'

'Oh, the effect lasts for about five hours. I'll stop it after five hours.'

'Are you *really* with me for five hours?'

'Yes,' he said.

'How exciting!' She clapped her hands. 'I love this room. I feel safe here.'

'Annabelle, it won't be in this room. It'll be downstairs in the clinic.'

'Oh, but that would be horrid! I don't want to be with sick people and nurses. I'm not ill. I'm doing this because I choose to. I'm *interested.* I want to experiment with LSD. I want to open *the doors of perception,* as you said. I just want to experience it in nice safe surroundings. I don't want to be in a hospital.'

'It's not like a hospital. It's a clinic. You need to be there to be supervised during the night, when I'm gone,' Andreas said.

'When you're gone? I thought you said you'd stay with me.' Annabelle was apprehensive. She began to withdraw from him, shrinking into the cushions.

'I leave after you've tripped. I stop it with Largactil and Sodium Amytal. You'll get very drowsy and fall asleep. I will come and see you in the morning. The sister will ring me if anything goes wrong. I'm only five minutes away.'

But Annabelle would not look at him.

Eventually she raised her eyes.

'Is it true that one can kill oneself on LSD? I've read that people fall out of windows thinking they can fly, or walk in front of cars. It removes your defences, your sense of self-preservation.'

'It isn't true.' Andreas was looking at her in a strange way. 'I thought you weren't afraid of dying,' he said coldly.

The sudden change in Andreas unsettled Annabelle. He appeared stern, cold, unsympathetic. This was a new side to him.

Annabelle shivered and said feebly: 'I think I'm more frightened of life.'

'Yes.'

His *yes* was judgemental.

9 Eros and Psyche

No matter how much apprehension Annabelle felt at the thought of seeing Andreas again, all this was swept away when she stepped into his room and realised he had been waiting for her. She wore a creamy white suit. The jacket fitted tightly around her slim torso and pushed her breasts up to the silk scarf draped loosely around her neck.

Andreas stood up quickly to welcome her then waited for her to sit down.

'Do you feel better since you've been taking the anti-depressants?' Andreas asked. There was a hopeful note in his voice.

Annabelle crossed her bare brown legs—the skirt of the suit rose up. She watched his eyes and caught his desire.

'No,' she said, unfurling the scarf, tossing it to the side to reveal more of her cleavage. 'Perhaps for a few weeks but I find I'm back where I started. The worst time is the morning. I find it difficult to make any decisions. I'm confused and lost. Sometimes I go back to sleep. I sleep, so I don't have to make a decision.'

'You have made the decision to sleep.'

'It's a safe familiar decision. My parents were frightfully immature, fearful and neurotic. They wouldn't let me play with other children. They tried to bribe me with toys and books to stay at home. Not bribe really—I had no choice, no say. I wasn't allowed to ride a bicycle or a horse, or study ballet which I loved. I had dreams of becoming a ballet dancer, like my mother. They told me dreadful things would happen to me if I left home—I would get run over, have an accident, or some horrible man would kidnap me. Then I was sent to the convent. The nuns were worse with their ridiculous restrictions. You see, doctor, I lack certain life skills—how to comport myself with others.'

'They were projecting their own hostilities upon the environment, the hostilities they unconsciously felt for you.'

'Yes, I was a great disappointment because they had wanted a boy. The most chagrined was my grandfather. As my father was his only son and ours was a patriarchal family, he was bitterly disappointed that I wasn't a boy. He never forgave me. Never ever spoke to me, not directly, anyway. He would talk about me, refer to me always with sarcasm in front of relatives, as though I didn't exist.' Annabelle shrugged the hurt away. I didn't care.'

'But you did care. You were constantly humiliated, constantly rejected by the adults.'

'There was one uncle who was really kind to me. He seemed to like me. He was a champion fencer. I think that's why I took up fencing. I learned it at drama school, when I was studying to become an actress. I could have made it to the Olympics, Tex, my teacher said, even though he used to call me *dog's breakfast,'* Annabelle smiled.

'Even he humiliated you!'

'There was a story my great-uncle told me which I found fascinating. It was about a freak he had seen at a sideshow in Paris when he was a young man. This creature, this freak, was horribly deformed, with growths all over his skin and one in the middle of his brow, like Cyclops. When he took his hood off, people fainted and reeled in horror ...' Annabelle stopped in the middle of telling her story. 'Fancy remembering it now. After all these years.'

'You thought you were a freak because your grandfather didn't love you. Perhaps even your dear uncle intuited how you felt. That's why he was prompted to tell you such a story. You felt responsible for your father's disappointment that he hadn't provided his father with an heir to the family name,' Andreas said.

'I still feel a freak sometimes, with people. They avoid me…'

'Men are afraid of beautiful women. They find them very threatening. Sometimes they become impotent.'

'Yes,' Annabelle nodded.

'And performance means a lot to a man, especially with a beautiful woman. So the more frightened a man is, the more likely he is open to failure. Impotence is his way of expressing his hurt and anger, or the rejection he feels. Sometimes men are hostile towards these women, resenting them because of the sense of inadequacy they experience, so they try to put them down.'

'You've been horrid to me,' Annabelle said, taking advantage of the situation to reproach him.

'Yes, I know. It's not like me,' Andreas said, lowering his head. But when he looked at her again, he saw something in her eyes and felt she had forgiven him.

'You're a goddess, you know? You remind me of Psyche. Poor Psyche.'

'Why poor Psyche? What happened to her?'

'You don't know the story of Psyche?'

Annabelle shook her head.

'Would you like me to tell it to you?'

She nodded vigorously.

'Let's see,' Andreas began, taking his time, enjoying holding Annabelle's attention, and her sense of anticipation. 'One day, Venus was very angry with Psyche, so she left her on top of the mountain for Death to be her husband. Now Psyche was ravishing, far more beautiful than Venus but although she was perfect, she had no suitors, while her sisters had all married early and spawned several children. Anyway, there she was, left at the top of the mountain for Death to be her husband. Then Venus began to feel bad about what she had done so she sent her son Eros, or Cupid as he's also known, the ancient god of love, to the top of the mountain and told him to shoot an arrow into Psyche so that she would fall in love with Death and not be afraid. But Eros had a dark side. The arrows he carried, together with his bow, were either tipped in gold or in lead. The gold incited acute desire, the lead killed it. When Eros arrived at the mountain, he pricked himself with a golden arrow and fell in love with Psyche. So he called the West Wind and asked him to take her away. After that Psyche was never the same, even though she married Eros and became Goddess of the Soul, because she had experienced Death at the top of the mountain.'

Andreas could tell from Annabelle's expression that she was enthralled by his story-telling. It pleased him no end.

'Tell me more. I love it when you tell me stories,' said Annabelle, stretching languidly on the cushions.

'There are women who posses this inherent quality, which although seduces men, also frightens them,' Andreas said.

'Sometimes, they really want to hurt you ...' she said.

'Go on,' Andreas sensed there was something Annabelle wanted to tell him.

'I ... was ... raped,' she said. 'That sounds so melodramatic.'

Andreas held his breath.

'Go on, Annabelle.'

She shifted uncomfortably in her seat, pulling childish faces, wanting to minimize the histrionics of what she was telling him.

'It was at a party last year. I was a bit drunk and very sleepy. I get drunk easily, one or two glasses. Ridiculous! Anyway there I was leaning like the Tower of Pisa, with my eyes closed, when this good friend of David came across and put his arm around me and told me that I needed some fresh air. Well he was a doctor, a professor, at the university so I thought he knew best. We walked out in the fresh air and I began to wake up. When he came to where he had parked his gold Mercedes, he opened the door and shoved me inside, in the back. I was surprised at first—didn't realise what was happening. I began to struggle but he was very strong and seemed to be in quite an emotional state, sobbing and saying how he had been in love with me for years. I felt sorry for him but I still kept trying to get away. There was so much aggression. He kept calling me *bitch*. It was horrid. I was scared. I thought he wanted to kill me.

'He tried to force his penis inside me but he couldn't manage it—he was too big, too hard, and I was dry. He thrust violently, tearing me.

'When it was over, I tried to get away from him. He began to say it was all my fault, that I'd seduced him, that it was the way I dressed. Funnily, I didn't argue, I almost believed him. I ran straight to the bathroom and washed myself. I screamed when the water and soap touched me. Then I went to look for David and told him I had a headache and wanted to go home. David asked me why I was limping. I told him it was because I had blisters from my new shoes. I didn't tell him what had happened because I was afraid of consequences. I didn't want David to find out about his best friend. He would have felt hurt and betrayed.

'Mostly I was ashamed and didn't want anyone to know. I think I was suffering from shock. But what could I do? It's difficult when you know the person and everyone thinks that he's a very decent member of society. I mean if he's middle class, clean and educated, one of you, it's not the same as if some dirty, scary-looking stranger rapes you. You can't very well stick a knife in that person or shoot him, now can you? Because you know him and trust him, you can't imagine that he would do that …'

'You would have liked to kill him?'

Annabelle was silent.

'Perhaps. I felt angry afterwards. But what could I have done?'

'You should have reported him to the police!' Andreas said.

'As if they would have believed me. I knew the man, I was semi-drunk, I had accepted his offer to go for a walk with him in the dark.'

'You should have reported it. He could do it again,' Andreas insisted.

'I didn't want to go through a court—have some imbeciles asking me salacious questions about what it felt like, etc. I'd probably lose my temper. There aren't any effective laws to protect women. I'm told they're coming. Who knows when? Besides, I survived. My injuries healed. It was desire, a moment of passion, whatever you want to call it on his part. Anyway it was an interesting experience. Material for a would-be-writer. Quite exciting, really,' she said, looking at him with a strange expression, challenging him.

'Yes, I thought that was what you were trying to tell me.'

Annabelle stared at Andreas in disbelief. Then trying to cover her hurt with anger, she flared up.

'That wasn't what I was trying to tell you at all! It's my way of coping. If I can't express the way I feel, I cover up or adapt. I resolve it by saying to myself that it was an exciting experience, so that I don't go under, or become a victim. I don't have to go on feeling helpless about something I can't do anything about. I have done the same with my husband.'

'Your husband's raped you?'

'All men do, one way or another. Some men don't know the meaning of *No.*'

'Not all men. I've never raped anyone,' Andreas said.

'That's what you believe,' Annabelle responded. 'Oh, I forgot to mention. The rapist won't be doing it again. He killed himself shortly after that night.'

Andreas stared at her coldly.

'You turn men's love into weapons. They expect the worst from you. They want you to destroy them so to please them you oblige.'

'I'm not really a destructive person,' Annabelle said, trying to defend herself, wounded by his sudden attack.

'You're trying to be a good girl, aren't you?' Andreas mocked her.

'You hate me. You must find me quite abhorrent.'

'No,' he said.

'Oh, why doesn't someone put a bullet through my head? I'm so tired, I feel a hundred.' She was disheartened and disappointed with Andreas. But mostly with herself.

'They'd be up for murder.'

'They shoot horses, don't they?'

'Some. The lucky ones. Some they flog to death.'

Annabelle withdrew, crossing her arms and her legs, turning away from him. She fidgeted then floundered under Andreas's observation. But his mood changed and soon he was looking at her with the gentleness she loved so much—quite different to the cold, sarcastic stare she had just experienced. Or the unbalanced one she had glimpsed, which had frightened and excited her at the same time.

Annabelle was studying him too, employing his method of detection. She was a sharp learner and was watching Andreas out of the corner of her eye as he played with his wedding ring. He kept slipping the ring on and off. She wondered whether he was aware of what he was doing, or if it was his subconscious desire to make love to her. Perhaps he wished to rid himself of his wedding ring, symbol of his unsatisfactory marriage.

Annabelle set a trap. She began to copy Andreas's movement, pretending to be unaware of what was happening.

He watched her with interest. A few minutes later, he drew attention to her hands.

'What are you thinking, Annabelle?'

'Why, nothing,' she replied, with a certain innocence.

Andreas smiled, a knowing confident smile.

'Your gesture,' he indicated, drawing attention to her hands.

'I don't know,' she said, her eyes inviting assistance. 'What does it mean?'

Andreas shifted his weight in the armchair and rubbed his hands.

'Well, it can mean that you want to get rid of your wedding ring, or your marriage. Or it could have another meaning. Look at what you're doing with your fingers and your ring. What does it remind you of?'

She looked down at her hands.

'Oh!' Annabelle blushed on cue.

'Exactly!' Andreas exclaimed with satisfaction. 'What are you feeling now, Annabelle?'

She hid her face behind her hand.

'What are you feeling now, Annabelle?' he repeated.

'Sexy?' she volunteered shyly.

Andreas nodded, satisfied.

Annabelle was tempted to thank him, or make him feel foolish but she kept quiet, pleased with her secret knowledge of him.

The observer had become the observed.

10 Tripping in Light and Darkness

Annabelle had been staring enraptured, at the luminous being, the *God* she had experienced under the effect of the hallucinogenic drug.

Andreas was sitting across from her, hands clasped, two fingers on his lips, his attention totally centred on her. She marvelled at what she had been through and Andreas had been there beside her, a witness, but also a participant on her journey. It had been her first LSD trip and, she believed, the greatest adventure of her life.

But Annabelle could not stare forever at the sun so she turned away from him towards the window. A brace of wild ducks was rising in the sky.

'I wonder what sort of journey they'll have,' she said, tilting her head and following the birds until they were gone except for one who was flying all alone some distance behind. 'He's not going to make it,' she said.

'Why?'

'Because he's weak. And it's a perilous journey all the way to Russia or Turkey, or wherever they fly. They arrive exhausted and are shot by hunters.'

'Annabelle, I'd like you to tell me everything you remember of your trip, every detail.'

Andreas waited patiently for Annabelle to begin.

She took a deep breath and levelled her attention on him.

'I arrived at 5.30pm and you still had a patient with you. I became suspicious, you were keeping me waiting, playing power games. And that was before you gave me the drug.'

'Go on,' he said.

'When you emerged twenty minutes later, you weren't very nice, you didn't even say hello. You just asked why I hadn't been to see the sister about being admitted. You reproached me further by telling me they were waiting for me. How was I to know where I should be?' she chided.

Andreas was contrite.

'I'm sorry, sometimes one is pompous when one is trying to hide one's real feelings.'

'One, one, one! How *very* pompous, indeed. Anyway,' she shrugged, 'my paranoia increased when I went downstairs to the clinic. I didn't want to trip with nurses and crazy people around. I read that you should take LSD in beautiful surroundings with people you love. I was very disappointed. You joked with the nurses, you couldn't even be reassuring, you were so self-absorbed. The nurse asked me a whole lot of silly questions such as: 'What is your religion? Whom do we notify in case of death?' They even weighed me, took my temperature and blood pressure. All that intimidation stuff that goes on with hospitals and the medical profession to reduce people to an infantile state. I tell you, if they'd tried to put me in one of those stupid hospital smocks where your bottom is exposed, I would have walked out. In the animal kingdom, the subservient ape presents his bare bottom to the dominant male. How powerful the doctor or therapist must feel when such a pitiful creature appears before him. How convenient!'

Andreas listened attentively, nodding in agreement.

'I was beginning to feel confused and demoralised. This wasn't at all how you said it would be. Then you walked in and I could feel the excitement. The nurses were all a-twitter with your presence. You seemed arrogant. I'd never seen you like that before. You did something nice though. You wrapped an orange towel around the light which transformed the room giving it a sensual glow.

'When you gave me the injection I felt as though a volcano erupted inside me. So much was happening! Extraordinary! I was being torn in all directions. It was during those first moments of panic that I sensed a change in you because I couldn't really see you. I had my face buried in the pillow.'

'You were thrashing around on the bed. An abreaction,' he explained.

'That change in you,' she continued, 'I felt it strongly. You went from professional egotism and control, to suddenly caring about me. You no longer hid behind your public persona. You took off your coat and loosened your tie. Then you began pacing back and forth while I raged. I heard you murmur something, as if you were speaking to someone. I think you were a bit concerned with what you had helped unleash. You had your arm over your head and one hand on your waist, like this,' she said, duplicating his gesture. 'And you were pacing like a trapped tiger. I felt sorry for you. I wished I could help but I was out of control.

'Then you took my arm and tightened the strap. You tried to give me another injection but I fought you. You worked fast and efficiently. You said to me, 'Let me take the edge off.' But the needle felt like a knife.'

'You screamed like a hurt child. You threw quite a tantrum,' Andreas said.

'I'm sorry. I was held down and given lots of injections when I was little because I was often sick. How long did it last? Ten minutes?'

'Forty minutes!' Andreas said. He seemed pleased, amused even, to have witnessed her reaction. Perhaps he thought he could break her defences.

Annabelle looked at him in disbelief.

'Oh, I'm so sorry,' she said.

'Time distortion under LSD,' he explained.

'Next morning I was looking at the tray with the used ampoules, and I noticed that next to the Lysergic Acid ampoules, there were some others…'

'Ritalin. That's what I was giving you at intervals. Although it's a stimulant normally, it has the paradoxical effect if someone is in a hyperactive state of slowing them down. One of the side effects of Ritalin is to suppress sexual desire but you've thoroughly disproved that,' Andreas said.

Annabelle gasped, remembering the astonishing thing that happened.

'I was filled, overwhelmed by the most intense, agonising sexual desire! I've never experienced anything like that before. Not ever! I wanted, *you*. I wanted the feel of your body, the weight, the smell, the sound. How I love the sound of your voice when you try to soothe me. *Your gentleness is so powerful*, I said, do you remember? That was when I imagined you making love to me.' She stopped suddenly, a frown appeared on her brow.

'What is it, Annabelle?'

'You asked me, 'Who am I? Look at me, who am I?' Who on earth were you supposed to be? Marlon Brando?'

Annabelle had seen *Last Tango in Paris,* twice.

'Your feelings were very strong. Your body seemed wracked with desire. But then you began to whimper like a child.'

'I felt it here, in the middle, in my belly. You told me to press into it. You had your arm resting on me, and you were pushing down into me. Then I wanted you to be *inside* me. I raised my gown.'

'Did you find the therapy helpful?' Andreas appeared cautious suddenly.

'It was fun, wicked. It was *wicked!'* She curled up on the settee, giggling, scrutinising him, inviting him to join her in their secret. But he refused to give anything away. 'Why did you stop my trip? Why did you give me Largactil so soon? Most trips last eight to thirty hours I read. Were you trying to protect yourself?'

'I had to stop it because you started anchoring. After five hours you don't regress very much and it isn't very useful. And because there's a danger of the other person becoming enmeshed in the trip and that makes it hard then to be objective.' Andreas was almost defensive. 'What else do you remember, Annabelle?'

'Events seemed to move very fast, at a million miles an hour. There were so many movies whirring inside my head, playing all at once. I wanted to talk to you, to share and communicate so much, but my mind was going faster than my lips could say the words. By the time I'd say something, I'd be completely carried away by another thought. Every word became a lifetime experience. If I thought *cold,* an entire documentary about the word would begin. My brain was this huge encyclopaedia with emotions. Within a second, I would have lived a life in the North Pole as an Eskimo *and* a Polar bear. I could feel the icy burn of steel pierce my body in a medieval joust. I became an orphan abandoned on a cold wintry street. It's strange how a lifetime of experience comes into your full understanding of a single word. But it must have been odd for you sitting there watching someone living through all these invisible worlds.'

'I look for signs. I have to concentrate for those five hours. I watch your face, expressions, body language, breath, sounds you make. Emotions. All these tell me about what's going on inside of you.'

'You asked me, 'Who am I?' It doesn't pain me or shock me to face up to it. You could have been my father. Part of you was, but I also saw you as a man I like. *Un Homme Qui Me Plait.* It's the title of a French movie. Of course, you may find it difficult to accept.' Annabelle was watching the effect her words were having on Andreas. But there was something she needed to know. 'What did you say to me when you took me on your lap?'

Andreas shook his head.

'I don't remember. Why?'

'I adored sitting on your lap, your arms holding me. It's almost the greatest feeling in the world,' Annabelle said.

'Why, almost?'

'Because making love with you would be the best.' Annabelle gave a sudden little cry as she remembered. 'You said, 'It must have been very difficult for your father.' *And* you had an erection.'

Doctor Zill balked, lost his composure for a moment. He shifted in his seat, ran his hand over his head and smoothed down his tie.

'I wanted you to treat me as a woman. I said, 'I love your beautiful lips,' tried to touch them and kiss them. But you behaved like a nervous parent, patting my bottom and dismissing me with a, *now, now*, and putting me back to bed.'

'It was the erotic love and driving passion of the child that you experienced.'

'It was mine!' Annabelle protested.

Andreas felt helpless to console her.

'You loved the pictures of the horses on the wall...' he said.

'I love horses ...' Annabelle broke off, shivering. 'They scare me also. All that flesh and muscle completely out of control. The ultimate symbol of male sexuality.' As Annabelle talked, she began to evoke some of those images. 'The horses were covered in gold and silver and they began to prance and dance. When I looked at you, you were king, priest and magician. The Sun God! And then ...' Annabelle stopped, as though she was remembering something extraordinary. 'I had an even more beautiful experience. I saw you as the Russian prince in *War and Peace*. You were dressed in a white and gold uniform, preparing to ride your white horse into battle. An amazing thing happened—both rider and horse turned into a magnificent white wave galloping across the surface of a luminous pale-green sea.'

Annabelle stopped. She held her hands over her lips to stop herself revealing a thought.

'What is it Annabelle?' Andreas said.

Annabelle hesitated.

'*André* is the Prince in *War and Peace* who is wounded and dies. It's very sad and tragic,' she said.

'Is he your favourite character in *War and Peace?*'

'Yes, he is. But it was you, all the while during my journey, whatever being you became, whether I had my eyes open or shut I was aware that it was *you* because you are all this to me.

'You were the devil, too. King of the Underworld. You looked positively evil at one stage. But you didn't scare me. Funny, I almost wanted you to take me with you to hell, like Persephone. The thought of dying occurred to me when I heard glass shattering outside. I may have imagined it as well because I noticed later that all the glasses and carafes are made of plastic.'

Andreas nodded.

Her eyes were inviting him to conspire with her. She enjoyed playing at being mysterious, sensing the *frissons* she sent through him. 'I'll tell you a secret, my dear doctor. Just between you and me—there's a dark side, a very *black* side to you. An aberration. I recognise it, for we are twins in our darkest souls. I have known you before. And forever.'

For a moment Andreas seemed to be caught off guard. Annabelle had seen something within him which he refused to acknowledge yet feared its existence.

He laughed, trying to conceal his fear.

'You're cute!' he said.

'What a drippy thing to say,' Annabelle rebuked him.

'Sorry, I was lost for words,' Andreas said. He had a pained expression. Then he added, in the other language they shared: '*Qui s'excuse, s'accuse*. Oh, damn!' His efforts were only going to add to his awkwardness. But again he laughed out of a feeling of excitement tinged with despair.

'*Mon pauvre docteur*,' she said. 'You suffer too, thank god!'

Suddenly Annabelle gave a breathless cry as she remembered more. 'You touched my breast and it was fantastic! Why did you not make love to me then?' she asked in earnest.

'I'm in a position of trust, Annabelle. I can't betray that trust, you know that.'

'All noble, touching sentiments, Andreas. But they're meaningless,' she said. 'Anyway it's not the whole picture.'

'You don't understand. There are professional ethics to consider. I couldn't make love to you even if I wanted to. In all my years of medicine, I have never touched a patient.'

'So you said before. Yet you touched my breast and my tummy here,' she revealed, remembering what had occurred.

'I was trying to increase the pressure in that area, where you hold your feelings—your heart and your stomach,' Andreas said.

'I didn't know I came here for sex therapy.'

'You don't believe me?'

'No. Because you arose strong sexual feelings in me for *you*. You were testing me because you weren't certain. You wanted reassurance that those feelings I had were for you.'

'For the parent, Annabelle. Your father.'

'You're not my father. My father loved me!'

But Annabelle could not stay angry for long. Not when he was looking at her with eyes full of sadness. The Russian melancholy touched her deeply.

'Why did you leave me?' she asked in a soft voice.

Andreas looked down. She could see he was overcome with feelings of inadequacy. His task was difficult. He must have felt he was not equipped to help her. There was the fear of failing her.

'I had to,' he said.

'Couldn't you have stayed an hour longer?'

'You were angry when your father left you to go to his mistresses.'

'Leave my father out of it!'

Annabelle sat for a while ignoring Andreas. But the desire to unburden and share things she had never spoken about made her continue.

'I used to feel as though my world crumbled whenever he left. I became invisible, insignificant. I'd run out into the street crying and looking for him.'

'You loved him very much,' Andreas said. He got up and went across to her as she rose to leave. He placed his hand gently on her shoulder. 'This is only the beginning. I'll see you next week.'

11 A Gift

Although Annabelle had been coming to the Bollingen Clinic for a year now, she always found the waiting unbearable. A week was a fiendishly long time in between sessions. All her life Annabelle had waited for someone. All those years, so much of her life spent in vain. Why was it never the other way around with David, Andreas and her father?

Annabelle lived for those afternoons when she was due at the Bollingen Clinic. She would prepare herself for Andreas like a bride, or, a mistress. Clothes were an absorbing preoccupation. She delighted in seeing what effect each gorgeous creation had on him. Annabelle could be a siren in a sensuous 1930s crepe dress from an op-shop; a young girl in a Victorian camisole and lace petticoat or patched up jeans; the mysterious lady in black velvet; or the whore in red. She would be *all* women to Andreas and seek to satisfy every one of his desires.

Annabelle bought Andreas small gifts too. Perfumed soaps, so he would think of her every morning when he lathered himself under the shower; jars of French jam, or peach-flavoured tea imported from Harrods; a glass wind chime; a rose-quartz crystal heart; books and incense; sweets and exotic fruits from up North. She also composed poetry, wrote letters and put down thoughts on paper when she did not have the courage to speak them.

She arrived at the Bollingen Clinic that day, full of spirit and expectation. She had not felt such intense happiness and self-assurance in a long time.

Annabelle paused transfixed at the door of the consulting room. Andreas was wearing a black suit with a black shirt and a pale blue-grey tie, which matched his eyes. He looked arresting—the black, a contrast to his Nordic looks. She was about to swoon.

He extended his hand to her in the familiar handshake, his eyes intent on hers. She was conscious of the heat rising in her cheeks, inflaming her.

Annabelle held out a small gift. Andreas took the exquisitely packaged box from her, gold on a white design with pink rosebuds, and brought the soap to his nose to inhale its perfume.

'It's glycerine and roses,' she said. 'I thought perhaps you might have used this brand in your home in Switzerland.

'You'd like to bring me back my childhood. I'm touched, Annabelle. How sweet. Thank you.'

Again, Annabelle felt faint when he praised her.

Andreas waited for her to sit down.

'Any thoughts?'

'A lot. I left out a few things about my LSD trip, so I wrote them down in my notebook.'

Andreas took the book from her and began to read:

I wanted so much to find what I was looking for and you were trying to help me. We came close several times. You said: Let yourself go, Pet, let yourself go. Did you know it's old fashioned and can be regarded as a put down to call a woman that? But of course, you wouldn't know that—it's your foreignness. I loved it just the same.

I was trying to seduce you. I raised my gown. Or was I trying to hide from you? I felt small and lost in the gown. You said that I was the most beautiful gift you had ever been given. I saw love in your eyes. You held my hand and before leaving, I said that'd I'd like to make love with you and you replied: No, you wouldn't. And when I asked you why, you said: You know. But I don't know. You kissed my forehead and whispered, The answers lie within us. You seemed almost ashamed of yourself, as though you were trying to tell me you weren't worthy of my love.

You spoke of the Alchemist's search for golden youth, Jeunesse d'oré. I think you were feeling quite old. Did you speak to me in French to try and trick me into believing you were my father? My father gave me gold when I was young. When I grew up, he took my bracelets away and sold them to pay his gambling debts.

I saw men as cannibals, golden cannibals, a paradox, don't you think?

Their hunger is so voracious, devouring, insatiable. It scares me. I saw myself beginning to shrink at one stage, until I was about three years old. But when I touched my face it felt like the face of a very old woman. My fingers went right through my skull, from the present to the future and beyond. It was both frightening and fascinating at the same time. It made me realise how little time we have and how much has already been wasted.

You shrank too, dear doctor. You became a baby in my arms. I think you desperately need to be mothered. I don't think you received enough love when you were a child. Poor, poor Andreas. You touched my breast and it was thrilling. You touched my breast... You touched me. Thank you for holding my hand.

Andreas closed the notebook, sighed and looked at her. Annabelle's face was burning. She regretted confessing so much.

'What about your sexual feelings?' he said. There was a noticeable tension in his voice.

'I remember the strawberries. I wanted to give them to you because the nurse had brought you a cup of coffee and you were eating some awful biscuits. I had all these maternal feelings for you. Then a wonderful thing happened. An image appeared. I was in a beautiful villa, in a nursery with a glass domed ceiling, a Victorian conservatory. There were blue butterflies and delicate flowers etched on the glass panels. Exquisite pink climbing roses, in bud, outside the window. I could smell their perfume in the warmth of the afternoon sun. A cot stood near one of the open windows. I'm not certain if there was a baby in it but I saw a young woman dressed in a long white lace dress walking in the garden. Her hair was loosely tied with a ribbon. She had a pink satin sash around her corseted waist and she carried a parasol. Suddenly I had a strange feeling—one of giving birth and at the same instant of being born. I experienced it all at the same time. It was extraordinary. I think it was motherly love I felt for you.'

'But you withdrew from it,' he said. 'You recoiled from the responsibility of having someone dependent on your love. You don't believe you are capable of loving, or worthy of being loved!'

'It's true, I never gave myself to anyone completely.'

'Including your husband?'

'Especially my husband,' Annabelle said.

'Except Daddy. You gave to Daddy and he hurt you. So you seduce men and then reject them by not giving them everything.' Andreas suddenly looked awfully defeated. 'It's late,' he said, 'and I have to see another patient.'

Annabelle rose from the settee and quickly gathered her things. She was about to leave when she hesitated for a moment.

'Oh, I almost left this behind,' she said, taking her notebook away from him. She looked into his eyes and gave him a knowing smile. 'I read that's a ploy patients use who have a crush on their therapists so they have an excuse to return before waiting a whole week.'

'You left me this,' he said, holding the gift she had given him.

'Goodnight, Andreas,' Annabelle said, her smile promising him other delights.

'Goodnight, Mrs Eichler.' His, was a weary but affectionate smile.

She realised that one of the things she liked about him was that he sometimes managed to stay a step or two ahead of her. It was important. It made her feel safe.

12 The Whore

It was exciting arriving at the clinic not knowing what to expect. How would the next session unfold? Andreas's black suit had thrilled and surprised her. What would he do next? How long could he resist her? Fate had brought them together. Why?

'Annabelle! You look like Susie Wong in your lovely cheong-sam and those flowers in your hair,' Jess the secretary exclaimed, clapping her small hands. She was a tiny bird-like woman with intelligent eyes that twinkled with harmless mischief, like a favourite aunt.

'What are they, frangipani? Are you one of those Flower Children, a hippie?' Her fingers fluttered nervously around the flowers in Annabelle's hair.

Annabelle laughed and would have liked to explain to Jess that there was more to being a flower child than wearing flowers in your hair. Most of the hippies she knew were committed to change—ending the war in Vietnam, women's rights, children's rights, animal rights, gay rights, saving the environment.

'They're tuberoses,' she said. 'Here, have one, Jess,' Annabelle said, raising her arms above her head and reaching for a flower.

'Don't disturb them. You look so lovely. Thank you. Where's the mirror? I want flowers in my hair, too,' said Jess, struggling to pin a tuberose in her sparse flapper bob. 'There! How does that look?'

'Simply divine,' said the doctor, approaching. He appeared in good humour and winked at Annabelle.

'You're teasing me, now. He always teases me. Beware of him, Annabelle, he's as harmless as a sabre-toothed tiger.'

'Thanks for the warning,' Annabelle whispered, as she followed the doctor to his room.

'You look very alluring …' he said, his eyes sweeping over her body.

'I've just been told I look like a Chinese prostitute,' Annabelle said laughing.

Andreas held up the coin he had been playing with. There was a hole in its centre.

Something about the way he was handling it, twirling it between his fingers, aroused Annabelle's curiosity.

'What is it?'

'It's an old Chinese coin. Take a closer look.'

Annabelle leaned towards him, enough for him to inhale deeply her scent.

'Oh!' she broke off, laughing nervously, blushing. 'I see a naked man and a woman in a compromising position.'

'It's brothel currency. They used such coins to pay for their pleasure in ancient China.'

Annabelle was beginning to enjoy the game. She looked down at her outfit—the red and gold sheath with a split up the thigh.

'What a strange coincidence. I've never worn this dress before.'

'Jung called it *coincidental synchronicity*. This afternoon you wanted to be an exotic creature skilled in the art of giving pleasure.'

'But I didn't know …'

'You are very ingenious at making a man feel good. You encourage them to talk about themselves whilst you listen to them with your beautiful limpid eyes. You nod and exclaim breathless encouragement. It's very seductive, you know? The dominant role is very seductive to a man. But you must see me as your doctor not someone you have to seduce. Now let's do some work. Any new thoughts lately?'

Annabelle was reluctant to relinquish the air of sexual excitement Andreas had created. By showing her the symbol of lovemaking, she understood he wanted her to share his arousal. He was still holding the coin playfully between his fingers, as if trying to hypnotise her.

'Annabelle, we must work,' Andreas said.

She shook herself awake.

'I was thinking how I see myself sometimes as a set of Chinese boxes. I go on opening box after box, here in these sessions and under LSD. I know there is one that I can't open. It's almost as if deep down I can't be reached. I'm afraid of failing you.'

'You mustn't see it like that,' Andreas said. 'See it more as a kernel, a seed that will grow with time. It's always difficult when you're learning and changing. You feel that you're not getting anywhere but you are.'

Annabelle was experiencing that familiar feeling of hopelessness.

'No, I think I'm beyond help.'

She sat very still, very quiet.

'Are you angry with me, Annabelle?'

Annabelle did not answer straightaway but after a while, she kicked off her shoes and tucked her feet on the settee, content to have Andreas's attention.

'I was disappointed with you because you disapproved of me last week when I came here, after I'd been with my friends. I behaved badly, but I expected you to understand, to accept me. *Unconditional positive regard*, as Carl Rogers would say. It's what the therapist should give the patient, *n'est-ce-pas?'*

'I've asked you to stop reading books on psychotherapy. It's best if you don't. You mustn't think too much. It stops you being spontaneous. Anyway, what makes you think I disapproved?' Andreas said.

'You did.'

'Why would I disapprove, Annabelle?'

'Because I came here late, and tipsy.'

'You were unreachable.'

'You resented it. It's called possessiveness. Control. Whatever.'

Andreas sighed. 'There are ethics in my profession. You don't accept people if they come to a session drunk or under the influence of drugs,' he said.

'Oh, but it's all right if they're doped by the medico—as long as the *doctor* has prescribed the drugs, because that means *he* is in control. After all, isn't he God Almighty, all powerful, omnipotent and omniscient? At least, that's his delusion.'

'You were unable to concentrate and that made the session useless. I should have thrown you out.'

'*Thrown me out*? Isn't that rather excessive, doctor?' Annabelle castigated him. 'If you'd done that, I wouldn't have returned,' she bluffed.

'I know. That's why I didn't,' he said.

'I wrote you a letter. It's childish and silly.'

'Do you have it with you?'

Annabelle nodded.

Andreas held out his hand.

'Show me,' he said.

Annabelle opened her bag and pulled out a piece of paper and handed it to him. Andreas took a deep breath.

Dear Doctor,

You make me feel helpless, hopeless and trapped. You patronise me and sexualise me. And you assume too much. You're self-centred and vain. There is no passion in you, only cynicism. You're old. And please don't say, Well, you're angry with me, because it makes me mad! I'm sick to death of this farce, this fantasy and fallacy that you are someone special. You think you are but YOU ARE NOT! You're just like everybody else.

And I thought foolishly you were a hero.

Signed: me.

Andreas folded the piece of paper and put it down on the table beside her.

'What's a hero to you, Annabelle?'

There was a trace of weariness in his voice covering up the hurt he felt.

'A lover of freedom and justice. Someone with passion and imagination who although is afraid, doesn't let fear stop him doing what he wants to do. Not to believe in the improbable is to give up and die.'

Andreas waited, then spoke gently.

'Why are you here, Annabelle?'

'I'm here because of a cerebral curiosity, doctor. That's all.'

'You're certainly very angry. What else makes you angry? Go on, tell me,' he said, trying to be brave.

Annabelle gave him a withering look. They sat in silence, she in her closed defensive position, and Andreas sitting opposite with his hands on the armrests of his seat, inviting her to reveal more of herself.

'You should be angry more often,' Andreas said, encouraging her to talk about her feelings. 'It does you a lot of good.'

Annabelle turned away from him and looked at the sooty clouds forming in the sky.

'I was shot at in New York, on a train, on the way to Washington. I was sitting opposite David and the train was passing through Baltimore. Suddenly the window beside me shattered. Luckily I wasn't hurt, just a few small cuts. The conductor came by. 'Must have been a bullet,' he drawled in his Southern accent. It seems it's quite a common occurrence.' A look of bewilderment came over Annabelle's features. 'What on earth made me tell you such an irrelevant story?'

'Fear, I suspect. Fear at being angry,' Andreas replied. 'You see, nothing is irrelevant. Everything is linked. Everything has a meaning. It is the basis of psychoanalysis. Freud called it *free association.*'

'Did I ever tell you about how I used to go shooting with my father?'

Andreas shifted his body in the big leather armchair settling in comfortably. He shook his head.

'I was probably too ashamed of having been a witness to such a disgusting spectacle. Hunting is very big in Spain. Even their stupid King goes shooting elephants in Africa. My father had a *galgos*, like every hunter. The hunters regularly string up their *galgos* with wire, by the neck, to die slowly and painfully. Punishment for not being a good hunting dog. Or sick or old. Tens of thousands of dogs die this way, each year. It's *tradition!* I stopped getting attached to the dogs, because of what happened to them.'

'Go on, Annabelle.' Andreas's voice was ever so gentle. He noticed her chin was trembling.

'I should have told him to stop but I was afraid of displeasing him. I didn't want him to not take me with him on these walks through the woods. I just wanted to be with him. Often, he would show me how to do it, how to hold the gun, his cheek pressing hard against mine, his body against my back. He had me aim and shoot. I didn't want to do it. I didn't want to kill. But that's what *he* wanted and I always had to do what *he* wanted.'

'You're very upset by that memory,' he said.

'I feel sick. It's abhorrent. I couldn't hurt a creature now. I even hate fishing. I don't eat animals. If you love someone, you trust them and do whatever they want you to do.'

'If you're a child, that is.' Andreas said.

'I have to go,' Annabelle said, rising quickly. The room was closing in on her, it felt like a prison, she was finding it hard to breathe.

'Strange that you began by telling me how you were shot at, and now you tell me about your father. You identify with the animals he killed. I want to prepare another LSD session for you.'

'No.'

'Yes, Annabelle. I must.'

* * *

Doctor Zill soon arranged for Annabelle to have a second LSD session. It would be one of many over a three-year period. He would later tell her how desperate he had been to help her break through her impenetrable defences, and how he had hoped the drug would have brought about the necessary changes.

'I had been counting on that. Indeed, I had longed for a miracle,' Andreas had said.

* * *

Was that the sound of a baby crying in the distance, or was it a crow? Annabelle wondered, as she brushed her hair in front of the mirror.

Annabelle had arrived early at the Bollingen Clinic and went straight to the bathroom to arrange herself. It was a ritual she performed whenever she felt unsure of herself—just as animals preen themselves if frightened or in pain. From the bathroom window, she watched the harbour city sparkle as darkness fell and the lights came on. A loaded ferry carried commuters bravely across the water.

Annabelle found the room she would occupy for the next LSD session and switched on the light. A stark fluorescent blinked crassly into life. Annabelle flinched and tried another switch. This time a reading light came on, so she turned off the fluorescent and sat waiting on the bed, like a bride for her groom, in her Victorian nightdress. It was a favourite item she had found in an antique shop. She had admired the exquisite lace work on the garment. It must have been part of someone's Parisian trousseau. Now, as she played with the lace and ribbons at the neck and wrists, she wondered about the woman who had worn it before her a long time ago.

The sheet beneath her buttocks felt stiff and cold. When she lifted it, Annabelle uncovered a piece of reddish-brown rubber. For the incontinent, she assumed.

It was not a crow. It was an infant and it was still crying in the distance.

Suddenly he appeared. Andreas. The doctor. Followed by the nurse with the syringes and the ampoules.

The nurse switched on the fluorescent light and took care to explain to Andreas before leaving the room that one syringe contained Ritalin and the other Largactil.

Andreas seemed distracted. He asked her to repeat what she had just told him.

'Wouldn't it be comical if you gave me the Largactil first, by mistake,' Annabelle said, when they were alone. 'I'd fall asleep and you could go home to your wife.'

'That's not really what you want is it?'

Andreas cracked open one of the ampoules. He handed it to her as a keepsake after he had drawn out the liquid.

Annabelle twirled the glass shell in her fingers.

'Pure Sandoz, from Switzerland,' she said, reading the lettering on the ampoule. 'Not like the stuff they sell on the street.'

'The best, for you,' Andreas said.

'Thank you. I'm so glad I came to you to acquaint myself with LSD,' she said, giving Andreas a complicit smile.

'I'm glad too.'

Andreas took her slender arm in his hand. The gold bracelet was in the way. Annabelle wore it above the elbow. He slid it up her arm and fastened the strap tightly. Then he injected slowly. It made her whimper and bite her lip.

When he had completed the procedure, Andreas switched off the stark fluorescent and wrapped the towel around the reading light. The room became a golden cocoon.

The drug began its effect. Annabelle's heart beat faster. The muscles in her buttocks contracted and a strange sensation, like an electrical charge, shot through her moving up from the perineum, into the womb, stomach, chest, heart and up to the brain. She had an intense awareness of each cell in her body—could *see* inside as well—it was red, wet and very crowded—like the world was becoming. It too would destruct one day.

The baby was still crying.

'It's crying its heart out,' she tried to tell Andreas. 'Can't you hear it? It's going to die. It can't survive. There, it's quiet now. Everything is silent.'

Annabelle was cautiously curious as she looked inside her mind. She became a baby seal, all furry and white, with soft brown eyes. The hunter came with his nail-studded club and bloodied her. He skinned her alive, robbing her of her white coat, and left her to die on the ice, right there, in front of her mother's helpless gaze. Annabelle the seal, screamed in pain.

Soon Annabelle was weeping real tears, the first in a very long time.

'It hurts to cry,' she said to Andreas, as each sob felt like a blow.

The lace on the gown had torn. It looked like a knife slash, exposing her skin—the bloodied flesh of the seal.

'Why are you crying, Annabelle?' His voice was kind and gentle.

'I'm crying,' she uttered between sobs, 'because I'm frightened of you, Andreas. Because I'm trapped now. Because losing you would be unbearable. I foresee my suffering, and it is immense. I'm going through it all, the agony of loving. What else do you want from me?'

The doctor hurriedly prepared an injection.

'This will take the edge off,' he said, desperate to reassure her and relieve her pain.

But Andreas had trouble finding the vein in the dim light. He tried again, probing with the needle.

She looked at him in horror.

'How can I trust you if you hurt me?' she asked.

He sat back with relief when the drug took effect.

'How are you feeling, Annabelle? Who's there? Is it me or your husband? Or is it your father?' he almost pleaded.

But she could not reassure him or alleviate his torment.

'I'm blindfolded. There's a white veil—a gauze bandage over my eyes.'

'Who blindfolded you? Take the veil away, Annabelle. I'm here with you. You're safe with me. Take the veil away, darling.'

'No, the veil must stay!' Annabelle said, a hostage now of the narrative unfolding in her mind. After a while, she began to nod as if in agreement with an invisible power. 'I see now what I am. Worthless. Underneath the clothes, the siren's hair, lives a *nothing.* I'm on a convict ship. The English are ridding themselves of those misfits, sending them as far away as possible. To the end of the world. I'm below deck in the hold, a stinking cramped place filled with sickness, cruelty, despair. But I'm not even worthy of being a human, not even a desperate criminal or a pox-ridden whore. I'm too unimportant to be one of those wretched creatures. Instead, I'm a bug, a small insignificant bug, on the floor amongst the bile, blood and dysentery.'

There was silence, except for a tick-tock sound. A bomb. No, just a small clock Andreas had brought with him.

'If I am nothing, why is it that I feel so much pain? And why do I weep, Andreas?' Annabelle spoke calmly. She had anchored for a moment.

Andreas reached out to her, took her in his arms and sat her on his lap. He held her, wanting to comfort her.

Suddenly all the pain in Annabelle's world vanished and was replaced with a joyous feeling.

'Oh, Andreas, I want you so much. I ache for you,' she said, stroking him between the thighs, feeling his penis harden. She raised her gown. He caressed her stomach. Annabelle stretched and gurgled like an infant.

'This is ridiculous, absolutely ridiculous, I'm not a child. I'm a woman, Andreas,' she said, then trying to sound serious, added: 'I desire you as a woman!'

'I want you too,' he groaned. 'It's agony for me but I can't break the trust. If I'm to help you, I can't take the bait. I'm exercising incredible self-control. If I broke that trust, you would never be cured.'

'I don't believe you,' Annabelle said, standing up on the bed balancing precariously, alarming him. As he rose to save her, one of her arms swung around and hit him across the face.

Annabelle was more stunned than Andreas. She crumpled slowly, disappearing into the billowing white gown.

'I'm sorry, sorry, sorry,' she cried, hiding her face.

'It's all right, Annabelle. You didn't hurt me.' He lifted her up so that she could see him and be reassured.

'Oh, but you look sad. Please don't be sad, Andreas. Why do you look so sad, Andreas?'

'Because if you love someone, you have to let them go. I have to let you go, Annabelle.'

'No!' she cried. 'Please don't. We were meant for each other.'

He smiled gently, reached up to stroke her cheek burning with love.

'You seem to have come off your trip now, Annabelle. Would you like something to eat?'

'There are some strawberries over there in my bag,' she replied.

Andreas found a napkin wrapped around the strawberries. He undid it carefully, selected one and placed it on her tongue.

'Mmm, it's delicious. And the perfume, I never knew strawberries could smell so good. I want to put one in your mouth too, Andreas.'

Andreas closed his teeth playfully on her fingers and Annabelle squealed with delight.

'How did you know I played this game with my father? You see? You know everything. Your reactions are perfect, your smell is right. I'm fussy. I don't like smells but I love yours—it's clean, it's you. Unique.' She lifted her chin, wanting to inhale his essence deep within her.

Annabelle let out a scream. Andreas jumped out of his chair. She had covered her face with her hands. Andreas meanwhile had noticed that some of the strawberries were crushed into the white damask napkin and had stained it bright red.

He grabbed hold of Annabelle and began shaking her. But she kept screaming: 'No, no, no. It's a secret, I promised.'

'Who did you promise? What is the secret? Who did you make the promise to?'

Annabelle shrank away from him.

'Your voice is ugly,' she said, shaking her head and holding her hands against her ears. 'You sound like a judge. Leave me alone. I won't tell anyone. Never! I'd rather die.' Annabelle made a slicing gesture across her throat. 'I'm going to die and you won't be able to reach me.' She waited for the blood, she imagined, to drip onto her chest.

'I'm dying. All is calm. All is peace. All is white. Silent night. I'm a nun. A white witch. A bitch. A destroyer. I can destroy you. I know. You know it too. Are you afraid of me? Please don't be. I'm holy. I'm pure. Pure as a nun. I'm a nun like Héloise. Huh!' She turned around calmly and asked: 'Why do I feel like Héloise, Andreas?'

And he answered: 'Because Abelard was castrated.'

* * *

Andreas focused his attention on the disconsolate figure in front of him. He realised something he had not seen before. It intrigued him. He no longer saw her as the seductress she pretended to be.

'You're frightened of sex, aren't you, Annabelle?'

She began to weep softly.

'Why are you frightened?' he asked.

Annabelle remained silent, choking back the words that longed to escape.

Andreas thought of the words of an analyst he admired: *The greater the love, the deeper the secret, and the less chance or risk of it ever surfacing to the conscious level. And so many a loved one is protected.*

'You must have loved him very much,' he said. There was a yearning in his voice but she did not hear it.

'Yes, oh yes. And he loved *me*. So much love, I've never seen so much love. He wanted me to die for him.'

'You've never loved anyone else, including your husband? What are your feelings towards me?'

Annabelle did not answer. She kept her eyes fixed on the picture of wild horses on the wall, avoiding him. She could sense his despair but she could not reassure him.

Andreas in turn, was shattered by her new remoteness, her unavailability.

'Don't you love anyone?' he asked, his voice breaking. He waited but no answer came. Andreas dropped his head in his hands. 'I'm spent,' he said. 'It's getting late. I'd better give you some Largactil, then you can sleep.'

'Please don't go,' Annabelle suddenly implored him.

'I'm tired. Tired and broken,' he murmured half to himself.

'Please stay. I'd love you to stay.'

Annabelle had anchored again and was being attentive, looking at Andreas with adoration.

'Why?' he asked, confronting her with a look that seared her in its intensity. 'I'm an ageing, overweight failure with few illusions about myself.'

'You're wrong. I think you're beautiful!' she cried.

'Heigh ho. Yes. We're beautiful people in ugly bodies who are destroyed by the things we love.'

Annabelle was powerless, unable to say what he wanted to hear. She had often assumed the role of seductress, but it had been play acting. Now, wanting desperately to be real, she found herself failing badly and was overcome with a deep sorrow. Tears filled her eyes again. 'Oh, Andreas, if only you knew how I feel about you. You are my *god*,' she blurted.

Andreas's countenance changed at once. He felt elated, alive. He was young again. He had longed to hear those words from Annabelle. It was a dream.

'Oh, but I do. I do, my darling,' he said.

'You do?' she asked, looking bewildered.

'I accept your feelings, for me!'

Annabelle was surprised.

Andreas reached out and clasped her face in his hands, pushing back the damp hair from her brow.

'You're brave, Annabelle. You've worked hard tonight.'

Annabelle smiled sweetly at him and he was overcome with such tenderness that he kissed her fully on the mouth. She gasped, breathless and incredulous at what he had done. At last, all her repressed feelings were released and she began to respond to his embrace, which seemed endless and magnificent.

He pulled her down into his lap again and she touched his face tenderly.

'Darling Andreas,' she whispered holding on to him, luxuriating in the rich emotions flooding them both. It was as if someone had thrown a magic web over them, uniting and protecting them—a web spun from gold, with diamonds and pearls woven into the threads. Annabelle was lost in the sweeping romance of a film kiss, tempered by the remains of the drug in her system.

Andreas released her slowly with a long sigh.

'Please stay. Please stay the night,' Annabelle said.

Andreas struggled with his tiredness. It had been an exhausting week. There were problems at home.

'I'll be back in the morning. Let me tuck you into bed. I won't give you any more injections, you seem to be coming off your trip. Get in under the blankets,' he coaxed gently.

Annabelle reached up and put her arms around his neck, kissing him. He held her long in the embrace not wanting to separate from her.

'Sweet dreams, my love,' he said, as he finally released her.

He picked up his coat and swung it over his shoulder, like the young man he had become.

When he reached the door, Annabelle tried to engage him a moment longer.

'I'll never forget you,' she whispered.

Andreas paused with his hand on the doorknob and blew her a kiss.

'Whatever your name is,' she added.

⋆ ⋆ ⋆

Not long after Andreas left Annabelle, a nurse in an orange pantsuit came into the room. She looked at Annabelle with curiosity.

'Doctor told me that your bedclothes are damp,' she said.

'I sweated a lot.'

'I'll make the bed for you with clean sheets if you'd like to sit in the chair while I make it. I'm Beryl, by the way. I'll get you a cup of tea in a minute.'

'Thank you. I'm Annabelle.'

'What are you here for?' Beryl asked.

'I took LSD.'

Beryl nodded.

'We had someone here last week who overdosed on heroin.'

'I'm not here because I took LSD. I wanted to try it,' Annabelle attempted to explain.

'Excuse me, someone's calling,' the nurse said, as she left the room.

Annabelle caught a glimpse of herself in a mirror behind the door. She approached carefully, peering at the image. It was a strange effect, as if the eyes, mouth, nose and ears had been thrown into a pool. Everything kept moving around, floating away, then coming together again, refusing to belong to her.

At last, the fragments settled and she became whole again. It left her with a new insight into appearances—how beauty or plainness were just like the skin on a nut— impermanent, fragile, dispensable and ultimately did not affect the substance or nutrition of the nut.

Soon, the nurse returned, carrying a tray on which sat a bright yellow cake topped with three inches of pink frosting. She advanced with the plate towards Annabelle, who was staring in astonishment at the psychedelic cake.

'Lucky, aren't you?' said the nurse.

'I don't think I'm hungry.'

'Why don't you enjoy it? Some people have all the luck.' She had a tattooed heart on her arm with *Sandy* written on a banner above it. 'I wish I had some of that stuff. Wonder if there's any left,' she said, picking up the empty ampoules and sucking hard. 'Do you want anything else? My boyfriend's waiting for me. Got a Kawasaki and we're going for a spin along the Esplanade. Will that be all now?'

Annabelle nodded.

As the nurse was leaving the room, she turned to Annabelle and said with a knowing wink: 'Don't you worry. The doctor will soon be with you.'

13 Seduction

Annabelle imagined Andreas waking, just as she had a moment before, with the first rays of the sun nudging against her bed at the Bollingen Clinic. Perhaps he lay in for a while and thought of her, too. Did his wife sleep beside him and would she want Andreas to make love to her? How would he feel about his wife after last night? Would he oblige yet think of Annabelle instead? Now that he had kissed her it was as though they were lovers. Again she wondered what it would be like to make love with Andreas. A knock on the door interrupted her thoughts.

'Come in,' she said, sitting up.

'I'm Tina. Did you sleep well? Would you like some breakfast?'

'Tea and fruit, please,' Annabelle said, sinking back on the pillows.

'By the way, Doctor Zill rang to say he'll be late.'

The very mention of Andreas's name made her feel euphoric. At the same time, she had the familiar sinking sensation of being let down, then abandoned. He probably regretted what had happened last night. She was not going to see him again, he was stalling, trying to find someone to replace him. Annabelle curled up, shrinking into herself, pulling the bedclothes over her head—and nearly missed hearing the knock on the door.

'Hello,' Andreas said.

There was a look of concern on his face.

Annabelle froze holding the sheet in her clenched fists.

'I didn't think I'd see you again,' she managed to tell him.

She stared at him. She had never seen him in a Hawaiian shirt before, was not prepared for hairs on bare arms.

'You must not think like that, Annabelle,' Andreas said, taking her hand into his. 'Are you glad to see me?'

'Very much,' she nodded, to give conviction to her words.

'I'm sorry I'm late. I had some errands to do for my wife. She gave me a list. Look, here it is, *Return library books, go to butcher and supermarket etc. etc. etc.* I wanted very much to be with you but she has every minute of my life organised I'm afraid. I never realised it until now,' he said, looking into her eyes, losing himself in their depth. After a while he said: 'Would you like to come to my room?' His voice was soft and engaging.

Annabelle nodded again.

'I'll make you some chrysanthemum tea. Do you have anything to wear over your nightdress?'

'The white kimono.'

'Good. Come with me, Annabelle.'

* * *

Her bare feet barely carried her over the carpeted floor as they walked from one wing of the building to the other. Annabelle was flying.

Being Saturday morning, most of the doctors were away playing golf. It was very quiet at the clinic. As she hurried behind Andreas, Annabelle suddenly caught sight of a black shape on the wall—two moths, like two black hands stuck together, end to end, their fat cylindrical bodies pulsating.

Annabelle gave a little cry as she stumbled on the hem of her gown and nearly fell. Andreas turned around and grasped her arm.

'Is your husband calling for you,' he asked, unlocking the door to his surgery.

'He's busy, at a conference. I'll get a taxi.'

'Sit down, relax. I'll make tea.'

'I'll help you.'

'You're my guest, Annabelle.'

Andreas brought out two porcelain cups with a red and gold dragon design. The teapot was nesting in a silk-padded cane basket with a tiny brass lock.

'That's so pretty,' she said, admiring the basket. Annabelle tilted her head to one side and looked up at him. 'But tell me doctor, do you often entertain women in their nighties in your consulting room?'

'I don't. This is unusual. Very unusual. But then, you're a most unusual person.' He stopped what he was doing for a moment and stared hard at Annabelle. 'The truth is, I haven't been able to get you out of my mind since we first met.' He shook his head a few times, uncomprehending.

'We were destined to meet. Everything else was mere camouflage. Including all those sessions about my childhood,' Annabelle said, in a playful, half serious manner.

Andreas sat down and fixed his expression on her. Annabelle tried to deflect his attention by letting her eyes wander to the antics of the lorikeets in the trees outside. But she could feel him pulling her back.

Finally Annabelle turned her head and met his look. 'What drew you to me when you first saw me?'

'Your eyes, they reminded me of a startled fawn,' Andreas said.

'Are you a hunter?'

'No, Annabelle. I don't kill animals.'

'I'm glad,' she replied. 'I could never love a man who killed animals.'

'You loved your father.'

'I was a child then. I had no choice.'

Andreas's gaze intensified.

'Every time I look at you, Annabelle, I'm overwhelmed. I don't know what to do.'

'I feel the same way, Andreas.'

Andreas rose and moved towards Annabelle. He bent down and kissed her upturned face. Then he lifted her and drew her close, taking her into his arms. He kissed her with all the desire he had suppressed ever since they met, yet his kiss was soft, tender and luxurious. She had never been kissed like this before, never felt herself dissolve so completely into another being.

Soon Annabelle was responding to his embrace. Andreas slipped the kimono off her shoulders and it fell to the floor. Tentatively, he lifted the nightgown over her head and stepped back, a strange sound escaped from his throat.

'My god, you're beautiful,' he gasped.

Andreas placed Annabelle's naked body on the settee and lay on top of her. His kisses and caresses continued.

Annabelle was in a daze about what was happening to her. She had longed for Andreas, and now that he was about to make love to her, felt totally disconcerted.

Andreas made a movement to enter inside her, but he ejaculated prematurely. The loss of his erection caused him terrible anguish. He groaned, mortified, seeking comfort against her cool skin.

At that moment, Annabelle wrapped her arms around him and murmured loving words to reassure him. She began to feel her power, the power to disarm such a man. The man of charm, position and authority had become something soft and harmless in her hands.

* * *

Soon after, they made love again—and it was very different. A miracle. A transformation. Annabelle had worked her magic with Andreas, soothing, cajoling, encouraging, until as they lay in each others' arms, he began to stiffen again.

Andreas was not going to rush it. Forget *time*, the unwelcome guest.

He had placed the blanket on the carpeted floor so they could lie together more comfortably, kissing, touching, wondering at the sensations that arose from those secret parts of themselves.

Andreas took hold of Annabelle's legs and spread them apart. He kissed and caressed the softest part of her thighs then gently opened her up. He held his breath, marvelling at what he was about to possess.

A shiver ran through Annabelle's body.

'What are you doing to me, Andreas?' she gasped.

'Like petals of silk,' Andreas murmured in her ear, as his fingers found the silky moistness and opened her up further. She undulated, moaned and called his name. He waited and watched the emotions he elicited cross her face. He wanted to watch her face forever, he said.

When Annabelle had settled, Andreas carefully positioned his erect penis so he could penetrate her. He paused and waited for her surrender, then thrust past the point of resistance.

His confidence restored, he journeyed deeper into her being with each stroke, completely bathed in the sensation of being with her.

'Andreas,' she cried out his name, again and again. Annabelle was succumbing, and surrendering to the terrifying and immensely pleasurable sensation of being swept up in his passion.

* * *

His mood was dark as he began to put his clothes back on and thought of the rest of his life and what awaited him. Andreas pulled Annabelle gently to her feet and helped her dress.

'Come, my love. I have to leave now.'

'Oh, no!' she cried. 'Please, not yet!'

Andreas held her tightly in his embrace.

14 The Taboo is Broken

It had been three days since the incredible and improbable had happened. Andreas had pierced Annabelle's defences. The memory of his kisses and his lovemaking had left her tossing and turning in bed like a ship of peril in an advancing storm.

She had not slept for three nights but was not the least bit tired when she shimmered into the clinic, a rapturous and radiant young woman, eager and excited about each moment that lay ahead. She could hardly wait to see her lover.

Annabelle was wearing a velvet maxi coat with gathered sleeves and a fitted waist. Four buttons kept the top part of her body covered. When she moved, the coat swung open to reveal a mini chartreuse silk and lace slip. She wore gloves and black knee-length boots with high heels.

The door was closed when she arrived. Andreas still had a patient with him. Annabelle sat between the office and the waiting room which was being painted, and tried not to breathe in the fumes. Or listen to the chatter from the office which was unsettling her.

'All his women patients are in love with him,' Shirley was talking on the telephone. 'They're always finding excuses to ring him. Sometimes they hang around here waiting to catch a glimpse of the doctor. They say all patients fall in love with their obstetricians, too. I suppose it's the power. He's a terrible flirt,' Shirley continued. 'Oh, here he comes with Frida, I'd better hang up.'

Annabelle turned around to see the woman accompanying Andreas. She thought she had seen her before in the grounds of the Bollingen with a number of children running amok in the flower beds. A breeder—the Earth Mother type.

All her fears drifted away when she saw Andreas, and she forgot about Frida, and all the other women supposedly in love with him. Annabelle followed Andreas to his room. As soon as he closed the door he took her in his arms, kissed her and held her, rocking her gently to and fro.

'I can't tell you how happy you've made me my darling. I haven't stopped thinking about you, wherever I am, whatever I'm doing. It's madness, absolute madness. I've made love to you a hundred times.'

Finally Andreas released Annabelle from his embrace.

'I think we should do some work,' he said.

'Can't we make love, again?' she said.

'When Jess and Shirley go home. We must work, though. Any thoughts, Annabelle?'

'Why did you tell me that I did not value myself?'

'Because you don't. People see you as a beautiful body they want to make love to, but you want them to love you for yourself and you don't believe you can be loved. It's like the rich who think people are after their money. They constantly want proof they're being loved for themselves. Sometimes they try to hide their money, pretend they're poor. Are you all right?'

'I'm getting a migraine,' Annabelle said, shading her eyes from the light. 'It must be the paint fumes.'

Andreas looked concerned.

'Who are you angry with?'

'I'm not angry. I'm happy. Look at me. Do you remember how I would sometimes sit here and not say a word? And now look at me,' she said, trying to sound cheerful.

'Bubbly, like champagne.'

'What a sappy description,' she said.

'I'm sorry,' Andreas said, stung by her remark.

'Don't be. You have a right to be yourself. Why do you shake your head like that?' Annabelle asked.

'Because you remind me of my sister.'

'What's she like?'

'A bitch. But she has lots of style.'

'Why is she a bitch?'

'She's cruel. She finds my wife, Jean, a bore. Intellectually inferior.

My sister is married to a peer. Whenever Jean has visited her in London she hasn't felt very welcome. Jean comes from working-class roots. The class system is a curse.'

'Appalling,' Annabelle agreed.

'After my father finished his work for the League of Nations in Geneva, he was invited to England, by the Socialists. He was full of ideals. Sadly my Russian mother did not hold the same views as him. She had a terrible temper, always fighting with my poor father.'

'Who took care of you, Andreas, when they were fighting?'

'I did. I had a nanny,' he paused briefly, his features clouding over as he remembered. 'I had a governess, too,' he said quickly. 'But I was never very little or helpless,' he added with false pride.

'Young children aren't capable of taking care of themselves,' Annabelle reminded him. 'They need to be looked after. Loved.'

'I was very self-sufficient. If things got really bad, I'd take myself off to the roof in order to get some peace,' he said.

'Like Jung and his tower. So this is your rooftop.'

Andreas looked at her. His face broke out in a boyish grin. 'Sometimes you stun me,' he said. 'I realise now that all my life I had been waiting for you. Someone who understood me, just like you do.'

'Sometimes you puzzle me, Andreas. Are you manipulative, crazy, bad—or wise and brilliant? Perhaps you are all these things.'

Andreas nodded. 'We are all shattered beings. Each one of us, made up of a million different moments. We spend our lives searching for that time when we were whole, before we became fragmented.'

Annabelle knelt before him and put her arms around his waist, laying her face in his lap. His smell was warm and familiar. Andreas stroked her hair. He lifted her chin and looked at her. Annabelle saw a great deal of anguish in his eyes.

'What has made you so melancholy? Don't be afraid of me, Andreas. We are exiles together, birds of passage. I have always known you and always will. You said true love never dies, that it can be felt forever. We'll always be together even when we're apart.'

'My darling,' Andreas said, kissing her lips, lifting her up to his lap and seeking her breast.

'I'd like to switch roles now,' she said, gently pushing him away. 'I want to take care of you. Be your doctor.'

He laughed. 'You're so adorable.'

Annabelle moved across to the leather armchair.

'Tell me,' she said.

He looked at her, a smile on his face, accepting the reversal of roles.

'Tell me about yourself, Andreas.' Her voice was soft and encouraging.

Annabelle was prepared to walk beside him as his thoughts drifted to another time, another place. Andreas described a room in a grand hotel in Switzerland with plush sage-green carpet, silk taffeta curtains bunched to the floor, mirrors, marble, and sheets of crisp waffled cotton in the bathroom. The late-afternoon sun filled every space with its golden dust and carried in its warmth the perfume of tuberoses. A pale climbing rose spilt bountiful blooms over one side of the balcony.

'I was seven,' he said.

Annabelle saw the boy standing in front of the open French window, looking beyond, to the lake that reflected the sad blue-grey of his eyes. Further still, to a time when he had paddled his boat bravely, waving, searching for an instant of recognition, for someone to witness his existence. But the adults at the edge of the lake had been preoccupied with their own games, with their little seductions and their grand dissatisfactions.

Andreas described his mother's voice, drifting towards him—a lifeline out there on the lake. The others were busy with the wine and the food spread out on white damask cloth on the grass. He could see his father lying on the Persian rug in one of his melancholy moods, looking out over the water. He waved and called: 'Pappa! Pappa!' But his father did not notice.

* * *

'Annabelle, my darling, what are we going to do? I miss you so terribly and want to spend more time with you.'

He reached out, pulling her gently towards him, sweeping her long hair aside, kissing her neck, seeking her breast, hungry to possess her.

'It's so difficult being apart, Andreas,' she said, caressing his forehead. 'I ache, *burn* for you. I think about you every moment. I lie in bed in the morning trying to imagine you waking up. I follow you getting ready, showering, dressing, eating your breakfast.'

'I do all those chores, feed the dog, wash and medicate my son, get breakfast. Drive my daughter to school.'

'Do you think of me before you get up? Long for me? Make love to me in your fantasies? Do you masturbate?'

'No.'

'Why not?'

'I keep myself for when I see you.'

'I'm disappointed. I had this vision of you wanting me, calling out my name as you came. The Taoists don't ejaculate. They can have orgasm without ejaculation. There's a book I've heard about, *The Tao of Sexology.* I'll get it for you,' Annabelle said.

'I have so many dreams, my love. My dreams keep me alive.'

'Tell me about them.'

'Tell me about yours,' he said, resuming his doctor's role. 'What do you dream about, Annabelle?'

'I dream about making love with you.'

'All the time?' he asked.

Annabelle nodded.

Andreas looked enthralled.

'Aren't I shocking?' she said. 'Me, the frigid one. Until I found you.'

'What else?'

'I dream about being free and fearless, like a dolphin. And about saving the world because we're here on this planet and it's important we do something worthwhile. But I don't know yet how I can help.'

'Would you like a drink? I got a bottle of vodka especially for you.'

'Oh yes,' Annabelle said. She loved the idea of having a glass of vodka with Andreas. It would relax their inhibitions. Something was holding them back, but they did not know what it was.

Andreas stood in front of Annabelle, offering her a glass. When she reached for it, he playfully placed it down on the table out of her way, and tried to kiss her. But she eluded him. He tried to kiss her again, succeeding, leaving her breathless. Andreas held her face in his hands, studying it carefully, looking into her adoringly. Annabelle tried to pull away from his scrutiny.

'You're really quite shy,' Andreas said.

'It's my convent upbringing. I wanted to be a nun.'

'What a waste that would have been.' He emptied his glass. 'Come here, Annabelle,' he whispered to her.

He caressed her breast. Then his hand moved under her skirt, playing, probing—making her shudder.

'Oh, Andreas,' she sighed, gazing into his eyes, marvelling at what was happening.

'You're trembling,' he said. 'What do you see in me?'

Annabelle searched for words to express the love she felt for Andreas and realised how difficult that was. Erotic love too, was a foreign realm for Annabelle. Until they met.

'Let me count the ways …', she said, hoping not to make a fool of herself. 'You're beautiful, gentle, perceptive, sensitive, acutely intelligent and educated. You're from another world, another time, another sphere. You fill me with the most ravishing sensations. And you held my hand during my amazing journey with LSD. And more, there is much more I cannot express.'

'You're crazy, my love,' he whispered in her ear, as he began to undress her. 'My god, the last two days have been hell. I've wanted you so much.' He, too, was shaking with desire.

'Andreas, Andreas, Andreas,' she cried, as he pulled her skirt up, removed her underwear and spread her legs, lifting her up so that she straddled with one foot on each of the two arm-chairs. He touched her with his beautiful long fingers, caressing, delving, exploring, keeping her in a state of exquisite, painful tension. When she was weak and wet and could not stand up any longer, he lifted her and held her, kissing her lips, her neck, her breasts. Annabelle wrapped her legs and arms around him, and he carried her across the room and laid her down on his leather clad desk. He caressed the soft small curve of her belly, parted her legs and pleasured her with his tongue. Then holding her waist with both hands, he took her with long, slow carnal thrusts.

15 The Love Hotel

In 1977, four Palestinian terrorists hijacked a Lufthansa airliner and demanded the release of 11 members of the German terrorist group, Baader-Meinhof (also known as the Red Army) from prison.

Roman Polanski was arrested and charged with a number of offences and faced life imprisonment. The offences included: rape by use of drugs, perversion, sodomy, lewd and lascivious behaviour upon a child.

In France, they executed the last person by guillotine.

And in New York the Trade Centre was completed.

None of these events captured Annabelle's imagination for long. She was completely in the thrall of her affair with Andreas.

Annabelle's heart beat recklessly as she ran up the escalator of the Regent Hotel. She was late having had to wait for her husband to leave home before she could dress for her secret assignation.

Her lover was standing in the middle of the foyer looking somewhat lost. Annabelle hesitated for a moment, holding her breath—looking at a part of the dream which was coming true. They would be together for a whole day, locked in a glass tower, in the centre of a throbbing city and no one would be able to reach them.

She touched Andreas gently on the sleeve. He flinched.

'Have you registered?' she asked.

'No, I was waiting for you.'

'You thought I might not come?'

'The thought did occur.'

'My darling,' Annabelle said, her heart bursting with love for Andreas and his insecurities.

'I'm slightly nervous,' Andreas said.

'I can see that,' she laughed, squeezing his arm. 'Would you like me to register for you? Except the house detective might think I'm a call girl picking up a rich client and might demand a cut of my earnings.

Could be rather exciting!'

'No, wait.' Andreas held her arm pulling her back. 'I'll do it.'

'You're nervous about something people do all the time. I booked the room in the name of Kennedy, as you asked, although you don't look remotely Irish to me. I think you'll have to find a more convincing alias next time.'

Annabelle stayed close to Andreas at reception lending him support.

A young woman in a plum hotel uniform smiled enigmatically at the attractive man who seemed to be suffering from anxiety.

'Do you have a reservation, sir?'

'Yes.'

'Under what name please?' she asked.

Andreas hesitated in the grip of confusion. 'Kennedy!' he said.

'How long will you be staying with us, Mr Kennedy?'

'Until tonight.'

'One more thing, sir. Could I please see your licence?'

'I'm afraid I haven't got it on me.'

'That's all right,' she smiled. 'Here's your key, your room's on the thirteenth floor. Have a nice day.'

* * *

'My heart's pounding,' Andreas whispered in Annabelle's ear, trying to suppress the mounting excitement he was feeling.

'I know,' Annabelle said. 'I can hear it. Everybody can,' she teased him.

'Does it really show?'

'It's written all over your face what you're about to do. You wicked man.'

'Good. I'm beginning to enjoy this,' Andreas said, with a new defiance.

They entered the lift with a group of businessmen attending a life coaching seminar with an American guru famous for his fire-walking sessions. The men pressed the button marked *Rooftop.*

'You look smug,' she whispered with complicity, 'like the cat who swallowed the cream.'

Andreas arched his brows, giving Annabelle a mischievous look.

She, rolled her eyes heavenwards.

* * *

'Should we have a *do not disturb* sign on the door?' Andreas asked.

'Absolutely!' Annabelle said. Then she gasped and pointed.

'What is it?'

'A bed! A real bed. At last!' Annabelle threw herself upon it.

'No more skinned elbows or carpet burns,' Andreas added.

He lunged playfully after her but she rolled out of his reach.

'I'm a slippery eel,' she taunted.

'More of an agile pussycat,' Andreas said. 'Come here, Annabelle, darling.'

'No.'

'Why not?' he asked, a perplexed look crossing his face.

'I don't feel like it,' Annabelle said, moving towards the window to look out at the view.

'I see.'

Andreas looked concerned for a moment. Then he brightened up.

'We're going to play games, are we?'

'No. It's just that it feels strange here. I'm used to your room. Anyway, we usually drink vodka before making love.'

'Would you like me to call room service?'

'I don't drink at ten o'clock in the morning. Only alcoholics do that.'

Annabelle was being contradictory. It troubled Andreas. He wondered whether it was a mistake to have brought Annabelle to the hotel.

'Would you like some music? I brought my cassette player,' he said.

'What have you got?' Annabelle peered into his bag.

'John Williams.'

'No,' she said, with a dismissive hand gesture. 'I'd hoped you'd brought Russian music. Music makes me sad, anyway. I can feel the pain of the composer.' Annabelle turned her back on Andreas and looked down at the world below. 'All those poor people, working at jobs they don't like.

It makes me feel guilty when I think of them. Do most people suffer from guilt?'

'Most people don't think like that,' Andreas said.

'I'm just a depressive,' she said. 'Or maybe other people just can't face it because it's too awful.'

'Perhaps you envy them for being happy.'

'I can't believe they're happy,' Annabelle said, looking intently at the people in the street in their sombre clothing. She was trying to gauge their mood by their pace, the tilt of their head, the position of their shoulders.

'Sure they are,' Andreas said, approaching Annabelle. 'I saw a cheery sort-of-person just now on my way in. A clown, playing the flute, brightening up the morning for the office workers.'

'You really think the clown is happy?'

'Of course. Happier than you are my dear at the moment.'

'All clowns are tragic,' Annabelle said, her eyes wistfully searching for the splash of colour among the grey asphalt down below.

'The sadness comes from you, my darling. It's what you project onto the world.' Andreas sighed. 'I wish I could take your pain away.'

He was standing behind her at the window. Andreas placed his hands on Annabelle's shoulders and spoke tenderly to her. 'Why don't we undress and get into bed? We don't have to make love. I'll just hold you in my arms.' He turned her around, lifted her chin so that she could look into his eyes.

All her protests were a fearful reaction to the depth of feeling he could arouse in her. Andreas succeeded in awakening not only Annabelle's erotic fascination but also her curiosity about what lay beneath the surface, the dark side.

'I'm sorry. I feel rather foolish,' she said.

'You seem to regress, playing games to hide your fear. Sometimes you sound like a child who doesn't want to be interfered with.'

'Don't try to analyse me, please!' Annabelle commanded Andreas with a stern look. 'And I'd like you to leave my father out of the picture from now on. I'd like you to stop hiding behind him.' Her expression softened. 'Let's just be two people, a man and a woman who love each other.' On impulse, Annabelle gave Andreas an affectionate kiss on the cheek. Andreas pulled her towards him and kissed her, his mouth lingering on her lips until he felt her weaken and succumb to his embrace.

He picked her up and carried her to bed where he slowly began to undress her. She slipped under the sheets and waited for him to join her.

'Have I told you how I dreamed of you after the first night we met? Every night, for three months, I thought of you and waited for you to appear at the Clinic.' Andreas said, taking her in his arms.

'Were you certain I would come?' Annabelle asked, thinking back to the moment when she had first walked into his room and seen the expression of unadulterated delight on his face.

'I wanted you so much—I probably made it happen. All that wishing,' Andreas said.

'I don't think we have much say. The Buddhists believe people come into our lives for a reason. To teach us something we need to know. What can you teach me Andreas? What can I teach you?'

'We'll find out in time, I guess,' he said, sounding grave, clasping her to himself, as if to protect her from harm.

'What did you dream about me? Did you lust after my body?'

Annabelle wanted to provoke Andreas into further admissions.

'Yes, and that,' he said.

'What did you do to my body?' Annabelle said, slowly caressing him.

'Explored you with my mind,' Andreas said, trying to hold himself back, taking Annabelle's hand away from where it was heading and kissing it.

'Is that all?' Annabelle pretended to be disappointed.

'Kissed you, a thousand times, felt you, touched you, made love to you, a thousand times more,' replied Andreas.

'Oh,' she moaned. 'I'm starting to feel sexy, Andreas.'

'Sucked you,' he said, pleased to incite a reaction.

'Sucked my cunt,' she said putting a finger in his mouth.

'Yes, your sweet cunt juices,' he gave her a gentle bite.

'Vampire!'

'We are all vampires hungry for blood, or love, my darling.'

'You can't have my blood, but you can have my juices,' Annabelle said.

'I want all of you. Everything!' Andreas said, throwing off the sheet. 'And I want you to come, Annabelle. I want you to orgasm when we fuck. Time and time again.'

Annabelle gave a little wail of protest.

'Why? You know I can't. Isn't it enough how you make me feel? I swoon when you touch me, Andreas. I love everything you do. You are so gentle, so loving, so enthralling. You never hurt me no matter what you do to me. It's as if your love protects me, speaks to me, shields me from pain. Not like the others—big, brutish and hard. I hate that. It's rape! But the way you…'

'I know I'm not exactly what you'd call well-endowed,' he interrupted.

'Oh, my darling, you're wonderful! We're perfect for each other—a perfect fit. The way you make love to me, how you touch me, is pure love. I've never been touched like that before. It's astonishing. But I can try to climax if you really want me to with my hand.'

Above all Annabelle wanted to show Andreas how much she loved him, even if she was not capable of yielding completely to his demands. She was so thorough with her caresses and her kisses, playing with him, sucking him, arousing him, that she hoped he would forgive her other failings. She raised herself and straddled on top of him, intending to pleasure him. But he could not resist taking hold of her and lifting her on the tip of his erection, with the now familiar pause before penetration, waiting for her surrender, then thrusting the whole of his sex into her. It always made her cry out, fear or surprise, even though she expected it. He held her buttocks, moving her hips around his cock.

'Come, Annabelle, come, darling.'

'Please don't,' she protested. 'I can only do it with my hand. There,' she said, touching herself, pressing and moving her hand in a circular motion until they both cried out and Annabelle's body folded over his in an exquisite faint. They remained connected, inseparable, until the light outside began to fade.

* * *

Andreas and Annabelle woke up from their sleep with caution. They marvelled at the hours they had lived through. How long had it lasted that faint? The delicious death?

As Annabelle withdrew her cheek from the hollow at the base of his throat, Andreas's arms unravelled from around her body and their bellies parted like two halves of a shell. The eyes were the last to relinquish the lovers' regard.

After bathing and dressing, they found their way to the restaurant because they were hungry. The waiter showed them to a secluded booth and they sat in silence. Only their eyes spoke of where they had been and of what they had done.

Later, they walked arm in arm through the city, careless, like intoxicated lovers. How could anyone deny them their happiness?

When they wandered into a cinema where a soft-porn European film was showing, they did not stay. The love-making on the screen was crude and remote from what they had experienced.

Andreas hailed a taxi and, as Annabelle kissed him and clung to his neck, he whispered the words she wanted to hear: 'Today was the most beautiful day of my life.'

16 A Grand Mal

Annabelle handed Andreas a piece of paper. She had just arrived for her session and he could not quite analyse her mood. Andreas began to read what Annabelle had written and gave a sigh of relief—he had somehow imagined it would be an attack. One could never tell with Annabelle—she could be contradictory, unpredictable. He read the note again, savouring what she had written:

As you kissed my lips and your hand rested on my breast, you took me to the very source of my pleasure. I experienced ecstasy pure and intense. With every touch, you overwhelmed me and filled me with the most astonishing feelings. I tried to tell you this and you said to me: Have you ever thought what you've given me? And I answered: No, I can't see me, I think I'm made of air. But touch me again, this time I'll know I'm real.

'My love,' Andreas said, crossing over to her. 'My love,' he murmured again.

Annabelle took a deep breath, filling her lungs with his presence, nestling into his body. Andreas sat down in the armchair, cradling her in his lap. She took his hand and guided it beneath the folds of her skirt.

They sat together for a long time in the shadowy twilight, listening to the song of a bird before it settled down to roost. A distant clatter of dishes and pans came from the kitchen below, where the evening meal for the residents of the Bollingen Clinic was being prepared.

A loud knock at the door interrupted their reverie. Annabelle quickly moved away from Andreas, landing on the settee, where she hastily composed herself.

Andreas brushed his hair back and switched on the lights. He opened the door. It was Jean, his wife. She had decided to come to collect him.

He tried to block her view of the room, of Annabelle, with his frame but Jean was suspicious. She craned her neck, peering around, trying to see who was with Andreas. Andreas knew his wife did not trust him. Jean feared someone would steal him from her just as she had taken him away from his first wife and children. She stood on her toes and finally managed to catch a glimpse of Annabelle.

'I'm not ready yet,' Andreas told her. 'I've got a patient. You don't have to call for me. I'll walk home.'

'I'll come back for you in half an hour,' she insisted.

He closed the door and grimaced like someone expecting a punishment.

'She's on the warpath. I don't think she believes I was at the meeting on Friday. Neither does Shirley. Apparently they tried to contact me at the hospital and couldn't find me.'

'Friday cost you a lot of money in cancelled patients, hotel, dinner, parking, etc.'

'It was worth it, Annabelle,'

'At that cost, I don't suppose you can afford to do it very often,' she said.

'My accountant tells me that I have to cut down even more. I'm practically bankrupt. Also, Jean wants my daughter to go to a finishing school in Switzerland. All madness.'

'How on earth does someone who earns as much as you do get himself in such a financial mess?'

'I don't know. I have a thing about money, as if I don't deserve it. Some kind of guilt.' He waved the subject off, wanting to change the conversation. 'We don't have much time and you haven't done any work. We need to work, Annabelle.'

Annabelle sighed. It was all too disheartening—but she would do her best to please Andreas.

'I tried to find out why I become so scared when my husband gets angry with me. I think it's because I'm reminded of my fear as a child when my father was angry and threatened to leave us. That would have been a catastrophe—I would have been stranded with my mother.'

Andreas nodded.

'Good, Annabelle.'

‘Thank you, doctor.’ Annabelle fell silent for a while. Then she looked up at him. She had something to tell him. ‘I’ve got a problem, doctor,’ she said with a wan smile.

‘Tell me.’ Andreas shoulders stiffened. His face showed concern.

‘David wants me to have a child,’ she said. Her look was beseeching. She was hoping he could help her with her predicament.

‘Don’t! You’re not ready.’

Annabelle sighed with relief. She could now tell David what the doctor had told her.

‘Thank you,’ she said. ‘I don’t feel capable of mothering a child. At least not yet.’

Andreas walked over to Annabelle and sat beside her on the settee. He raised her hand to his lips. He glimpsed the love in her eyes which mirrored his.

‘I must go now. Jean will be waiting for me. If she saw you again, she would find you very confronting and become even more suspicious, making things very difficult. She’s despondent about our son. We had a stressful weekend, he had an epileptic fit, a *grand mal* and we had to call the ambulance. It was all very distressing, especially for my daughter, growing up in an atmosphere of sickness at her age when she should be having some fun, it’s no place for a teenager our home.’ Andreas covered his eyes with his hands brushing away tears.

‘You’re so brave. Most men would have crumpled under the weight of your problems. Yet you’re still capable of smiling and loving.’

‘We must roll with the punches, my love. Every event, every situation in which you may find yourself has a positive value, even the drama, even the tragedies, even the thunderbolt from a calm sky ... or something,’ he said, waving his hand in the air. ‘Sorry, don’t know who said that.’

‘You’re so wise. You remind me of a beautiful Buddha. It’s your eyes, their shape, yet they’re pale, my blue-eyed Buddha,’ Annabelle said, as she put her arms around his neck and kissed Andreas goodbye.

How she hated the separation. Her only consolation was the knowledge that he suffered too.

17 Prometheus

It was almost three years since Andreas and Annabelle had become lovers. Their relationship oscillated between moments of ecstasy and deepest despair. Neither of them knew what they really wanted. Or if they did, they were too frightened to articulate it.

Andreas reminded Annabelle of Prometheus, whose efforts to improve human existence result in tragedy. Cursed by Zeus for stealing the fire, he is bound to the rock to be tormented, and have his liver eaten every day by the vulture. Annabelle felt sorry for Andreas but also helpless and angry at how he had allowed himself to arrive at such a position. He was bound to his ailing son, his suspicious wife, his alienated daughter, his patients, the controlling women in his office, his dismal financial situation and, of course, to her.

All these stresses were not without their consequences. Annabelle worried how they could be affecting Andreas. But she too was sickening. She had a pain in her right side, under the rib cage.

'You're full of ambivalence towards me,' Andreas was saying, seeking reassurance as he felt her listlessness and waning interest.

'I'm sick. I've got a fever,' she whispered, trying to justify herself.

Andreas seemed not to have heard her.

'How are you getting on with your husband?' he enquired.

Annabelle sighed and rested her cheek on her hand, holding her head up. She felt feeble and feverish. 'Why do you always ask? I don't ask you about your wife,' she said, wishing the session would end.

'As your doctor, I'm interested. I want to see you happy,' Andreas told her, fiddling with his collar as if it was bothering him.

'Huh!'

'What's wrong, Annabelle?' Andreas asked, despairing, unable to appease her.

'I told you, I'm sick. Physically and emotionally. I'm not getting therapy, just drugs. I need a doctor.'

'I am your doctor!'

'I can't burden you with my problems. You have enough of your own. I'm just upset that I've lost you as my therapist. I'm torn between the two of you. I love you, and I also need you as my doctor. When I see you, I want to make love with you, but then I don't have analysis. It's difficult.'

'I'm worried about what you're saying, that you've lost me as your therapist. I've been giving it a lot of thought, Annabelle. I think that we must work, rather than make love. I want you to know that I care for you as a person and I want to help you. So that we're not tempted, I think you should change your appointment to an earlier time when my secretaries are still here. We'll try to be alone once in a while, when you can get away from your husband ...'

'No!' Annabelle said, shaking her head at his suggestion.

Andreas made a helpless gesture with his hands. At the same time, a look of relief spread across his face.

'We must work now,' Andreas said, pleased by the intensity of her outburst.

But Andreas had planted the seeds of doubt about Annabelle's desirability as a woman.

'I don't believe you really like making love to me,' she told him, her eyes narrowing with suspicion. 'You're afraid of the feelings I provoke in you, that's why you really want to stop. Perhaps you don't find me sexy anymore.'

Andreas shook his head.

'You're wrong. I adore making love to you. I want you all the time. You're beautiful to make love to. Everything about you is thrilling to me. Your softness, your cries, how you feel when I'm inside you.' Andreas paused for a moment. 'You know, you're teaching me a lot about myself. You've made me think deeply about a lot of things. It's strange that you should fear being rejected by me. I would never hurt you.' He had a slight smile but his eyes were sad. 'You know, our fears are similar. We're so alike, you and me.'

'We are long-lost atoms, come together, linked for eternity. Remember?'

Andreas looked at Annabelle. She lifted his spirit, filled him with hope. He could dream on.

'I do,' he said.

'I just want to make love with you,' Annabelle said, in a subdued voice.

'I want to prove to you that I don't use you,' he said.

Annabelle had stopped listening. She rose and went across to Andreas, leaned over the armchair, her breasts touching him. She slipped her hand inside his shirt and caressed the hair on his chest, playing with his nipples. Her hand moved down his body.

'Annabelle, we mustn't …'

'See how hard you are here? Your body wants me and you shouldn't deny yourself the pleasure. I can't stand martyrs.'

'No. We can't do this.'

'Yes, Andreas, we can.'

He could hold himself back no longer. Beaten by desire, he seized Annabelle and cast her against the settee. They tore at each other, stroking, devouring, sighing.

'Oh,' he moaned when they were spent. 'Oh, damn.'

'What's the matter?' she asked.

He moaned again, holding his forehead. 'I was so full of good intentions.'

'Stop it. Don't spoil it, please,' she said, taking one of her lace handkerchiefs and pressing it between her legs. 'When it was so good.'

'Annabelle, Annabelle, what are we going to do?' Andreas said, reaching for her and holding her close. 'Will the gods punish us?'

'*In time*,' she said, sounding like the Oracle.

* * *

Two days later, Annabelle was in bed with a temperature and a persistent ache in her side. The pain was acute, as was her yearning. She needed Andreas, longed to hear his voice. But it was not possible, psychiatrists did not make home visits. She had hoped Andreas would come and see her, especially as her husband was away. Instead, he sent a general practitioner, a Doctor Dyball.

Annabelle was surprised at how quickly the GP came. It occurred to her that he may have been a patient of Andreas, which would have explained his eagerness. She might say some nice things about him to his analyst whose approval he most probably craved.

When the doctor arrived, Annabelle was alarmed. And when Byron, the neighbour's dog she was taking care of, barked at him, she became a little frightened. Byron was a good barometer of character. There was something sinister about the doctor. Apart from the fact that he was flustered and sweating profusely, the lenses of his thick glasses magnified his dilated pupils, adding to his crazed appearance.

'What's wrong?' he asked.

When Annabelle explained her symptoms and told him she had a chest infection, mentioning the fever and the ache in her side, he shook his head.

'You, my dear,' he intoned, pointing a dirty fingernail at her, 'have a case of acute appendicitis. It's plainly obvious.'

'It feels more like a lung infection,' she said. 'I have a pain in my side when I breathe.'

'That's what they all say. I've removed dozens of appendixes. It'll have to come out, my dear.' His eyes narrowed as he waited with arms akimbo for her to say something. 'We can get you into a private hospital by tonight, and tomorrow morning we'll whip it out. Just be good will you and do as you're told. Don't be argumentative! Lift up your nightie for me. I want to give you an internal examination, just to make sure there's nothing else wrong down there.'

'No!' Annabelle cried, sitting upright and pulling the bedclothes up to her chin. 'I need a second opinion.'

The doctor's face became uglier. He spoke through clenched discoloured teeth.

'My dear, it would be a complete waste of my time. But if you must, if you really insist …' He made a dismissive gesture with his hands.

'Who do you have in mind?' he asked.

'Eichler,' she blurted out. 'Professor Eichler.'

'A relative?'

'Yes.'

'I don't know him.'

'He's my husband, he's away but he's coming back tonight.'

Doctor Dyball was not pleased. 'If that's the way you want it, I wash my hands completely of this case. I'm warning you though, you're wasting time. You'll be dead if you don't listen to me.' With those parting words, he wrenched his black bag off the bed and exited from the room with Byron, the deaf-rescued-runt collie from the pound, snapping at his heels.

Still shaking from her experience, Annabelle called David at his hotel where he was speaking at a conference. He, of course, was unavailable. She would have to wait until he got her message.

On his return, David arranged for Annabelle to have a chest x-ray. When he examined the x-ray, it confirmed what he already suspected. It was pneumonia. One of the first lessons medical students were taught was how to distinguish the pain in the lower right side of the lung from the pain of appendicitis. He then rang the GP and blasted him for endangering his wife's life. Pneumonia was an expeditious assassin.

Annabelle did not respond immediately to the antibiotics, much to her husband's concern. David wanted her to be hospitalised, under the care of a colleague, but Annabelle's reaction was so extreme at his suggestion that he arranged instead for her to be cared for at home. She simply did not trust doctors.

For days, Annabelle remained in a feverish state of exaggerated perceptions and confused feelings. She recalled the tender way Andreas had made love to her and yearned to be with him. Annabelle replayed only the beautiful scenes from her LSD sessions—there was the time when she had worn a peach-coloured satin night dress from the 1930s—seducing him. She felt his caresses again, his hand running along the curves of her breasts, stomach, thighs. She burned with fever. He never came.

18 The Necrophiliac

Two weeks later, when Annabelle had recovered from pneumonia, she strode into the doctor's consulting room in her pale tan knee-high boots. She was in a humourless mood.

'How are you?' Andreas asked with false composure.

'How dare you recommend that mad, incompetent, moronic doctor? Is he your friend or a patient of yours?'

'He rang me and said you had appendicitis and that you were being difficult,' Andreas said, trying to defend himself.

'He's an odious buffoon! A fucking lunatic! A danger and menace to society!'

'He's a doctor to *high* society,' Andreas said, trying to appease Annabelle.

This infuriated her further. 'I don't give a fig about high society! I'm not like your wife! I know why you recommended him. Because he's *ugly*. You're insecure and jealous and vain, and you're afraid of any man touching me, so you sent that psycho who would have operated on me for something I didn't have. I would have died because my pneumonia was not being treated.'

'He's not that bad, surely?' Andreas said, hoping to minimize the situation.

'He's Frankenstein and Dracula rolled into one. He wanted to give me an internal examination. Not bloody likely! Over my dead body. Yes, he'd probably jerk off over my dead body. I bet he's a necrophiliac. You can tell by looking at him. He fucks cadavers!'

Andreas tried to stifle nervous laughter.

'You don't give a damn about me,' Annabelle continued, in a subdued tone. 'You wouldn't care if I died. I think you wanted me to die.'

'I'm sorry. I made a mistake.'

'Why did you not come and see me?' she blurted, full of hurt and reproach.

'I couldn't. It would have been unethical. What would your husband have thought?'

'He's never there. Besides, he wouldn't have minded if you showed that you cared about me as a person instead of letting me die. You could at least have telephoned.'

'I did, but David answered. So I hung up.'

'You would have been happy if I died. You would have been rid of me. You could have returned then to your moribund existence.'

'No, it's not true. I suffered too. I was concerned but I knew that David would take good care of you and that you'd get well.'

'What made you so sure? I was pretty sick, you know? David was quite worried at one stage because the fever wouldn't break.'

Andreas fell silent. He did not know how to answer to Annabelle.

'I'd like you to find out why you became so sick,' he said, finally.

'I caught pneumonia, that's all,' Annabelle said.

Andreas shook his head.

'One doesn't catch pneumonia. You gave yourself pneumonia, Annabelle,' he explained.

She looked at him with undisguised fury.

'How could I give myself pneumonia? Why would I do that?'

'That's what we have to find out. What were you needing, Annabelle?'

'What do you think, doctor?'

'What did you want from me?'

'Oh, Christ you're so dim sometimes. *Love*, of course.'

'What does love mean to you?'

Annabelle looked at Andreas with despair.

'Doctor asks his patient to define *love* to him because he doesn't have a clue,' she said, in a theatrical aside, as if she was speaking to someone else. 'Why should I educate you? I'm *paying you*.'

An angry silence followed. Annabelle set about demolishing the lace on the edge of her underskirt.

'Often, when people need something,' Andreas began, 'and they don't know how to ask for it or go about getting it, they make themselves ill. They can induce headaches, ulcers, backaches, asthma, colds, even heart attacks. I have patients, unhappy housewives, whose children have grown up and left them, and whose husbands don't love them anymore, dying of cancer. They've given themselves cancer instead of changing their unhappy state. A woman with breast cancer said to me: 'My husband was a real bastard all the years we were married. Now that I've got cancer he's really nice to me.' Men do it too. One patient, a man in his fifties, divorced his wife and is living with a de facto who harangues him about getting married. He's not good at saying no. The other day he walked into a hospital and said: 'I think I'm having a heart attack,' and promptly collapsed. The doctors fortunately resuscitated him. His doctor's advice was that he mustn't be stressed about anything and to take it easy. It was easier for him to give himself a heart attack than to say: 'No, stop nagging me.' It's important to remember that if we have the power to make ourselves ill, we can also heal ourselves. What is it you want from me that you're not getting, Annabelle?'

'I don't believe in asking.'

'You think that if someone loved you enough, they would be able to guess?'

'Yes.'

'It's best to ask, because often they can guess wrongly. That can make one very angry.'

'I could never ask.'

'Why not?'

'Because people don't like being asked. Besides, one doesn't necessarily get what one wants,' Annabelle said.

Andreas bowed his head.

'You never ask me for what you really want, either,' Annabelle added.

'It's true. I'm afraid of rejection,' Andreas said.

'We're both cowards, then.'

Andreas appeared lost and despairing. He needed a drink to relieve the tension he was feeling.

'Would you like a vodka?'

'Why not?' Annabelle said, running her fingers through her hair, sweeping it aside in an impassioned gesture.

Andreas reappeared from behind the screen with the bottle of vodka he had taken out of the freezer. He sat beside Annabelle, offering her a glass. She raised it to her lips and swallowed the liquid. It was like melted gold, she imagined, running down her throat and through her veins. She leaned back against the cushions.

Andreas was staring at her with a strange, intense expression, trying to engage with her.

'God, I've missed you, Annabelle. You've taken over every aspect of my life. I think about you constantly. You cause me a lot of trouble.'

'I'm glad,' Her response sounded heartless.

'I'm telling you that I love you. Do you understand? I love you Annabelle.'

Annabelle gazed into his eyes. The chilled liquid she had swallowed was thawing her out.

'I'm afraid of you, Andreas. Afraid that I could want you so much—and when you didn't come to see me, I felt I was dying.'

'I'm sorry. I couldn't come,' he said, sounding full of contrition. He knew it was something he would regret for a long time. A mistake. Or was it?

'Last time I was here I saw a woman. An inmate of the asylum,' Annabelle said, with a note of sarcasm. 'I didn't have my car and was waiting for a taxi. She came staggering to the front of the clinic in a dressing gown, barefoot. She looked terrible, as if she was falling apart. Drunk, or drugged. Her face was all doughy, her hair wild. A look in her eyes, as if she had been to hell. Two of the male nurses came and carried her back inside. I was shocked. I thought she could be a patient of yours. I imagined she was like that because of you. Perhaps she had been in love with you and you broke her heart.'

Andreas frowned, puzzled. 'It must have been Eleni,' he said, finally. 'She was tortured and raped by the police in Greece when the Colonels were in power and she was a student radical. So that's it! You decided I was such a destroyer of women that you wanted to die rather than face me again. My poor darling.'

Andreas took Annabelle in his arms and kissed the top of her head. He held her just as she had longed for him to hold her when she had been ill.

* * *

The room at the Bollingen Clinic was a vessel, carrying them across landscapes of tribulation but also breath-taking peaks of erotic love. It was there that Andreas had revealed parts of himself to Annabelle he had kept secret all his life.

Andreas had chosen to name the clinic after Jung's original tower which he built on the upper shores of Lake Zurich. Bollingen had become Jung's retreat after his traumatic break with Freud, his father figure. It was to be: *a place of maturation—a maternal womb—in which I could become what I was, what I am, and what will be.* Andreas had suggested the name for the clinic because it was a symbol of psychic wholeness—a place where Jung had felt reborn. Andreas believed it would be healing for patients to discover the meaning and make it their own. It had not occurred to him that it was what he needed for himself. Until he met Annabelle.

Bollingen had also been a place of seduction, where Jung brought his mistress, Antonia Wolff. She had been a twenty-two-year-old patient of his, who, later, became an analyst. Antonia remained Jung's mistress until his death—forty years later.

'Annabelle.' Andreas's voice was like a caress on the back of her neck. She turned, and immediately her spirits began to rise.

'I'm sorry to have kept you waiting. It's been a stressful day. We've had a few crises at the clinic, and Jess has had to go to a doctor's appointment. But come now,' he said, inviting Annabelle in.

Andreas closed the door to his room and reached to turn off the air-conditioner.

'I had to switch it on because one of my patients smokes. Sorry about the smell.'

'Why don't you have one of those new: *Thank you for not smoking* signs? And if you hid the ashtray, your patients would probably be too timid to ask you for one.'

'I can't do that. I want them to feel totally relaxed here. They're under enough strain as it is,' Andreas said.

'I'm worried about you being affected by cigarette smoke. Do you know that other people's cigarette smoke can increase your risk of leukaemia seven times? I read it in one of David's medical journals.'

'I find your concern very touching. I've got those injections for you,' he added, with an enthusiasm that bemused Annabelle, although she was also apprehensive, as she did not like needles.

'What injections?'

'The ones I told you about. The androgens,' Andreas said.

His enthusiasm was having a cooling effect on her.

'You still think I need something to arouse me? I'm not sexy enough for you? Is that it?' It was not a question, more of a reproach.

'I worry because you don't seem to achieve orgasm through intercourse. I'm not satisfying you.'

'I'm …' Annabelle faltered. 'I'm afraid someone might hear me in here. I could be very noisy.'

'Could you now? Like a Japanese lady? They say they scream like peacocks.'

'Yes,' Annabelle nodded.

'You mustn't worry about making a noise. I can easily explain it away if anyone mentions it.'

'I get tense here and I'm worried about your wife. She could be standing outside the door, listening,' Annabelle said, squeezing her hands together and despairing. But Andreas was blind to her discomfort.

'That's why I want you to have those injections. I want you to be satisfied, I want you to feel lots of pleasure,' he said.

'You want everything!' Annabelle burst out, angry that he could be insensitive to her feelings. This was a new side to him. He had always been so aware, so deeply perceptive and protective. He was discounting her feelings now, as David always did. It disappointed and frightened her.

'We'll start the first injection today. It'll hurt a little because it's been in the fridge. But come, Annabelle, hop on the examination couch. I'll make love to you afterwards. What do you think of that, making love on the exam couch? Face down, please. I'll try not to hurt you,' he said.

Annabelle whimpered when the cold liquid was injected into her buttock.

Andreas rubbed the area with his hand to help disperse the liquid. 'It hurts a little, I know,' he added. Then he kissed and caressed her buttocks and spread them apart, inserting his tongue in the small tight fissure. His other hand slid underneath, to the front, touching her, surprising her, shocking her.

'Turn around,' he said. 'Are you comfortable?'

She nodded and crossed her arms over her face.

'Come now, don't hide from me,' Andreas said, gently taking her arms away from her face. 'I want to watch you,' he said, rasing her legs and giving that familiar thrust which helped him complete the action of penetration and elicited a cry from her. 'There, now,' he said, as he resumed a slow rhythm. 'You feel so good, so good inside. It's exciting isn't it Annabelle, making love on the examination couch? Almost sacrilegious. Like making love on an altar.'

'Yes,' she whispered, overwhelmed and fearful at how wicked she had become—wondering what the punishment would be.

* * *

'He's waiting for you,' said Jess, having finished for the day, as Annabelle passed her on the stairs running late for her appointment again.

Annabelle stopped outside the waiting room and watched him. Andreas had come to look for her. Annabelle enjoyed spying on him. After a while, she sashayed up to him. Andreas tried to appear as though he was not bothered that she had kept him waiting but he could not resist saying: 'You're late.'

'I'm sorry,' she said.

'Late people are angry people,' Andreas said.

'What are early people, then?'

'Early people are anxious,'

'And those who are on time?'

'They're obsessional.'

Annabelle looked at him. Her eyes narrowed and the warmth disappeared from them.

'It seems to me as though one can't win with you shrinks. It's as if it's very important for you to have labels and jargon and explanations for everything. Then maybe you'll feel in control. Superior. I read a very good description of narcissism: *The need for dominance, admiration and an exaggerated sense of entitlement*. You must all feel powerless deep down.'

'Why are you twenty-five minutes late? It doesn't leave us much time,' he said, ignoring her critical analysis.

'I had an interview. For a job as an interpreter. A medical interpreter, working for doctors and lawyers—insurance and compensation cases.'

'It doesn't sound like something you'd enjoy,' he said.

'You're probably right,' she said. 'But I need to do something to earn a living and be independent.'

Andreas rose from his seat and went across to be beside her on the settee.

'My darling,' he said, taking her in his arms, pacifying her. 'It's true, I feel powerless deep down. I feel I'm living on the edge of a precipice. I've always thought it stupid the way some people tend to do things that get them into trouble. But I think I understand them now.' Andreas sighed and would not let her go when she tried to break free. He held her and she succumbed, surrendering to him, leaning back against his chest. They watched the sun setting in the distance. Andreas brushed back her hair with his lips, stirring her senses, and began to recite in her ear:

Come to the edge, he said
No. We are afraid
Come to the EDGE
No. We might fall.
COME TO THE EDGE
… and they came.

… and he pushed them
… and they FLEW!

19 The Realm of the Senses

There was a battleship in the harbour. The Navy was practising manoeuvres, catapulting rocket-like objects into the air. They kept flopping back into the sea.

Andreas was waiting for Annabelle. The secretaries had left and he was sitting in his room, reading the newspaper when she arrived. The door was open, and at first she hesitated to enter, frightened he might be angry with her, but fear gave way to rebelliousness and a desire to solicit a reaction from him. She wanted to let him know that he was not the centre of her life.

'I don't feel like sitting down,' Annabelle said. She stood by the window looking out at the bay.

'Tell me why you're so hostile, Annabelle.' Andreas said.

'You don't understand me and you never will. I'm too complex for you. I'm not angry or aggressive—I'm passionate. I have strong feelings. Something you will never understand because you live your life in a strait-jacket.'

Annabelle caught an expression of anguish on his face.

'I've been away for three weeks,' Andreas said, in a subdued tone. 'Did you miss me?'

'No,' Annabelle lied. 'You attach too much importance to your *importance* to me. I was in Byron Bay, enjoying myself with friends—and some gorgeous American surfers who've escaped from the Vietnam War draft and are hiding there. We swam with dolphins, danced, smoked dope and went horse riding in the moonlight.'

Annabelle loved exaggerating, intimating things, so she could test Andreas's reactions. She wanted him to suffer, as he had made her suffer when he had gone on a trip.

'You must have your excitement, mustn't you?' There was a note of recrimination in his voice. 'You're a butterfly,' he added, 'no, a courtesan, born out of your time, breaking men's hearts. I thought so the first moment I saw you. In spite of everything, you succeed in remaining free, elusive. I'd love to be free, too.'

Annabelle looked at him and thought how wrong he was. She was not free. How could she be when she felt helpless, in love with him, and crippled with migraines? She was far from liberated.

'You seem to be angry with me because I enjoyed myself with my friends. I shouldn't have come today. I intended to ring and cancel my appointment but I left it too late.' Annabelle turned her back on Andreas and concentrated her attention on the grey battleship and the Naval games. Eventually, she moved away from the window and looked at Andreas: 'I thought only the psychiatrist's patient became angry and depressed when the shrink went on holidays, not the shrink himself if his patient was away.'

'You make me reveal myself,' Andreas said. Then frowning, he added: 'Where were you on Saturday? I thought you said you'd be back by then, that David was still in New York. I tried to ring you.'

'I didn't get back until Monday.'

'We should talk about things. I've got to help you, and I feel I'm not doing a good job at all,' Andreas said, rubbing his forehead.

'I can see the Olympic pool from here, where I swim. It's just across the water,' Annabelle said, looking into the distance.

'Whenever I try to pin you down, Annabelle, to take responsibility for a certain area in your life, we come up against a wall,' Andreas said. He sighed, looked at his watch. 'Your hour's up, I'm afraid.'

'But I haven't done any work, today,' Annabelle protested.

'That's true. You've spent a lot of time sabotaging and being rebellious.'

'Let's not talk, Andreas,' Annabelle's mood suddenly changed. 'I want to have fun—make love.' She was making a desperate effort to be light hearted.

'It's very difficult to talk about one's hostile feelings. You think you might make me angry, Annabelle. You've stopped trusting me.'

'I don't recall ever trusting you.'

'Be serious. Our relationship is fragile,' Andreas said.

'It *is* fragile,' Annabelle admitted. The realisation made her feel mournful. He was the centre of her life now. What would happen if he were no longer there? 'Oh, Andreas, help me!' It was a cry from deep inside her being. 'There are moments when I do trust you. And times when I love you so profoundly, that it hurts. It's unbearable how I love you sometimes,' she said, turning away from him so he would not see her distress.

'My darling Annabelle, my precious love.' Andreas swiftly moved across to where she stood by the window. He was behind her, holding and kissing her.

All her insecurities, disappointments and feelings of abandonment began to leave her. She leaned her head against his shoulder. Andreas buried his face in her hair.

Slowly, his hands began to lift her dress.

Annabelle sighed and bent forward, spreading her arms like the wings of a bird, resting them on the window sill. He was able to gaze on her exposed neck, she had swept her long hair to one side, offering him that secret and unseen part of herself.

It was not a bird she brought to his mind so much as a ballerina impersonating a bird—Anna Pavlova in *Death of a Swan.* It was an old favourite piece of film that had belonged to his father.

Andreas kissed her neck and allowed his hands to cup her breasts. He caressed her nipples and felt them harden. He sought other parts of her body, making her at times gasp and moan. He explored the silky wetness between her legs until he could hold himself no longer, wanting to be within her, joining in her essence. And when he did, calling out her name and holding her as though he would never let her go, she cried out like a ghostly creature in a forest.

'Why, oh why, is it so good with you Andreas?' Annabelle sobbed.

Andreas could not answer. He had entered deep into the realm of the senses and lost himself, long ago.

★ ★ ★

Annabelle wanted Andreas to see *The Last Tango in Paris,* a film which had caused a controversy because of some explicit sex scenes. She enjoyed provoking her husband's more conservative friends by telling them that *Last Tango in Paris* was a great film. They either looked at her aghast, or were titillated because the film's notoriety centred around a buggering scene with a packet of butter as lubricant.

It was a film of great depth, an examination of the human condition, made by a talented director known for his intellectual brilliance, himself deep in his own Freudian analysis with his psychiatrist. The use of the paintings by Francis Bacon in the opening credits was inspired, because no modern artist could express the pathos of human anguish like Bacon. It had touched Annabelle deeply when she first saw the film, and it touched Andreas too—causing him great distress.

They sat in the amniotic darkness of the small cinema, on very hard seats amongst an audience of anarchists, lovers and the raincoat brigade. Watching the film for a third time, Annabelle made an exciting discovery. Andreas reminded her very much of the ageing character played by Marlon Brando.

When the film ended, Annabelle turned and looked at Andreas, searching his face, curious to see his reaction. To her surprise, Andreas looked pale. Clearly, the film had unsettled him.

'Didn't you like it?' she asked, looking at him with concern.

But Andreas was not able to reply. He left his seat and went outside. Annabelle followed him and took his hand. Andreas held her arm as they walked through a neglected part of the city, where the last of the art-house cinemas remained. There were cheap hotels for country visitors and refuges for the homeless. Some Asian restaurants had recently opened nearby. They walked past the small theatre where a few years before, Annabelle had played Antigone, her favourite character. She had always loved Antigone because she was courageous, invincible and indestructible.

When they arrived at the smarter end of town, they stopped for a coffee and to talk about the film.

'It's very rich in meaning and symbolism,' Andreas said. 'A psychiatrist's dream. From the very beginning—when they meet in the apartment and he takes her—the way he holds her in his arms, like a father holds a child on his lap. And then, the anal games—anal sex—right through to the very end, when he puts her father's military cap on his head. It breaks the fantasy and the *taboo* is revealed, so she shoots him. The murder of the father is an Oedipal thing. She has to kill him.'

Andreas stopped talking and looked hard at her.

'It frightens me,' he said. 'I can see you, your destructiveness. That's why you wanted me to see it. You needed to warn me about your destructiveness.'

Annabelle was exhilarated that he understood her. 'We broke the taboo. I wonder what will happen to us?'

'We've embarked on a voyage into the unknown. It's uncharted territory. Not much has been written about it,' Andreas said.

'The gods will take care of us. They're kind to lovers,' Annabelle stroked his arm.

'Not in the stories I know,' Andreas said. There was a grim, unfamiliar expression on his face.

'They put them through some terrible tests, I know. But in the end, the lovers are reunited in some mysterious way or another,' Annabelle said, trying to cheer Andreas. But he was not amused.

'You think there are some hard times ahead?' he asked. He was testing her to see if she was prepared for consequences.

'All I know is that I feel a tremendous love for you, Andreas. You've been so wonderful to me. I'll never forget what you've done.'

He smiled and put his arm around her shoulders.

'Your existence confirms mine,' he told her, kissing her temple.

'Andreas, you're such a beautiful man,' she said, gazing deeply into his eyes.

'Heigh ho,' he said, wanting to minimise the intensity of the moment.

'You have a funny way of saying that,' Annabelle said. There was an expression of bewilderment on her small face that he found endearing.

She took such an interest in him. It filled his heart with acute joy.

'What?' he asked.

'*Heigh ho.* I sense a wistfulness. It's probably your Russian melancholy,' Annabelle said.

'You're too sensitive to my moods, my darling.'

'Of course, Andreas, because I love you.'

He shook his head slowly. 'I can't get over what a lovely surprise you are to me.'

'And I can't get over *you*. I don't think I ever will.'

'Tu es vraiment farouche, ma petite,' he told her.

'Qu*'est-ce que c'est farouche, mon amour?'* she asked, curious, not being familiar with the phrase.

'It's a paradox. Untameable, wild and shy. A wild shyness, like a deer in the forest, or a feral child.'

'What a lovely imagination you have, doctor.'

* * *

It had been six months since they had been to *The Last Tango in Paris.* Annabelle longed to see Andreas outside the clinic. But it was too difficult. There were chains holding him.

The room which Annabelle had loved so much now represented a prison, keeping Andreas inside. The secretaries, wife, patients, doctors and inmates of the clinic, were the guards, watching him in case he tried to escape.

Annabelle felt ambivalent about the clinic. But it was the only way she could be with Andreas. She was late again.

'Sorry. I got lost. I took the wrong turn. It's like a dream I have of never arriving. I've a dreadful headache, too. I can't function when I have a migraine. My judgement's impaired.'

'What are you afraid of Annabelle?'

'You always ask the same questions,' she said, feeling irritable.

'Would you like a drink?'

Annabelle looked at Andreas mystified, wondering why he was offering her a drink when she had a headache.

'Yes,' she said, feeling reckless, not caring if her head fell off.

Andreas disappeared behind the screen and returned with a frosted bottle of vodka and glasses.

'Why doesn't the bottle explode when it's frozen?' she asked.

'Because the alcohol is pure.'

Annabelle took two sips from the glass—and waited for the vodka to spread its icy warmth through her veins. It affected her instantly like a drug. She felt herself sinking deeper into the cushions. She loved vodka. It was St Petersburg covered in snow. Anna Karenina's fatal train emerging out of the fog. The movie *Doctor Zhivago.* Russian princes on white steeds, riding the crystal waves of her imagination.

'*André*,' she called, like a siren from the stories his grandfather told him. 'Why is it so good with you? Wherever you touch me, you seem to know where to touch. Your instinct is so right. I was frozen in a dark blue sea. You've brought me back to the sun'

Annabelle emptied her glass. Andreas removed it from her hand and re-filled it. But she did not take it from him. Andreas placed the glass on the table beside her. She looked at him, frowning and rubbing her temples. Something was bothering her.

'Is your head still hurting?' Andreas asked.

'Yes.'

'What's on your mind? Tell me,' Andreas said. 'What is troubling you, Annabelle?'

'You promised we'd do something together. Can't we meet for coffee or a picnic Andreas?' she said, suddenly becoming animated, hoping her enthusiasm would affect him.

'I don't have any time for myself. I never imagined I'd meet you. I've let others— my wife, children, secretaries—take over. My life is now filled up with the most mundane existence. I didn't care because I was dead you could say. I don't know what to do because I, too, want to be with you.'

'You've said all that before.' Annabelle felt dispirited with Andreas's excuses and subterfuges. 'I wrote a poem,' she added, rummaging inside her bag. 'It's called *Circle.*'

Andreas took the sheet of paper from her and walked over to his desk to retrieve his glasses. And began to read.

I love your face
flooded with emotion
You gasping for air as
You reach your climax
I love the way you desire me
and lust for me
Sitting on your lap
Rocking me like an infant
I love you sucking and biting
My nipples
The way you thrust into me
The things you do to me
which leave me stunned and
reeling under the impact
I love you
Who you are
And the Psychiatrist
What you look like
What you taste like
What you've been
I love talking with you
About Pushkin, Lao-tsu, Laing and Nabokov
And playing
Seeing The Last Tango
I love your madness, your recklessness
And your anarchy
You. Are an empty frame, a giant dangling puppet
A robot
You play with me out of boredom and despair
You are a helpless unhappy child battered by the
Women in your life
I don't wish to be part of it

I don't want to be a woman
I relinquish my sex

Andreas nodded.

'It's true, you're so right,' he said.

Suddenly he laughed. Annabelle had never heard him laugh like that before. It was a bitter, uncontrolled laugh and it distressed her.

'Please don't. Just help me, Andreas,' she said.

'Help you?'

'Help me not to be like the other women in your life.'

'You're not. I love you,' he said, reaching for her and closing his arms around her.

'If anything happened to you, I would want to die, too. I couldn't bear to live without you. It would be unimaginable. Unbearable. It's hardly bearable now. Do you know when I miss you most, Andreas? When I'm surrounded by people. If we're at a dinner or some other social function, and there's music playing, I miss you. I miss you in the morning and at night. It's as if my heart is missing, and there's a big hole in my centre, where my heart should be.'

Annabelle fell silent. She had said too much. But there was one last thing she wanted to tell him: 'I want so much to climb that mountain with you, Andreas.'

'What mountain?'

'The one I keep coming across when you give me LSD, where the air is rarefied, where the lammergeier soars high in the sky, and the alpine flowers grow in the most precarious of places, and you're the king of this pure and perfect realm,' she added dreamily.

'Jung wrote that you have to descend into the deepest and darkest depths before you can begin to climb to the top. You have to die to live again. But to suffer one's death and be reborn is not easy,' Andreas said, squeezing Annabelle close to his own heart.

They remained silent for a while, contemplating what was said.

Then Annabelle's thoughts moved to another subject that preoccupied her.

'Why did you leave your first wife?'

'I didn't love her. I woke up one morning after a drunken night to find myself married to her. We spent sixteen years together.'

'You spent *sixteen* years of your life with a woman you didn't love?' she said, pushing away from his hold.

'I was unfaithful most of the time, hopping in and out of bed at the hospital with the nurses. One day she rang me at the hospital wanting to know what I was doing. I told her I was having sex with the sister. She said: 'No, darling, seriously.' I said: 'I swear to you, I'm in bed with the nursing sister.' She didn't believe me, so from then on I didn't bother to lie. She just didn't believe me when I told the truth.'

'How extraordinary,' Annabelle said. But she could have said what she really felt. Appalled.

'One day, a friend of hers brought her rather attractive girlfriend along. I made a pass at her and within two weeks we were living together, and then after my divorce came through, we got married. Jean is very jealous and possessive. She's terrified because she broke up my marriage that the same thing will happen to her. She's got to know where I am all the time.'

'How stifling! Don't you mind?'

'I didn't really care. I went along with it, felt sorry for her insecurities. I squandered the fortune my grandfather left me. Nothing left now except mortgages and debts.'

'Your grandfather must have loved you very much,' Annabelle said.

'Yes.'

'If I could have one wish in this world, it would be that all the dead people one knew, loved and admired, could be brought back to life. Maybe even in spirit form. I was taught at the convent that God would do so on Judgement Day. But I don't want God's interference. I just want it to be private. To be able to see those dear ones and tell them how sorry I am for not appreciating them, and how much I love them and miss them. Sometimes you don't know the true value of a person, until they become a memory. I would love to start all over again and really get to know them. That's what I would like. Wouldn't that be lovely, Andreas?'

'You are very sweet, Annabelle.'

'What about your wife, Andreas. Do you love your wife?'

'No,' he said, with a puzzled look, as though he had never thought about it before. 'I never have. It's been difficult since Nick became ill. Jean can't look after him. I have to be around to lift him and give him injections when he has epileptic fits. He's almost a grown man now, and heavy. There's also my daughter. I don't want to hurt her as I hurt my other children. I didn't want any children the second time. One family was enough, but Jean was adamant.'

'I have fantasised once or twice about having your child,' Annabelle replied.

'It's common for women to do so. It's a primitive thing, particularly if they feel the male is going to provide and take care of things. Pure biology.'

'Also for men?' Annabelle asked.

'The desire to have children isn't as strong,' Andreas said. 'But it's there, I guess the urge for immortality.' He gazed at her with affection. 'I thought the idea of childbirth scared you,' he added, tickling the lower part of her stomach.

She took his hand away from her body and held it.

'Not if you were there holding my hand.' Annabelle played with Andreas's fingers, kissing them, intertwining them with hers. 'Nothing would scare me if you were there. Would you hold my hand, Andreas?'

'Of course,' he said. 'I delivered my last two.'

Annabelle pulled her hand away. She lay back on the cushions deep in thought again.

'Anyway, I'm on the pill,' she said with a shrug. 'Just fantasizing on my part. Safer to dream about something. It doesn't have to be real.'

'It's dangerous to live in dreams, Annabelle.'

'Some dreams are too dangerous to be made real, Andreas.'

A disturbing quiet settled between them. So much was left unspoken.

'Are you still frightened, Andreas?' she asked.

'No.'

‘Make love to me then. Over there, on the examination couch.’

‘No.’ Andreas was firm.

‘You want me, don’t you?’

‘I want you, yes. But it’s sacrilege.’

‘It’s what we both desire,’ she said.

Andreas rose, took Annabelle by the hand, across the room, and to the couch.

20 The Edge

Whenever David returned from an overseas trip, he always brought Annabelle a bottle of her favourite perfume, and copies of *The International Herald Tribune*. She loved to read the *Tribune,* not just because it was one of the very few quality newspapers in the English language, but also for being an important link to exiles and expatriates living in Paris and Rome. It gave her a connection to her literary ghosts.

The night before she was due for her appointment at the Bollingen Clinic, Annabelle read in the *Tribune,* that the distinguished founder and President of the American Psychiatric Association used to drug and rape his patients.

That night, she started drinking alone. Vodka, of course. She had never cared for alcohol, but since Andreas had first offered her vodka at the clinic, she associated it with him—and what happened in his room. And so Annabelle became an inebriate.

In another session under the influence of LSD, Annabelle believed she was in the grip of something cataclysmic. She felt a dense web spun by a malevolent creature was trying to keep the lovers apart, distorting and destroying their love.

It was sad, infinitely sad. And it was all her fault.

'I know what I am,' she told Andreas, after the LSD session, as she sat in her usual place on the settee. 'I saw it when I was tripping. I'm a black spider. I'm made of knives, glittering blades. I'm fire and ice. I'm from another planet. My body is encased in steel and deadly spikes, and I can rip apart anyone foolish enough to touch me. I don't trust lovers. I need a doctor I can talk to. But I cannot ring you because you are you, and I am your lover and it would appear as though I needed you and then you'd judge me and think I was demanding. Or worse, weak.

'I take handfuls of anti-depressants,' she continued, 'and eat all the things you told me not to, hoping to die. I think your psychiatry is a sham, an easy game of detection, facile, obvious, predictable. I play the game, I know the tricks. I stumble over words and fake mental blocks. I choose the words and images to trick you. I rock or hug myself, cross my legs and my arms, send whatever signals I choose to send. I can lead you to believe anything I wish. I even invent dreams to manipulate you, you know? Like Nabokov. You sit there watching me, listening patiently, waiting to pigeon hole me. One day you're a Freudian, another a Jungian, a Kleinian, or a Rogerian. Some days you try a bit of Gestalt, now you're reading Kohut. And so it goes. Sure, they all make sense, but the truth eludes you, a chimera twinkling in the distance, goading you on, out of your reach.

'The patient is far more cunning, my dear Doctor, than you imagine, and the clichés and platitudes don't really get you anywhere. The patient rages and suffers and wants more. I curse you and hate you because you cannot help me. Why can't you wave the magic wand or give me the potion I ask for?'

Annabelle waited. But Andreas had no answer. She felt sorry for him. She knew how impotent she made him feel.

'My head aches horribly,' she said.

Would he forgive her outburst? She would need to make amends for belittling him.

'I had hoped you'd ring me yesterday. What kind of lover doesn't call when he promised he would?' Annabelle was looking at Andreas with a mixture of love, contempt and despair.

Andreas gave a sigh of relief.

'You're angry with me because I didn't call you. I tried but I was interrupted. There was a crisis at the clinic.' He paused, wondering how he could reassure her that he loved her. 'The child believes that it's abandoned if it can't see the loved one. I'm here. I'm with you even when you can't see me. I'm here, Annabelle.'

'Oh, Andreas, I want to be with you, all day and all night.'

'I snore dreadfully my love, and crawl up to the bedhead, trying to get back into the womb. We had to put some padding because I kept hurting my head.'

'I would soothe you and hold you, and offer you my breast.'

'I know.' But he did not ask: *for how long?*

'It's got nothing to do with transference, psychotherapy, father, or the Oedipal complex. Really, it hasn't. I would have loved you no matter how, or what, or who you were when we met.'

'I almost believe that,' he said.

Annabelle gave an angry wail.

'Fuck! There you go again!'

'I'm sorry, I'm trying to be realistic, Annabelle.'

'Do you hate it when I swear? Do you think I sound vulgar?' she asked.

'I rather like it because you're being honest and passionate.'

'My husband hates it.'

'Yes, little girls aren't supposed to swear. And he treats you like a child. It's his way of keeping control over you. Except when he's away. Then you overcompensate by running away with your hippie friends and smoking dope. By the way, how is your relationship with David? When did you last have sex?'

'The other day, before he left.'

'What was it like?'

'Okay,' she said. Annabelle did not wish to dwell upon the subject.

'Did you enjoy it?'

'It was okay,' she said impatiently.

'It's probably those injections I gave you.'

'They must be having an effect. I notice it if I'm wearing tight jeans. I've been feeling quite sexy lately, even looking at older men.' She was going to make him regret his interrogation. 'I met a lovely man the other night. See what you've started?'

Andreas looked at her coldly. Unmoved. Or so Annabelle believed.

'My friend, Nicole, told me that she always has to fantasise when she's making love, even with a new lover. And she has lots of lovers. She said she fantasised about pornographic films and books. But I never need to do that when I make love with you, because I'm so turned on by what is happening in the moment. You're better than any fantasy.

Sometimes, though, when I read in the newspaper about a child having been raped or murdered, I get a strong feeling, as if I were that child. It's strange. Do normal people have these feelings?'

'It depends. You had a very early sexuality, a rather cruel one. Your father went too far. It's anxiety that makes you preoccupied with such things.'

'If I read an erotic book, like *Story of O,* I become sexually aroused.'

'Yes, you aren't going to lose yourself with an erotic book. It's safe. There's no responsibility of being hurt like in real life.'

'I have fantasies about what I think I want, but in reality it's different. It's confusing.'

'There's nothing wrong with a rich fantasy in order to enjoy something which you wouldn't want to enjoy in real life. Or maybe what excites you is what all that represents to you.'

Andreas was looking at Annabelle now with an intensity she found disturbing. There was something important he wanted to ask her. But he seemed nervous, hesitant.

Annabelle cocked her head to one side—waiting for him to tell her what was on his mind.

'Annabelle, if we lived together, how long would it be before you were unfaithful to me?'

Annabelle's face clouded over with emotion—fear, anger, disappointment. 'Ahhh! *If, if, if, if! If ifs and ands were pots and pans, there'd be no need of tinkers.'* She had played Shaw's *Saint Joan*. 'How the hell would I know? What a stupid question. I might not ever want to be unfaithful to you, then again, how on earth would I know how things would turn out? I'm not psychic.' Annabelle bit her lip, surprised by her outburst. She hated him for not trusting her. She felt like weeping. 'Why did you say that?'

Andreas looked pale and shaken.

'It was just a question.' Andreas glanced at his watch, then said rather dismissively, 'I have to go soon. I've got to see a patient of mine.'

Something in the way he said it fed Annabelle's curiosity. It was the proprietorial *of mine* at the end of his sentence.

'Oh?' she asked, raising her eyebrows.

'A young woman. She tried to kill herself. Slashed her wrists and throat. I think she did it for my benefit.'

Again, the chill in her veins, the way he had dropped those last words. She dared not ask any more questions. But she did not want the session to end, either.

'It's late afternoon. I hear David's car pull up. He's home early for a change. I wait at the front door with Byron, the dog I'm minding, in my arms. I wait and wait but he doesn't come. Finally I open the front door and peer over the wall. I can see the Porsche and David sitting behind the wheel. The picture I see is one of utter desolation. Every movement of his head spells pain to me. Should I run out to him and find out what the matter is, or should I leave him alone? Perhaps it's a private anguish. Perhaps, someone he loves hurt him, or maybe he's discovered what we've been doing, that I've betrayed him. I cannot stand the suspense any longer. I walk, heavy with dread to the car, clutching Byron. When David sees me, he smiles. I'm confused. He opens the door and I hear the voice of the radio announcer reading the evening news. He has been sitting in the car listening to the evening news. Half an hour later, I'm still shaken by the experience. I *invented* it all. All the pain. I saw it in front of my eyes even though it wasn't there. What hope is there for me if I see the world like that? David calls me a stranger. He says I'm from another planet.'

'Your pain is very real. I'm not helping you. I'm not helping you at all. I should have known that your analysis would be aborted. Worse, worse than that, I have made it …'

'Don't say that. Please don't say that,' Annabelle cried.

* * *

It was one of those beautiful sunny days, a perfect blue sky, swept clean by the wind— the Northerly, they call it—which kept the Sydney sky clear and unsullied. And Andreas was coming to dinner.

Annabelle had seen her husband off at the airport that morning. He was flying to New York for another conference. Then San Francisco and Las Vegas for some rest and recreational activity organised by the pharmaceutical company he was associated with. Normally she would have poured scorn on David's willingness to be bribed by Big Pharma. But now Annabelle did not care. Or rather, she only wanted to think about Andreas.

Annabelle drove straight to Taylor Square where she knew she would find the freshest produce from the Greek grocers along the strip. The menu she had decided upon for that evening included little courgettes soufflés from Elizabeth David's *French Provincial Cooking.* These soufflés were exquisite, and had originally been prepared for the writer by the proprietor of a lorry drivers' café in France. They would be followed by a seafood salad with a variety of fresh greens and mango. For dessert, she would serve one of her light chestnut crepes.

* * *

'You're early,' Annabelle lamented, quickly wrapping a sarong around herself, and then struggling to remove the rollers from her hair.

'Sorry, my love, but I told Jean I was going to a meeting at the hospital, and she knows they start at six. But you look wonderful with your hair done up like a geisha.'

'They're hair rollers!' she cried in dismay.

'To me, you're the most beautiful woman in the world. Nothing can change that.' He handed her a bunch of pink roses.

'How gorgeous, Andreas!' Annabelle cried, as she hugged and kissed him.

'I can't eat. I'm too excited,' Andreas said. 'I want to make love to you.'

Annabelle took him by the hand and led him upstairs to the bedroom.

'I won't be long,' she said.

Andreas looked around the room.

'So this is where David sleeps with his wife,' he whispered below his breath.

Andreas moved away from the bed to the French window seeking a distraction. He could see the harbour over the roofs of the terrace houses.

'Andreas,' he heard her whisper.

He straightened up, filling the frame. Music drifted up from somewhere in the neighbourhood. It was *The Skaters' Waltz*.

'*André. Andrei …*,' she called his name softly in French, then Russian. It was a mermaid calling—calling a sailor to his doom. He had told her how he had sat at his grandfather's knee after begging him to tell him once more the story of the Lorelei, the beautiful water sprites who lured men to their deaths. How he had loved him—and felt loved in return. Grandparents die too soon. Too soon.

What was the other name the dear old man had called them? The Russian name?

'*Rusalka*!' he said, remembering, exalted, turning and obeying the call. 'My little Rusalka!'

Annabelle stood in the middle of the room in a red silk kimono embroidered with gold and silver herons in flight. It was a Japanese wedding kimono. The birds were a symbol of happiness.

Andreas gravitated towards her. She would be his forever, one way or another. His hands were shaking as he took hold of her face, lifting her chin and kissing her lips. Andreas slipped the red kimono off Annabelle's shoulders. It clung to her body at the waist where it was held by a sash. He cupped her breasts in his hands and bent down to kiss them. When he heard her sigh, he pulled at the sash and it came undone, allowing the garment to fall to the floor. Then he carried her in his arms to the bed where he lay her down on the quilt. She sank through the softness, looking desirable and desiring. In her eyes, Andreas thought he saw reflected the longing, the love and the fear he always felt for her.

He parted her legs and pleasured her with his tongue. She called out his name over and over again, begging him to stop, yet not wanting him to end his enjoyment of her—or her of him.

Andreas undressed and leant over the bed, taking her gently towards him. She quivered under his touch, reached up to him, her arms encircled his neck. She cried and moaned, arched her throbbing body to receive him.

Their sighs and cries echoed from other lives in the corners of the room, until they were carried by the breeze across the water, over an imaginary mountain, and finally to a green and fertile plateau. They could have died, then.

* * *

The memory of that evening when he came to her home soon faded and she longed to be with him again. The weekly session was not enough. It *never* was enough. Annabelle longed to walk through a park with Andreas, lie on grass and look at the sky, or on a beach after a swim. To feel him beside her in the middle of the night—and in the morning, wake up in his arms.

'When Tuesday comes, I say to myself, I am going to see him, and I feel myself thawing. Being away from you is cold and bleak and barren. To be with you, like we are now in each other's arms, our hearts beating together, is glorious summer,' Annabelle was telling Andreas.

'Do you know what you've given me, Annabelle? A second chance at life. You make me feel emotions which I've buried since my childhood.'

'You expected the worst from me,' she said, caressing his cheek.

'I was afraid of you.'

'Afraid of *me*?'

'Of your power to beguile, to bind and excite, Annabelle. You're enticing and ensnaring, you know that?'

'That's not me.'

'Believe me that's you, Annabelle. You've disturbed my sleep forever.'

'Good,' she said.

'I love you,' Andreas whispered, kissing her lips. 'Oh, Annabelle, dearest one, I have so many beautiful dreams for us.'

'Tell me about them.'

'I want to take you abroad and show you off to all my friends and relatives. I want you to meet my sister. She would love you, you're so alike. See, our relationship is very incestuous in more ways than one.'

'It's very difficult to get away from this incest business, isn't it?' Annabelle said, shaking her head. 'Perhaps it's simply, *love*. Like the Jewish joke, '"Oedipus, Schmidipuss, what does it matter as long as you love your dear old mamma".'

Andreas laughed and it gladdened Annabelle's heart. There was so much seriousness in his life.

'Perhaps you're right,' he said.

'I read *Bond of Perfection*. I liked it and found it very moving. I'd love to read more of your sister's writing.'

'She wrote another book, I'll get you a copy, about her first husband. It's very moving. He drowned on a beach in Cyprus when his plane was shot down in the war. He was twenty-three,' Andreas said. 'When you meet Irina, you can tell her how much you loved her book,' he added, squeezing Annabelle closer to him. He kissed her neck, behind the ear, then worked his magic with his hands and his mouth, making her utter sounds he loved to hear. 'I want to take you to Switzerland, where I spent some of my childhood,' he continued, his fingers probing deep inside her, feeling her wetness, her nectar. 'I'd like to show you the lakes and the valleys and the mountains I knew. I'll take you climbing to my favourite mountain. I want you to meet my old schoolteacher, she's ninety-six and very bright still. I went to see her three years ago. She's got a marvellous mind, very *au courant* about what goes on in the world.'

'Oh,' Annabelle moaned, bending over, then straightening up as his hand moved up her body to her breasts, encircling her nipples. 'Andreas, could we stay in a beautiful hotel with huge iron gates and roses, lots of climbing roses and … Oh, my god, Andreas! What are you doing to me?' she broke off, pressing her back against his chest and his erection.

'I know exactly the one, my darling,' he interrupted, full of enthusiasm and sexual heat. 'I'll take you to Le Beau Rivage. It's the way you've described it. Maybe you've been there already.'

'In some other life, with you, yes,' Annabelle said, smiling mysteriously. 'Do you know what I wanted to be when I was little?'

'A courtesan,' Andreas said with a hint of disapproval, but also delight, which did not escape her. He lifted her buttocks.

'You're wrong!' Annabelle said, shaking her head, escaping his hold, and turning around to face him. 'Heidi! I wanted to be Heidi, the little girl who lives in the Alps with her grandfather and the cows. I wanted to have fair hair and blue eyes and freckles, lots of freckles. I love freckles, they make a girl look so pretty. The only freckle I have is on my wrist,' she sighed.

'Instead you came out looking like Bambi.'

'I hate the way I look.'

'I love it,' Andreas said kissing her eyes and her lips again. 'And China,' he continued. 'China will be opening up soon to the world. I want to go there. My dream is to give up my work and study Chinese medicine. Take it to the West.'

'And I will sit in the front row of the audience wherever you are in the world and applaud your brilliant discourses. I can see it. It'll be fantastic. I'd love that for you, Andreas,' Annabelle said, stroking his hair, cupping her hand at the base of his skull, feeling him relaxing into her caresses. 'Tell me more about when you were little, what you did, where you lived.'

'I want to enter your delicious cunt!' he said.

'And I want to know *everything* about you.'

Andreas sighed.

'We holidayed in the South of France in summer and the Swiss Alps in winter, for the skiing. Our home was always bustling with visitors—writers, humanitarians, philosophers and scoundrels. The scoundrels were usually invited by my mother. She did it to annoy my father. He felt ashamed about her Polish connection because the Poles behaved very badly towards the Jews during the war. He always believed the Poles were anti-Semitic, and of course he was right. It was jealousy, because the Jews had the best houses, were the most educated and artistic, and the women were beautiful. After the war, he donated money to Israel to make up for it. I gave a lot of my money too.

'I was sent to boarding school, to Bedales, where my father had gone—a smart, permissive type of school run on the philosophy of William Morris. We were never caned. If we were punished, we'd be sent to the kitchen to peel a sack of potatoes. Sometimes, it seemed as if nobody cared enough to get angry. I fell in love with a girl in my class. After months of torturing myself, I finally raised enough courage to write her a love letter. It was a disaster. She told me to get lost. I was shattered. I never forgot the feeling.'

'It probably started earlier, my love, this feeling of rejection,' Annabelle remarked.

'My little analyst,' Andreas said, affectionately biting her nipple.

'I don't want to ever hurt you, Andreas. I would rather destroy myself than hurt you.'

'You're adorable,' Andreas said, kissing her hand. 'Now will you let me fuck you?'

'*Heigh-ho*,' Annabelle teased, imitating his quaint old-fashioned phrase.

'You take me far, far away, from my cares and mundane existence,' Andreas said. He could hardly wait to be inside her. He tried again to reach her, probing, stretching her resistance. But even though she reacted to what he was doing with little cries, gasps and shudders, Annabelle held him off.

'Do you know Andreas, I think about you a hundred times a day. Sometimes, I see you the way you are when you make love to me, that first defining moment … like when an animal is slaughtered.' Annabelle pressed her hand against her mouth when she saw the expression on Andreas's face. 'How strange that I should associate sex with death,' she said. Then, trying to minimise the seriousness of what she had confessed, added: 'How Freudian.' When that did not make Andreas smile, she tried to justify herself by quoting Picasso: "To think about death is to be truly alive!"

But Andreas was not mollified.

'You think a man wants to take everything from you, don't you?' he said.

'You do! You want *everything*. I can tell, I sense it, especially when you make love to me. Your lovemaking is so thorough, so concentrated on *me*, instead of on your pleasure, unlike other men. You don't want to leave me anywhere to hide.'

'It's true. I want you. I want all of you. Don't hold back on me, Annabelle. Please don't hold back!' Andreas's eyes shone with that intensity which frightened her, while exciting her at the same time.

He began undressing her with feverish skill. He could undo the tightest knot in a second, a Houdini—and drew her down on top of his erection. Annabelle cried out but Andreas pressed his hand quickly over her mouth to stifle her cry.

'This is better than bouncing on Daddy's knee,' he whispered.

'Oh, yes,' she sobbed.

* * *

That night Annabelle lay in bed wondering about those beautiful heroic men, Andreas's father and grandfather. It was not just their good looks that were so seductive—these men were exceptional, stellar performers, much admired and sought after, men of brilliance, courage and ideals. Andreas had inherited some of their qualities, and yet had never achieved his potential. His life had been one of drawbacks, dreariness, failure. He could have done so much with the fortune left to him, yet he had squandered it all, except for what he gave away to his Jewish friends. It seems as if those men had done everything—received all the accolades, the love and the glory—leaving nothing for Andreas.

His love for her was now so powerful, so despairing, that he was resorting to dangerous games. He had bent himself out of shape, trying to guess what she wanted him to be, to please her, so that she would love him. It was madness. All this weighed heavily on Annabelle's mind. Most of all, it frightened her.

21 The Tao of Sex

When Andreas announced that his wife was taking their daughter to Switzerland to enrol her in a finishing school, he handed Annabelle the keys to his house. It surprised Annabelle, but she surmised it was for her convenience, so she would not be left waiting outside if Andreas was held up at the clinic.

They had both hoped David would leave the country too, for some of the time Andreas's wife was away, so they could at least spend the nights together. But Annabelle's husband was working on his research.

The Zill residence was a large, conventional old brick home on the North Shore, with a lawn that reached to the harbour's edge. Annabelle immediately noticed the sparse planting of trees and plants. It was an unloved garden. The unappealing pool was set in shadow and whenever it rained, funnel web spiders washed into it. Annabelle noticed a few floating on the surface. She shivered for a brief moment with revulsion at the black hairy, and deadly predaceous arachnids. The house appeared devoid of any personal touches. It could have been the home of a well-endowed institution. Annabelle thought Andreas's room at the clinic had more warmth and character.

Andreas had left an item on the coffee table for Annabelle. It had some meaning for him and he had been keen to show it to her.

It was an amateurish handmade children's storybook.

'H. G. Wells wrote and illustrated it for my sister and me. He hand coloured it, which apparently was a very unusual thing for him to do, as I don't believe he was very fond of children. He used to visit our home in Geneva. I think he was in love with my mother and was trying to seduce her.'

At the beginning, Annabelle was overjoyed to be spending more time with Andreas. He had promised he would take one afternoon off work a week so they could be together, and had arranged for his son

Nicolas to be cared for elsewhere.

Nonetheless, Annabelle was overcome with feelings of unease. There was a streak of decency, a remnant of breeding which she had inherited from her mother, along with the normal Catholic guilt from her convent days. It made her accept that it was wrong to endanger the marriage of a man with two teenage children—one seriously ill. She wanted Andreas for herself, but not at a price paid with other people's unhappiness. And of course, there was David to consider.

The thought of leaving David, as well as all the financial and emotional security he gave her, made her physically ill. Annabelle believed David would never betray or abandon her. She felt safe with him, sheltered by the umbrella of his fidelity. David, she reasoned, had come from a loving Jewish family, unlike Andreas, whose father had left a trail of wounded women and illegitimate children during his marriage. At the same time, there was a part of Annabelle, the *farouche* side that Andreas had identified, which longed for play, excitement and danger. Fired by her impetuosity, she could not travel fast enough that summer to meet him at his home .

As for Andreas, the idea of taking the whole afternoon off from work, to make love, play and rest, was unfamiliar and troubling. It was all new to him, especially laughter. Sometimes, Annabelle would tickle him or tumble with him on the carpet or on the lawn and he would laugh, surprising himself. There had been so much despondency in his life.

'Where's your dog?' Annabelle said, looking around the house.

'We gave him to Mrs Carter, the cleaning lady.'

'Oh,' she said, sounding disappointed.

'He's happier in her care,' Andreas reassured her.

But Andreas felt downhearted that Annabelle did not express a desire to meet Nicolas. Perhaps he had made a mistake describing his son as an overweight fully grown man in a wheelchair. And when Annabelle had asked Andreas if his son looked like him, Andreas had replied: 'No, he looks like Jean.'

'I feel guilty,' he said. 'My wife and I never spent much time lying in bed like this. It would have been self indulgent. I guess it's our generation, a legacy of the Protestant work ethic, doing something pleasurable is sinful and wasteful. Not quite true, I know,' he added. 'Protestant Victorian gentlemen spent a lot of time in the pursuit of sex ...'

'Seducing poor servant girls. Getting them pregnant. Bastards!' Annabelle interrupted.

'Yes, they were hypocrites,' Andreas said. He gave Annabelle a half-hearted smile. 'I'm afraid it's going to take me some time to get used to this. My life has been so rigid, so regimented.'

Andreas cleaned out the pool and they dipped into it and played games. Annabelle loved to swim through the arch he made for her with his legs. It was a game Annabelle had played with her father when she was a child. When she surfaced, gasping and laughing, Andreas took her in his arms and held her. His embrace was not sexual, although they were naked. And yet, no parent had ever held her that way.

Annabelle went inside the house to retrieve her sarong. She stood and observed Andreas for a while through the open window. His eyes were closed and his face was turned to the sun. He looked so pale, so much in need of those healing rays.

'*André*,' Annabelle called. 'Andreas, come.' She wanted him to feel her body again, in a sexual embrace this time.

Andreas responded to her call.

Annabelle was still standing by the window when Andreas walked into the bedroom. When she felt him close behind her, she dropped her sarong and bent forward, spreading her arms wide on the window sill as she had done once before, to remind him of the dying swan. He swept the hair from her neck kissing her nape, leaving more kisses down her back and into her sacrum. He spread her legs apart with his knee. When he fingered and played with her clitoris he elicited a reaction resembling a bird caught in the throes of death. How expressive of the French to call this moment *the little death,* he thought.

The instant Andreas felt Annabelle swoon and yield completely, he clasped her waist and pulled her close to him. She straightened up and turned her head towards him so he could kiss her face. When he felt her responding, and saw her steady herself by holding on to the window frame, he lifted her from behind so he could insert himself into her. She leaned back against him, helping him to move in deeper.

'Feel me?' he said. 'Do you feel me, Annabelle?' It was a request, a plea.

'Oh yes,' she cried. Her cry almost a sob. 'I feel you *so* much, Andreas.'

If the lovers are perfect for each other, according to the Taoist book, their hearts will connect during the act of intercourse, when the man's penis is aligned with the mouth of the woman's womb. The male heart has a nexus with the tip of his penis. The female heart has a bond with the bud of her womb.

* * *

Afterwards, Andreas told Annabelle: 'When we make love, I feel immortal. *You,* have the power to make me feel immortal.'

And she replied: 'And you have the power to make me feel beautiful.'

'That's impossible,' Andreas said. 'You already are beautiful.'

'*Heigh ho,*' Annabelle mocked, and was pleased when he laughed with her.

'Sometimes, Andreas, I wish people could see us together. I want them to acknowledge our existence, to witness our love. I want us to walk arm-in-arm down the street, like we did that time when we went to see *Last Tango*. I'd like us to sit in a restaurant, look into each other's eyes and for people to see us. Otherwise how do I know we're not an illusion? But most of all I want to sleep beside you for a whole night and wake up in the morning in your arms.'

'How can that be, Annabelle? You are David's wife.'

* * *

Later that afternoon, after the swim and the love-making, Andreas sat in a winged armchair beside the open window. But he was not gazing at the beautiful sunset and the white sails rollicking along the harbour. No, he was staring at Annabelle who was lying in bed.

'What is it, Andreas?' she asked.

Andreas did not answer immediately. Annabelle rose pulling the sheet around herself, covering her vulnerability. She went across to Andreas and took the empty wine glass out of his hand and sat on his lap, kissing his cheek, looking into his eyes, hoping he would open up to her.

'My father said something to me once that I never fully understood, until this moment,' Andreas said.

'What was it?' Annabelle coaxed, in an attempt to allay his discontent—and her anxiety.

'Actually, it was Tolstoy who said, 'The moment a beautiful woman makes a man the happiest of men, he becomes the most miserable.'

'Why, I wonder?'

'Because he's afraid of losing her. Because he doesn't believe he's worthy of her love.'

Annabelle sighed. She felt helpless, had no idea how to even begin to dispel Andreas's fears. She looked out of the window, wanting to escape. But her attention was caught by something in the distance, around the edge of the harbour—a dark figure among the rocks. It was being followed by a tiny creature. Soon, another and another feline appeared until the shadowy figure was surrounded by a bunch of wild, stray cats.

Andreas, who was watching Annabelle watching the cat lady, explained:

'That's the old woman who feeds the cats. She comes every day at dusk. She's been feeding them for years. She's getting too old for those rocks. One day she's going to have a bad fall.'

'And who will look after those poor hungry creatures if anything happens to her?' Annabelle lamented.

'They'll starve to death, I suppose.'

'Oh no!' Annabelle cried, covering her eyes.

* * *

Another time, Andreas closed the shutters in order to darken the living room so that he could show Annabelle the home movies he had promised her. As the old black and white rickety images materialised from the past, Annabelle held her breath and waited. When the camera finally found the little boy with blond hair, he seemed to bask in the momentary attention bestowed on him. He danced, waved, blew kisses—and fell to the ground. His sister came and took him away.

There were skiing holidays in Saint Moritz and summers at Cap d'Antibes. A few times the child reappeared, hoping someone would acknowledge his existence. There was an air of desperation about the little boy Annabelle found heart-breaking.

Annabelle sat close to Andreas, touching him, stroking his back, hoping to make up for that childhood neglect, although she sensed some things could not be healed. Nevertheless, Annabelle continued, kissing his cheek, brushing back his thinning hair from his forehead with her fingers.

'There's old Bernard Shaw,' Andreas was excited at showing her the famous people who had visited his parents' home. The amiable figure of the playwright with the white beard ambled then posed beside a lemon tree in a Versailles tub, on the terrace at the edge of Lake Geneva. 'There's Bertie Russell, and there I am sitting on Jung's lap. He had a very comfortable lap—like a bear—a very powerful and charismatic man. He made a lasting impression on me, I don't know why. Women loved him. Did you know that Jung was seduced, sodomised, by a friend, when he was a boy? By a respectable, highly educated man, whom he idolised and trusted?'

* * *

When the screening ended, Annabelle waited patiently for Andreas to finish spooling back the old film. Then she beckoned tenderly to him.

'Come Andreas, come darling, I want to teach you to be a little bit more selfish. Come with me,' she said taking his hand and leading him to the bedroom. 'Lie down on the bed. I'm going to make love to you, but you mustn't touch me, because when you do, I close my eyes. And I want to look at you. I don't want to miss anything.'

'That's going to be hard,' Andreas said.

He hesitated.

'Lie back, on the cushions,' Annabelle coaxed with a gentle and reassuring touch, until he surrendered into her hands.

She began by caressing his head—forehead, eyelids, ears, mouth. Then Annabelle moved down to his neck, chest, nipples—she stopped there, moistening them with her tongue and blowing warm air from her mouth. Annabelle continued down to his stomach and thighs, which she pressed apart. She kissed the inside of them, then took his penis in her hand, gently pushing the velvet skin back to reveal the pink organ which she placed in her mouth. Her tongue played with the tip. There she stopped because she did not want him to climax yet. There was more to do. Other places to pleasure.

Annabelle massaged the area around his perineum and was pleased to observe the arousal it evoked. Every time he reached for her, she brushed his hands away. Then she did something which made him gasp—after wetting her fingers in her mouth, she parted his buttocks and inserted first one, then two of her fingers, working them around, until she found the gland. This, she massaged slowly, lovingly until he shuddered and cried out her name in a moment of uncurbed ecstasy. No wife, mistress or whore had ever done that to him. No experience had ever electrified him with such a complete physical expression of pleasure.

'My god, Annabelle! What have you done to me?' Andreas said, drawing her to his chest, kissing her cheek and her temple.

* * *

Andreas was not home the next time she arrived at his house. Annabelle let herself in with the key he had given her for the first time, enjoying the thrill. She unpacked the meal she had prepared and then looked around, opening kitchen cupboards and the refrigerator, curious about the other woman, the mistress of the house.

There were no fresh vegetables or fruit anywhere to be seen. When she opened the freezer, she found it stuffed with meats—steaks, pork chops, sausages and salamis. There were also Sara Lea cakes and pastries. Annabelle was concerned that Andreas was existing on a terrible diet.

Curiosity drew her to the bedroom, to the bedside table to see what he was reading. She picked up a book, *The Greeks* by Euripides, and opened it where he had left a bookmark.

What are the Furies?
They are a kind of conscience.
They were engendered
In love that is poisoned
In feuds in the family
In the screams of tortured children
In bloodshed and violence
In cruelty and anger
In the stench and the venom
Of good things made foul.
They drive their victims mad.

The doorbell rang. Annabelle froze. She did not want to answer it in case it was a friend of Andreas's wife, or a neighbour. Instead, she tiptoed to the window and peered out. It was a woman about her age with a 70's frizz, dressed in patchwork layers and heavy boots. She rang the doorbell again, and again. Then she trudged around to the side of the house. Finally, to Annabelle's relief, she returned to her car and drove off. Annabelle thought that she had seen her before at the clinic but perhaps she was mistaken.

* * *

It had been a beautiful summer but it was coming to an end. Sydney seemed unwilling to relinquish days of brilliant sunshine and was weaving magic with the weather, holding back the cold. Andreas's wife would soon be coming back from England and the Continent.

Andreas had taken his glass of wine with him to the verandah, while Annabelle cleared the remains of their lunch. She always brought more food so that Andreas and Nicolas could have another nutritious meal. She was secretly glad that Andreas had arranged for Nicolas to be looked after by a friend for the few hours Annabelle was at the house.

Annabelle had noticed earlier in the afternoon *The Tao of Sexology* on

Andreas's bedside table. When she went to join him, she took the book along. She had bought it for him on her way to see him one day but had not had a chance to look at it.

Now, sitting outside, next to Andreas on the chintz-covered sofa overlooking the harbour, she opened the book.

'Do you know the *Five Virtues of the Penis*?' Andreas said. There was a twinkle in his eyes which always animated Annabelle.

She looked up at Andreas with a quizzical smile.

'No,' she said.

He took the book from her and quoted:

'*The penis is kind. It exists mainly as a tool to service the woman. Two: It's not selfish—it's certainly not about man's pleasure. Three: It's courteous and polite. It knows when to advance and when to retreat. It must be made into a source of happiness, not pain. It must not be used as a weapon to hurt another. Four: It is wise. It will do everything to please and satisfy a woman. Five: It is honest. It completes its duty.*'

Annabelle looked astonished. It was all new to her.

'I'm impressed,' she said.

'I'm enjoying it,' Andreas said. 'The Taoists were scientists who believed wisdom came from knowledge subject to scrutiny and deeper questioning. They held themselves to a higher ethical and moral standard. But here, pass me the book. I want to show you something.'

Andreas opened the book at a section he wanted Annabelle to see.

'Oh!' Annabelle cried when Andreas showed her the images of sexual intercourse.

'Take your pick. Would you like the Crane, Dragon, Fish, Monkey, Phoenix, Rabbit, Turtle or Tiger Sex?'

Annabelle was tongue-tied, eyes wide open. But disbelief soon gave way to amusement.

'All of them!' she said.

'All?'

'Yes!'

'How delightful,' Andreas said. 'Which one do you want to start with?'

'Tiger Sex!'

'In this position,' Andreas read out, *'the woman is on her hands and knees and the man is on his knees and penetrates from behind. Both are encouraged to move in a synchronous motion. The woman is encouraged to orgasm as much as it pleases her while the man is encouraged to withhold his.'*

Annabelle went down on all fours then sidled up close to Andreas, gazing into his eyes, rubbing the side of her head against his chest, nuzzling into him. She glided up to his face and rubbed her cheek against his, purring, seeking his mouth. Andreas stroked her head and kissed her lips. Annabelle licked his face.

Andreas laughed.

'You're more of a pussycat than a tiger!' he said.

Annabelle straightened up and sat back on her haunches. Her face had a look of earnest intensity. '*God created the cat so that man could caress the tiger.*'

'You're adorable,' he said.

Andreas could wait no longer. He wanted to be inside her body.

Annabelle gave a trembling sigh at his touch and turned away from him. She bent forward arching her spine, then flexing it in the opposite direction, like a cat. She moved her hips back so that Andreas could reach her.

Meanwhile, Annabelle had entered the spirit of the cat. She saw all their sufferings through the ages—the killings, rituals, hatred, ignorance, superstition and demonisation of the cat—and it was more than she could bear. She began to cry.

Andreas noticed and asked with concern: 'Why are you crying, Annabelle? What's wrong?'

'Nothing,' she said. 'Summer is ending.'

* * *

Andreas had learned to separate orgasm from ejaculation, the Taoist way, to prolong life and also to pleasure Annabelle. With this method, he hoped to satisfy her because deep inside he felt a failure. He took Annabelle into the house—she had cried out when she climaxed—and he was worried about the neighbours.

'They'll just think you've brought a peacock into your garden,' she said.

* * *

After their hours of lovemaking, Annabelle sat reading from the *The Tao of Sexology*. She was fascinated, then shocked to discover that all the positions for intercourse Andreas had shown her, directed that when the man penetrated the woman, he was to remain still, withhold his ejaculation, and let the woman do all the moving, all the rocking. The man was to encourage the woman to climax as much as she desired. Andreas had taken it one step at a time, guiding her, instructing her and encouraging her to move her hips as she felt it, while he had remained stable. Annabelle had felt awkward, she would need lots of practice.

All her adult life Annabelle had been conditioned to keep still. 'Don't move!' she was ordered right from the start. David liked to prolong his sessions with intercourse, by insisting his wife remain absolutely still. She realised that it was one more thing that had frozen her heart to him.

22 Shocking

One hot still summer evening, a Saturday, David invited Andreas and some of his colleagues to help him celebrate an award he had received. The perfume from the jasmine Annabelle had planted four years earlier, drifted into the house. It cascaded down the garden walls in clouds of pink and white flowers. Some of the guests found the smell intoxicating and moved away.

It was unlike David to appear completely self-satisfied as he was that evening—he had always been critical of himself and of others, although he disguised it well with audacity—but David's photograph, together with a story, had appeared on the front page of the daily newspapers. In celebration he had several glasses of champagne. After dinner, he whisked his wife into the middle of the lounge room floor to dance the tango. His friends cheered him on. When the music ended, he leaned over Annabelle and kissed her on the lips, hard and long. Annabelle felt humiliated by his sudden exhibitionism. David had treated her as an object in front of his friends, wanting to impress, perhaps even make them envy him. Annabelle feared he had another reason.

Andreas, who had been watching, paled considerably when David kissed Annabelle. His face and his silk shirt were wet with perspiration. He rose unsteadily on his feet and made his way into the garden.

As soon as she could, Annabelle joined him. Andreas felt clammy when she touched his cheek and she worried about him. Desperate to reassure him, she whispered in his ear: 'I love you.'

But when Andreas recovered, he left the party.

How Annabelle would have loved to run away with Andreas. Instead, she sat by the jasmine vine and wept.

* * *

That night, Annabelle lay awake, unable to sleep. Why had David invited Andreas to his party? What was his motive? Did he suspect Andreas and Annabelle were lovers? Is that why he had humiliated her with the kiss? But she was also angry with Andreas for accepting the invitation. After all, he had not come to the house when she had needed him most—the time she languished in bed longing for him and dying of pneumonia. Why now, to celebrate a meaningless award for David?

* * *

Annabelle stood hesitantly in the doorway of Andreas's consulting room, wondering what state she would find him in. She had tried to ring him, but he had not returned her calls.

Andreas was slumped in the leather armchair in the semi-darkness staring out the window. The rain was hammering onto the grey, still surface of the water. The Navy destroyer moored in the bay, was now an ominous presence.

'Hello, Andreas,' Annabelle said. There was a timidity in her voice, an indication of her state of apprehension.

He swung around but did not rise to greet her. On his lap lay an evening newspaper.

Andreas glanced up.

Annabelle waited for him to say something.

'I'm sorry I'm late. I was held up in traffic by the rain,' she said. The expression on his face made her ask: 'Is anything wrong?'

'Not at all. I was reading the paper, enjoying the break,' Andreas said.

'Did you think I wasn't coming?'

'The idea did occur to me. It's something I've anticipated from the start—that one day I won't see you again. I'm not afraid. I have it all stored inside me. No matter how far away you'll be.'

'I don't want to be far away from you,' Annabelle said, wanting to ignore the panic she felt rising within her.

But Andreas was no longer listening to her. He seemed preoccupied with other matters. He reached for the light switch on the brass lamp on his desk and held up the newspaper. On the front page was a photograph of a youth, handcuffed and flanked by two detectives.

'What's he done?'

'Killed a girl. Raped her, battered her and set fire to her. They found her body in the scrub. He's a deaf mute.'

'Oh god!' Annabelle said, not knowing what else to utter at the horror and the tragedy.

'He must have been very angry,' Andreas added.

For a moment Andreas's words struck terror in her heart. She was suddenly afraid of him, sensing his own murderous feelings towards her—that darkness he had managed to suppress so well. Wanting to help, Annabelle tried to lead him to that place he feared, and found necessary to isolate himself from.

'You're angry with me, Andreas,' she said gently, trying to appease him.

'I have no right to be. Besides, I never get angry, I've told you before. No, I guess I'm just weary and upset. I've had some bad news about my son—he's going to be in a wheelchair for the rest of his life—and a patient died on me this morning after I gave him ECT.'

'Shock treatment?'

'Yes.'

'You use shock treatment?' Annabelle asked in disbelief. ECT was a horrible procedure, terrifying, she had seen it done in films.

'I do, yes. It's used frequently in psychiatric hospitals with positive results. It's the best thing for severe depression.' Andreas sounded as though he needed to justify himself. 'Anyway, that's not what he died of. He was old and sick and I should have watched him after giving him the treatment until he came out from under the anaesthetic, instead of leaving him with an inexperienced nurse. There'll be a coroner's inquest and I will be called in front of the board and hauled through the ritual in front of my peers. His wife has every right to sue me for malpractice.'

'It was an accident, Andreas.' Annabelle was desperate to reassure him, and herself.

'No. We give hundreds of ECTs here at the Bollingen. It only seems to happen to me. This is my second death.'

'Second? When was the other one?' Annabelle asked, with a feeling of mounting dread.

'A few years ago. An obese man, same thing, ECT. Died under anaesthesia,' he said.

Annabelle was shattered. She felt like weeping. Did Andreas ever learn from his mistakes?

'I am responsible for those deaths, Annabelle.'

Andreas was in a fragile state of mind. How could she help him? She went across to him—touched him gently on the arm but he remained stiff and unmoved.

'It was an accident,' she repeated, but even to her own ears she did not sound very convincing.

'My friend Laurence gave up.'

'Who is Laurence, Andreas?'

'Another psychiatrist. We were together at the Tavistock. He killed himself after I left England. We have the highest suicide rate of any profession.'

'Why is that?'

Andreas shrugged. 'I suppose we're all crazy, unbalanced. That's why we're drawn to the profession in the first place. We want to get close to other crazy people so that we can study them and perhaps find the answers we are seeking to our own madness.'

Annabelle looked at Andreas and despaired.

* * *

There was more to come. Annabelle thought she could pinpoint the day and the incident which brought to a head Andreas's mounting distrust of her.

An arrangement had been made to meet around noon at his house. They arrived at the same time from opposite directions, engaging in a childish but dangerous game—driving towards each other at speed and swerving at the last moment to avoid a collision.

Annabelle had jumped out of the car shaking with laughter, ready to fall into his arms. But there was a yellow van parked outside, and instead, Andreas ran inside the house ignoring her. He seemed preoccupied that the painter was still there, and when Annabelle followed, he tried to hide her in the kitchen. Refusing to be pushed aside, Annabelle upset Andreas further by peering around the doorway and catching the young man's eye.

The painter winked at her.

'He's gorgeous!' Annabelle exclaimed, as soon as the young man left.

'Why?' Andreas asked tersely, looking in from the other room, where he was pushing the furniture into place.

Annabelle shrugged.

'He just is,' she said.

She soon regretted having provoked him—had not foreseen how her flippant remark might resonate with him.

While Andreas was making a telephone call to check on his son, Annabelle noticed a copy of Durrell's *The Alexandria Quartet* in his study. The set of novels had affected her deeply when she read them in her teens. Durrell's writing haunted her with its dark sexuality, coruscating prose, and the mysterious and seductive characters of a now vanished city, Alexandria. She held the thick book in her hands and opened it at a page Andreas had marked with a receipt from the jeweller—for the gold chain and heart he had given her. Three lines stood out, unsettling her: *There is no pain compared to that of loving a woman who makes her body accessible to one and yet who is incapable of delivering her true self—because she does not know where to find it.*

After lunch, Andreas brought out a hand-rolled cigarette from his shirt pocket. It surprised Annabelle as she had never seen him smoke before, except for the odd cigar.

'It's dope,' Andreas said, in reply to her quizzical look. 'A patient gave it to me this morning. He grows it in his apartment.'

Andreas lit the joint and inhaled deeply. He reached over and took hold of Annabelle's head with both hands blowing smoke into her mouth. Annabelle tried to protest—she did not enjoy marijuana as it sent her to sleep. Later, in the middle of making love, Andreas gripped her hard and stared into her face. He then let out a cry from the heart, terrifying in its intensity. 'I love you Annabelle. I really do!'

The nakedness of his revelation was shocking. He demanded that she love him in return, with the same madness. But she shied away.

Andreas would never forgive her for being afraid.

* * *

A few days later, Annabelle was sitting in his room at the clinic. It was a gloomy afternoon, another day of rain.

'In my dream, you walk away from me. You're all alone, in a bleak, colourless landscape, except for two bare trees on each side of the stony path you're on. You're wearing a long grey coat, like the one Marlon Brando wore in *Last Tango* … I want to follow but can't …'

'You mean *won't,*' Andreas said.

A disquieting silence settled between them.

'Are many of your patients affected by the weather?' Annabelle asked, desperate to dissolve the wretchedness they felt.

'Not just my patients,' Andreas replied. He looked strained and dispirited. He had not slept.

'How do the English manage, then?' Annabelle tried to start a dialogue.

'Look at them, they're so unhappy,' he answered.

'Still, they did manage to conquer half the world,' Annabelle reminded him.

'That's why,' he said.

'You're angry with me, Andreas.'

'Why should I be angry with you?'

'You're angry with me because I let you down.'

'I'm the one who let you down,' Andreas insisted. 'I betrayed your trust. I should never have made love to you. Making love to you was a betrayal.'

'I wanted you to make love to me,' Annabelle said.

'But you don't *love* me,' Andreas insisted.

For a moment he looked as though he would lose control, become enraged, hurt her.

'I'm having a slight identification crisis,' Andreas continued, in a resigned manner. 'For some time now, I've become rather mixed up with the countertransference. I realised it when we made love. At the peak of our lovemaking you cried, *Pappa*!'

Annabelle reeled, as though she had been struck. She tried to protest but succeeded only in making a strange sound in her throat. The blood draining from her head left her lightheaded and feeling faint.

'I don't believe it,' she said, shaking her head. 'I just don't believe you.' The silence which followed could not have been more acrid. Finally, Annabelle looked up at Andreas and asked: 'Did I really? Did I really, honestly say that, Andreas?'

He nodded gravely: 'Yes.'

Annabelle was still incredulous. He could be lying.

'That's okay,' she said brightly, trying to dispel despair. 'Why, only the other day I was reading in *Cosmopolitan* that when people make love and climax, they cry out all sorts of funny things, like: *Cripes! Hell! Jesus!* Anything and everything under the sun. What's so special about *Pappa*? We all do it. We're all the same.'

'No, we're not.'

'But our basic needs are similar. And our fears. We all need love and support.'

'Our defences differ. We develop diverse strategies to cope with our anxieties and our fears. *You* cut people off. *You freeze them out!*'

Annabelle detested his accusatory tone, but she hated silence even more. Surely things were not as hopeless as he was making them out to be?

'Your subconscious cried out *Pappa*. You mistook me for your father,' Andreas insisted.

'It's not surprising!' Annabelle sought to defend herself in the only way she knew—by striking back. 'Ever since I came to see you, you've tried to be my father. Over there, when you fucked me and rocked me on your cock, you told me it was better than bouncing on Daddy's knees. Don't you see? You gave me more of the drug, instead of curing me. You tried to brainwash me and enslave me. Because you loved me, you wanted to tie me irrevocably to you. You gave me this gold chain with the heart because I told you my father had given me one. You've tried to be Daddy to me. You've even tried to *out do* Daddy.'

'That was a big mistake of mine,' Andreas said. He looked humbled.

'It's all right, Andreas. I wanted you. I wanted you so much. It's all my fault. Really, it is.' Annabelle wanted desperately for him to believe her.

'I had the feeling that I was standing outside a closed door when I made love to you yesterday,' Andreas said. 'The dope we smoked made me more aware of what was happening. I despaired, just like others must have despaired. Just like your husband must despair. You're a destroyer, Annabelle!'

'I haven't destroyed David,' Annabelle said.

'I don't have his strength. Or maybe it's because I love you more than he does. He just uses you, for sex and to show you off. I don't think anyone has ever loved you the way I have. I know, because I know the depth of my love. But it will destroy me, I feel that now.'

'I would never destroy you, Andreas,' Annabelle said, her eyes filling up with tears.

Andreas would not be swayed.

'You would. In your subconscious, you wish to destroy me. You know how to do it. You have the power to do it.'

'Only if you give me that power, Andreas. I love you. I don't want to hurt you.'

'You castrate men!' Andreas said, determined not to be seduced again.

'It's not true. You held back too. You told lies. When I wanted so much to spend time with you, when David was away and you had a conference to go to, you defaulted. You told me that your wife and your secretary had decided it was not necessary for you to attend, that you could not afford to do so. We could have been together. Was I supposed to believe that you are so helpless?'

'It was true,' Andreas said. He sounded hollow.

'It may have been true that they forbade you to go. But what are you? A two-year- old? I don't believe you are that helpless. I believe you use it as an excuse. You're what's called *passive-aggressive*, doctor. Your secretary said you're about as helpless as a sabre-toothed tiger. I believe you had other reasons. You were afraid to spend four days and nights with me because you were scared we might get really close. We've never spent much time together. Do you realise that during all this time, we've never been together for a night? Even Romeo and Juliet had that!'

Andreas laughed at the comparison. For a moment Annabelle's heart leapt and she thought there might still be hope. But then he crossed his arms and his legs, and turned his face away from her.

'How ridiculous,' he said, dismissing her.

Annabelle was not ready to give up.

'That time, towards the beginning of our affair, when we were so happy,' she wanted to remind him, 'and we had just made love—you said to me that I was everything you had ever wanted and longed for. Then you astonished me by telling me that you would have to let me go. I couldn't understand what you were trying to do, what game you were playing. I had a feeling at that moment that I couldn't trust you because you couldn't trust yourself. I wanted you to be truthful with me, to say what you really meant, open your heart and treat me as an adult. Instead, you retreated and resorted to playing games. And when you saw how distressed I was, I sensed that you were happy, because you discovered the power you possess over me. The power to hurt me. I think you made the decision a long time ago that you would use your power, your famous charm, to hurt people instead of loving them. That's why you hurt your first wife and your children, and all the women you've seduced—as you're hurting Jean right now. Once you told me that we go through life making others feel like we were made to feel—mostly rejected, humiliated and unloved.'

'I did try to give you my love, yesterday,' Andreas said. 'I revealed myself to you and you wouldn't accept my feelings.'

'It's true. I guess it came too late. I realise now that I lost faith in you some time ago,' Annabelle said.

'When I crossed the line professionally,' he said.

'Yes. No! When you didn't come to see me when I was ill.'

But his heart now was closed to her heart.

They sat there in the darkening twilight, feeling utterly miserable, reeling at what had happened. It was as though they had lived on a splendid peak and now, having failed, were being banished to live the rest of their lives in lowly torment. It was punishment for breaking the *taboo*. The gods were angry.

23 A Slippery Slope

Annabelle lay in bed all morning staring at the ceiling in a state of shock. It felt like being in an accident, a train crash, and waiting to die. Perhaps she was already dead.

The ringing on the telephone eventually reached her, animating her. With great effort she reached across the bed to pick up the receiver.

But she could not speak.

'What are you doing?'

'Nothing,' Annabelle managed to utter.

'Would you like to have lunch with me?'

'Yes,' she said. Andreas's voice was bringing her back to life. Annabelle could not resist, did not want to resist. She needed to see Andreas.

'See you at the new restaurant, *Pavillion on the Park,* opposite the Art Gallery. Do you know it? I went there recently and it was very good.'

'What time?' Annabelle cried, panicking lest he hang up.

'One o'clock.'

Annabelle's heart sank when she looked at the time. It was twelve o'clock already, and she had not even showered. Andreas had hardly given her any time to prepare herself. Besides, her head was pounding and she felt ill. She sat for a moment on the edge of the bed and took a few breaths until she could stand up without fainting.

* * *

Andreas arrived at the restaurant fifteen minutes after Annabelle. He did not kiss her or touch her. His coldness made her nervous. She was not hungry but she ordered a salad to keep Andreas company while he ate. And she drank much more wine than she intended.

Soon Annabelle was beginning to regret having come at all. Andreas was telling her he would find her another analyst. He suggested Leonard Kew, his friend. He seemed very admiring of him. Leonard had left his wife after he had had a massive heart attack requiring open-heart surgery. But that had not stopped him sleeping with the odd patient, as well as his secretary—and a sister or nurse. He was taking a new experimental drug which was doing wonders for his libido.

Annabelle wondered why Andreas was boring her with the ridiculous tales about his friend's sexual feats. Was it out of desperation? Or to impress?

She did not conceal her distaste.

'What about the ethics of the profession?' she said.

'He's just enjoying the little time he has left,' Andreas said.

Annabelle was dismayed Andreas had not answered her question. This was the man he was wanting to send her to. She wondered whether Andreas was really serious. How far would he carry the masquerade?

'I'll find someone myself, thank you. I don't care much for the sound of your friend.'

The conversation came to a standstill. The air between them was filled with gloom and hostility. Annabelle looked around the restaurant so she would not have to meet Andreas's eyes. There was much laughter coming from the diners. They were the privileged ones who could afford to eat in a fine restaurant on a lovely green hill near the Art Gallery. An exhibition of Impressionists had arrived from Paris and was drawing the crowds in. They had been queuing under the colonnades and over the steps of the Art Gallery all morning.

Andreas was talking to her.

'You test people, Annabelle. You go on and on testing them, until you destroy them,' he said.

'How do I destroy them?' she said, weary and resentful.

'You're cruel. Your perfection, your beauty is cruel. You make a man feel helpless, flawed.'

'Is that why you're abandoning me, Andreas?'

Annabelle felt crushed, dispirited, wishing the trial would soon come to an end and she could escape from him.

'Yes. You would have destroyed me,' he said.

There was a new wretchedness about him she had not seen before. Annabelle almost felt sorry for him.

'We're not getting anywhere with this conversation. I need to get out of here,' Annabelle said, rising from her chair and almost falling off her high heels. It was not surprising. She was drunk.

'Where are you going?' Andreas asked.

'Home,' she said.

'Did you bring your car?

'No.'

'How did you get here, then?'

'I flew, stupid. On the wings of a dove.'

'I'll take you home.'

'No, thank you very much, doctor. I can look after myself.'

'You're drunk. I'll take you home,' Andreas said, gripping her arm tightly.

'If you so kindly insist, then you may,' she said.

'I'll take you for a walk around the park.'

'A promenade along the Corniche would be a perfect way to end this romantic *téte-a-téte* , don't you think? *Non*? Oops!' Annabelle almost stumbled headlong onto the concrete path but his grip restrained her. 'I'm afraid I shall have to remove my heels and walk barefoot in the park, as someone said.'

'Here, let me.' Andreas knelt down to undo her sandals.

Suddenly Annabelle was overcome with a poignant feeling of tenderness for Andreas. He seemed so caring kneeling on the ground before her. Surely all this unpleasantness was just an episode—it would pass in a moment—and then things would be the way they were meant to be.

'I love you kneeling at my feet,' she said, as she watched Andreas struggle with the delicate straps around her ankles.

'I bet you do,' he said, with a grim expression.

They strolled up to the Botanic Gardens overlooking the harbour. There were trees from all corners of the world. A large magnolia from Carolina scented the breeze with its delicate lemon essence. Tiny blue finches and yellow ones danced in the spray of a fountain. Bees sucked the nectar from the generous yellow centres of bohenias and gordonias. Couples strolled or kissed on the grass. There were picnickers, too, and lunchtime joggers, lawyers and senators from Parliament House, as well as office workers from nearby.

Still, people did look at the unusual couple walking together. He, a tall handsome man, dressed in a pale grey suit, his shirt unbuttoned at the neck. Andreas had removed his silk tie and stuffed it carelessly in his pocket. The woman, much younger, could have been his daughter were it not for a certain tension between them that spoke of a lover's quarrel. She projected an outward appearance of radiance in her white dress. Her slim legs carried her with the grace of a dancer, but she seemed to be held back by the man who was gripping her arm. If those who glanced their way with a touch of envy had paused for a moment longer, they would have noticed an air of reckless desperation about them.

They were not walking arm in arm, like lovers strolling in the park. He was holding her, to stop her from falling over. But the man seemed to relish the attention after a while. He walked with his back straight, swinging the woman's sandals in his other hand. Someone more astute, might even have suspected he enjoyed striking a pose.

It was hard to imagine on such a beautiful afternoon that summer was coming to an end.

Suddenly Annabelle grasped Andreas's arm to stop him walking any further.

'I can't. I can't go on,' she cried. 'I feel terrible.'

Annabelle was fighting an enormous feeling of dread engulfing her.

'Keep walking, it'll do you good,' Andreas ordered.

'Please let me rest. I can't go on. I feel awful.' Annabelle let go of his arm and slid halfway down the bank, almost in a faint, and lay face down on the cool grass.

* * *

When Annabelle opened her eyes again, it had grown cold and she was alone. She stood up shakily, shivering, feeling lost and bewildered.

She looked around for her sandals.

'He's taken my shoes,' she wailed to the wind and the sea. 'What will I do? How will I get home?'

As Annabelle swung around, she lost her balance and almost toppled over the edge onto the rock wall and the sea below.

'Good God!' Andreas gasped, grabbing her just in time. 'You could have been killed!'

'You stole my shoes!' Annabelle cried.

'I went to collect the car. Your shoes are in the car. Come on, I'll take you home.'

It was worse inside the car. Annabelle pressed a handkerchief against her mouth.

'I think I'm going to be sick,' she said. There was panic in her voice.

'Open the window,' Andreas spoke sharply to her.

Her stomach was empty, except for the acid wine. She leaned her head against the car window and keened.

'What have you done to me, Andreas? What have you done? What's happening for god's sake?'

'You've done it all to yourself,' Andreas said, looking severe. 'Will David be home?'

'No, there's no one. There never is.'

Andreas came over to her side and opened the car door. Then he rushed her into the house, half carrying her up the stairs to the bedroom. There he undressed her and put her to bed. He covered her and left in a hurry without saying goodbye.

Annabelle listened for a moment to his car driving away.

What a ghastly sound, she thought, before losing consciousness.

* * *

It was while Annabelle was brushing her hair one morning, staring at her face in the bathroom mirror, that she remembered something Andreas had said about his wife when he was showing her some photographs. Annabelle had remarked that Jean's hair was black in some but completely white in others. She had asked Andreas whether his wife had had a shock or an illness to explain why that happened. But he had said, 'No, her hair just turned white overnight.'

Now another alarming thought intruded—about the girl patient who had slashed her throat. Andreas had told Annabelle that the girl had done it for his benefit. She suddenly remembered with a chill that there had been a faint glimmer of a smile on his face when he said it.

But why had Andreas saved her? Why had he not let Annabelle crash onto the rock wall and the sea below on that wretched and harrowing afternoon in the park?

24 Dangerous Games

Several weeks passed since that afternoon in the park. Annabelle cancelled most of her appointments at the clinic, and was surprised when one of Andreas's secretaries, called. Shirley wanted to let Annabelle know that the doctor was concerned about her, and was wondering when she would be resuming her sessions.

It was enough to make Annabelle change her mind about her decision not to see Andreas.

Although Annabelle tried to look her very best for him, she arrived at the clinic in a state of emotional and physical disarray she was unable to hide.

'Have a drink,' Andreas said, handing her a glass of vodka, greeting her with forced cheerfulness.

The recklessness of the desperate, Annabelle observed.

Andreas sat down and took a large gulp from his glass. He had been drinking and smoking cigars—there were three butts in the ashtray.

'How are you?' he said.

Annabelle had the impression that Andreas was not really interested in her reply, but had something of his own he wanted to tell her.

'Fine, thank you. How are you?'

'Oh, I'm lucky to be alive, I guess.'

'Why? What happened?'

'My wife tried to kill me.'

'What do you mean, tried to kill you?' Annabelle said, alarmed, confused.

'Jean tried to kill me, by pouring LSD in my drink.'

'Why would she do that?'

'Because she's furious with me. When she got back from her trip she found some things around the house that shouldn't have been there—the receipt for your gold chain and other things. She threw me out.'

'What do you mean threw you out? It's your home, too,' Annabelle said, expressing indignation on his behalf.

'Jean bundled everything into two suitcases, including my shaving mug, then tossed the bags into the street. I had nowhere to go.'

Annabelle was shocked.

'What did you do?'

'I called Frida. She's been coming over to the house with her children while Jean's been away to help me look after my son. She's been very helpful. Used to be a patient of mine when she was going through her divorce. I told her that my wife had thrown me out. 'Come over,' she said. So now I've moved in with her.'

Annabelle sat immobile, frozen.

Andreas seemed to be studying her.

Finally she spoke.

'Is she married? I mean ...' But she realised too late how idiotic she sounded.

'I've just told you she went through a divorce. She lives in a rented house with her children. She's really marvellous with kids. Absolutely wonderful!'

'Did your wife really try to kill you?' Annabelle asked in disbelief. 'It sounds a bit melodramatic, slipping a potion in your drink. LSD was it?'

Andreas nodded.

'Jean rang me at Frida's on the weekend and asked me to come over to mow the lawn. When I got there, she met me in her negligé even though it was almost lunch time. She offered me an orange drink, then left the house. I found a note she had left for me. It sounded like a suicide note.'

More like a crass joke, Annabelle wanted to say. Still, she was prepared to listen.

'She was going to kill herself?'

'That's what she wanted me to believe. She was trying to make me feel guilty. I had told her once about LSD, how people can kill themselves because it releases us from the self-preservation instinct. So she thought that if she made me feel responsible for her death, I would feel guilty and kill myself. And she could have my insurance as well, because it would look like an accident.'

'How awful,' Annabelle protested. She was confused, and somehow sorry for him.

Her show of concern pleased Andreas.

'When I realised that I might be tripping, I rushed to the bathroom and looked through the drawers where I'd kept some drugs. I couldn't find the ampoule of LSD I had left there, so I went back to Frida's place and she looked after me. I began to relive an incident which happened in our home in Geneva. I started shivering uncontrollably, so Frida gave me a hot bath. It was wonderful. That's where LSD is like strong hash—it magnifies everything, the good and the bad. I'm really stunned at how things have turned out.'

Annabelle had become withdrawn. Her eyes were without expression. She could not move, nor speak. Her brain would not function.

But there was more Andreas wanted to tell her.

'My wife wants a divorce so we've started proceedings. I should have my divorce in a few months. My son will stay with me and my daughter wants to be with her mother. Nick is already calling Frida, 'Mrs Z,' after we visited him in hospital.' Andreas paused. He was watching Annabelle for a reaction. 'But tell me about yourself, Annabelle. After all, this is your session. How are you getting on with your husband?'

Annabelle tried to speak but her mouth was dry. She moved her tongue about, wet her lips.

'I hardly see him,' she said. 'He's away most of the time. But to answer your question, well, I suppose.'

'Good. We went fishing at the weekend. Frida and the kids love fishing. Her little girl, Greta, asked me the other day, 'Andy, what is love?''

'*Andy?*'

'I told her that love is going fishing and being all one family, and coming home in the evening and going for a McDonalds.'

'I hate McDonalds,' Annabelle murmured under her breath.

'Did you say something?'

'I hate McDonalds.'

'I've promised the children I'll take them to Disneyland.'

'Wretched compromises,' Annabelle said, thinking aloud.

Andreas did not enjoy Annabelle's remarks. He knew she could read him. He glanced at his watch.

'Look, do you mind if we cut the session short? I promised Nick I'd call in and see him at the nursing home, and Frida's waiting for me. Perhaps I'll see you next week?'

There was an unexpected crash. The glass had suddenly shot out of her hand and smashed against the window, scattering fragments like snowflakes across the room. It had disintegrated completely.

Annabelle looked amazed. Had she really flung the glass across the room? And with such force? She had never done anything like that before.

'Feeling better?' Andreas asked.

'No.' she replied, rising and hastily leaving the room.

* * *

That night, Annabelle lay in bed writhing like a poisoned animal. She wrapped her arms around her middle because that was where it hurt most. And the damned shivering, she could not feel warm, no matter how many cardigans, socks and blankets she put on.

Where on earth had Frida come from? She seemed to have dropped suddenly, smashed into their lives like a rogue comet. Who was she, anyway? Annabelle tried to recall the first time she became aware of Frida. It had been one afternoon in the waiting room at the clinic. She vaguely remembered a woman with a 1970s frizz hairdo, who seemed to occupy a lot of space with bags, children and noise. And the afternoon she trudged around the house looking for Andreas, before leaving in a battered Volvo.

There was another time when she had seen her emerge from Andreas's room with a tear-stained face and a red nose. Andreas had been beside her, kind and reassuring. How ironic. The one role Annabelle had never considered, indeed never even found remotely appealing, that of Earth Goddess, or Fecund Woman, was the one Frida personified perfectly.

* * *

For three years Annabelle had tried to be a model patient and not bother her doctor. But now the pain was excruciating. It was midday. Finally, Annabelle dragged herself to the telephone and dialled his number.

'Bollingen Clinic. Hello?' Shirley's high-pitched, nasal voice made Annabelle wince.

'It's Annabelle. Annabelle Eichler.'

'Annabelle. Hello!'

'I would like to speak to Doctor Zill, please, Shirley.'

'He's busy with a patient at the moment. I'll ask him to call you when he's free.'

* * *

Annabelle waited and stared at the telephone all morning. Her heart beat erratically. When it did ring, she panicked, throwing herself across the bed to answer it.

'Annabelle?'

'Yes.'

'What can I do for you?'

'I'm feeling bad, Andreas.'

'Are you taking the anti-depressants I prescribed?'

'Yes.'

'Take some Valium, then. That might help.'

'How are you Andreas?'

'I'm so happy, I can't tell you.'

'So you say.'

Annabelle hung up.

* * *

The self-defence classes Annabelle enrolled in were to give her confidence. She learned to defend herself anticipating and deflecting blows, striking back with deadly accuracy. Annabelle also practised meditation and yoga, and sought out a good herbalist and acupuncturist. Massage, too, helped. She exercised and went for long walks, touched trees, talked to the birds, saved stray kittens and found homes for them. And she read, book after book, searching for answers to human behaviour. Annabelle was determined to survive.

When she felt ready, she went back to her sessions at the Bollingen Clinic.

'You're looking very beautiful,' Andreas said, when she arrived for her appointment after an absence of eight weeks. She wondered whether he was disappointed, perhaps he had hoped she would look terrible, suffering for him.

'Cut the clichés and the seduction,' she swiftly replied, striding past him. She imagined herself a samurai.

Andreas followed her, watching with apprehension and some fascination.

'Don't patronise me, either,' Annabelle added. 'Let's get one thing straight. I pay you, so from now on I don't wish to discuss anything that is irrelevant to my analysis. That is, I don't want to hear anything about *you*. I don't care if your wife comes after you with a hatchet, or your girlfriend wipes your behind. *I* can say anything I want because it's my analysis and I'm paying you to listen.'

Andreas had been holding his breath. He let it out in a long sigh.

'That's exactly what I've been trying to get you to do. This is the first time you've been really angry here,' he said.

Annabelle ignored him.

'I really want to talk about a subject which is very important to me,' she continued. 'My marriage. David loves me. I want to get through all this so that I can function better in my relationship with him. Women want status and everything that comes with it—shelter, comfort, and protection. Money too. Especially money. That's what what's-her-name is after. Have you told her you don't have any? She's pretending to take an interest in your son, promising she'll take care of him, but she's using you. You've been tricked, Andreas. You'll see. She'll put your son in an institution as soon as she has you in her grasp. You're going to be tied by your balls for the rest of your short life. When you could have been free ...' she added.

'I can never be free. I have a sick son who requires 24-hour help. You talk about freedom, but you're confusing the issue. Being an adult is fulfilling one's role, accepting one's responsibilities, having children, not denying yourself your sexuality.'

'You've hidden behind your responsibilities all your life.'

'And you've deprived your husband of children, and punished your father by denying him grandchildren.'

'You're wrong. It was a selfless act. I did not trust myself to be a good mother. I was very badly parented, and a deprived child becomes a depriving adult. My decision not to have children was to protect the unborn. I was in touch with my instincts enough to see it, like the female kangaroo who withholds the foetus if there's a drought and the surroundings aren't favourable for survival. But what would you understand? You've fathered and made miserable four children. That is a hellishly selfish and irresponsible thing to do.'

Annabelle's words rained down on Andreas. He was beginning to look grey, defeated.

But Annabelle had a long way to go before his annihilation was complete.

'Do you remember the young man I mentioned that I met at a friend's place in the country? He rings me now every day. Wants to come to see me. His friends have left since President Carter pardoned all conscientious objectors to the Vietnam war. But Beau's decided to stay. He keeps wanting to come and visit me. I keep telling him, No, Angel (he looks like an angel), but he refuses to listen, so to appease him I have promised to go sailing for a week with him, when David goes away again. He reminds me a teeny weeny bit of you—he's American but he has a similar background to yours—a Swedish father and a Russian-Polish mother. He too, lived in Switzerland during his childhood. His father is a banker. Do you know what I love most about Beau? His passion, his persistence and perseverance and...' she broke off giggling, hiding her face behind her hand, 'his staying power. He sweeps me off my feet and carries me to bed. He's an unbelievable lover. We made love the whole weekend. He has incredible energy. He only needs to touch me like this,' she demonstrated by delicately pressing a button on one of the cushions on the settee. 'And bang! Off I go, fireworks! *Les feux d'artifice.* Amazing how things have worked out so well for both of us.' Annabelle paused for a moment, moistening her dry lips. 'I have some photos Nicole took of us. Would you like to see them?'

Annabelle did not wait for an answer. Instead, she reached inside her handbag and took out a stack of photographs tied with a red ribbon and placed the bundle on the side table next to his armchair. Andreas could look at them later, when he was alone.

There was a tense silence as they stared at each other, unflinching. Annabelle hated herself. She was being cruel, fake, playing a role. But Andreas had been insensitive and heartless, too. She hated him.

'Do you still want me to come and see you every week at the appointed time?' she asked, waiting for the *coup de grace*.

'I do,' Andreas said. His demeanour was grave now.

Annabelle drew back, momentarily disarmed by his reply.

'Fucking masochist,' she snapped.

There was another uncomfortable moment while they glared at each other like two wounded warriors after a long and bloody combat, not knowing how to end it.

Finally Andreas cleared his throat.

'Well, you have embellished your story,' he said.

'What do you mean?'

'There's a lot you've left out and a lot you've put in. Life isn't like that.'

Annabelle looked into his eyes.

'You would know because it's the same for you,' she said.

'You'd like it to be?'

'I know it is.'

Annabelle turned her back on Andreas and watched her reflection in the window. After a few minutes, she swung around.

'I detest you. You're such a pathetic egotist. You're no more than an opportunist. You're cynical and shallow. And you're a bad doctor, you kill people. You're an absolute failure. You're hopeless in bed too, inadequate. You're floppy and flappy all over. You can hardly hold an erection. But you know what I hate most about you? It's the fact that you're a weak man, easily led and dominated by women you don't love. You're a deadly-passive-aggressive-narcissistic-sociopath. You try to impersonate my father, control me and make me jealous, like he tried to do, like you all try to do. You're all the same, so very, very predictable. You make me sick.'

Annabelle's words kept flaying Andreas.

'You look tragic,' she said, after a while.

'You're angry with me,' he said.

'You must be used to attacks from angry patients, as any therapist must experience,' she told him.

Andreas attempted to swallow before speaking again, with difficulty.

'This is the first time anyone has said such things to me. And it's you Annabelle, saying them.'

'It's all piffle,' she said, turning her back on him.

'I don't think anyone else has ever accepted you like I have, Annabelle. You, the person, not the sexual object. Wanting to help you as I have.' Andreas's voice was now steady, gentle, while his insides were butchered.

'You've got a funny idea of helping someone who's drowning. I'm sick of this. I want to go home. This is a boring and useless session.'

'You're angry but you still won't let go. You hold yourself back. Even when you threw the glass at the window, you were frightened to break it, so you threw it in the corner.'

'That's not true. I threw it at the window glass,' Annabelle said.

'You aimed for the wooden frame, so that it wouldn't break. It's an old stage trick. I learned it at Oxford in the theatrical society. I wanted to be an actor too.'

Annabelle was thrown in a state of confusion. What was his game now?

'I'm certain that the glass hit the window. I wanted to break it.'

'Then why don't you?'

There was a long silence while Annabelle tried to fathom what Andreas had just told her.

'You really want me to break the window?' she asked in disbelief.

'Go ahead.'

It was a very large window with a huge expanse of glass. She would probably be killed. Decapitated, most likely.

Annabelle looked at Andreas. He was smiling.

Then, as if in a dream, she watched herself in slow motion lift the coffee table. Ashtrays, Kleenex and the pottery ornaments the patients made for the doctor came tumbling down at her feet. With a final effort, Annabelle reached up towards the darkening sky and the silhouette of the Moreton Bay fig tree. There was a tremendous impact of metal against glass. She reeled back, her senses obscured for a moment.

When Annabelle recognised her surroundings again, she saw herself and the area where she was standing covered in glass. There was glass on the settee too, on the carpet and on Andreas's desk. But there was no rush of fresh air from outside as she had imagined there would be.

'It didn't even break,' she murmured in disbelief. She sank down on the glass- covered settee, by some miracle not cutting herself.

'You couldn't even do that. You didn't succeed in breaking the coffee table, either. The glass top fell out and broke by itself. You couldn't let go,' Andreas said.

Annabelle stared at a piece of broken glass at her feet and then looked up at Andreas, seeking reassurance that he cared about her. But it was not forthcoming.

'I can't even cry,' she lamented feebly.

'I know you can't.'

'I had three near-accidents driving over this afternoon.'

But Andreas was not interested in excuses or near misses. He remained unbending, unsmiling.

'I won't be here next week. I'll see you in three weeks' time,' he said. 'I'm going on holiday.'

Annabelle rose slowly and moved towards the door. She tried to pull it open but she had no strength left. She felt helpless—without hope—like an abandoned child.

Andreas did not rise to assist her.

* * *

When the sound of Annabelle's footsteps had faded away, Andreas reached for the photographs on the small side table. He could not stop himself shaking as he tried to undo the red ribbon. The photographs spilled over the table and unto the floor, amongst the shattered glass.

There was one of Annabelle in a white bikini. Annabelle with a fair-haired, fit looking young man holding hands and running into a wave on a beach, followed by two Afghan hounds. The next photograph captured the young couple after their swim in an embrace. There was one of them driving off in a white ute with the dogs and a surfboard in the back. They went horse riding in a rainforest; sliding down a waterfall half naked into an emerald pool; dancing to a rock band in what looked like a pub; and smoking cannabis from a glass contraption.

Andreas bend down again to gather the rest of the photographs. He cut his fingers on the fragments of glass scattered on the floor. He took out his handkerchief and wrapped it around his bleeding hand. He picked up a photograph taken in a bedroom showing Annabelle and her young lover sitting close together on a four poster bed—the young man had his hand around her waist and his lips were on her neck. Annabelle's hair was dishevelled, and a strap of her short silk chartreuse slip had dropped off her shoulder, revealing a certain portion of her naked breast. The bed was in disarray, as if a great deal of activity had occurred there.

The photos had been taken by Annabelle's friend Nicole—and carefully staged by both women. But Andreas did not know that.

Annabelle expected Andreas to be shocked by what he saw, but she also knew this would soon be replaced by feelings of anger, deep hurt, helplessness, self-pity. Perhaps he would hold his hands up to his face and weep uncontrollably. How angry would he be? Enough to want to kill her?

25 Sex and Power

Annabelle wanted to cancel her session with Andreas, but her need to see him was greater than her pride. To add to her distress was the ubiquitous presence of Frida. She was sitting in the waiting room, crocheting a multi-coloured blanket when Annabelle arrived.

Just as Annabelle was hesitating outside the room, determining to turn away and leave, Andreas appeared.

'There you are, Annabelle. Come in,' he said, ignoring Frida's presence.

Annabelle resisted for a moment, but when she looked into his eyes, she capitulated.

Once they entered Andreas's room, Annabelle was impassioned. She turned sharply to him and said: 'Your landlady's been hanging around like a bad smell. Aren't you paying her enough rent? I think she's been waiting for me to arrive to see what I'm wearing. She's spying on us. Why don't you tell her to fuck off? Or at least to stay away from the surgery. It looks messy having one's landlady hanging around. I hear she gives you hell about me. I suppose she wants you to stop seeing me altogether?'

'You know she's more than my landlady,' Andreas said.

'I beg your pardon, girlfriend, how could I forget? Silly me!'

'I'll have to speak to Shirley and Jess. I don't want any gossip around here,' Andreas said. He was frowning, looking annoyed.

'Why, you thrive on it! Everybody knows everything about you. The whole Bollingen Clinic is tuned in to your fantastic soap opera, waiting breathlessly for the next ridiculous episode.'

'You're very angry,' Andreas said.

'Am I?' Annabelle feigned surprise.

She sat down and composed herself, folding her hands in her lap, crossing her ankles neatly in front of her.

'That's a beautiful dress you're wearing.'

'It's Edwardian. Very old and frail. I feel like that myself.'

'You don't look it.'

'Always keep your armour shining. That's my motto,' Annabelle revealed.

'You believe that?'

'Looks *are* everything. It's been shown in psychology experiments, don't you know? A person who looks clean, respectable and attractive is supposed to be regarded in a better light than others. Their passage through life is made smoother. Even though they may be fiends!'

Andreas chose to ignore her cynicism.

'And what have you been doing with yourself?' he asked.

'I've written you another poem. Not a very nice one. I think that might be an understatement.'

Andreas put his hand out. Annabelle noticed it was shaking. She took her time searching for the sheet of folded paper in her embroidered silk purse. Since he had been living with Frida, Annabelle was quick to note that Andreas had stopped wearing a suit and tie. Instead, he wore an unflattering mustard coloured sports jacket meant for a much younger and slimmer man.

Andreas put his glasses on to read the poem.

I hate you
for betraying your origins
being a coward
giving up on me
becoming the man you've become
humourless, dead, old, a bore, a tragedy queen
for your fear and hatred of women
you false subjugation to them
your inability to think for yourself
or stand on your own two feet
your incapacity to act of your own free will
your lack of imagination and spontaneity
your fear and failure to take what you want

your self deception, the lie you call living
your attraction to disaster
your collection of miseries
for discounting you and me
for being an underdog
for your obsession to control me, your insistence
on my orgasms
for being a shocking liar and a hypocrite
and a whingeing, cringing coward
a dissembler
but most of all for not being true to yourself.

Andreas folded the piece of paper and handed it back to Annabelle.

'I notice you only keep the nice poems. The ones that aren't so flattering, you hand them back. How narcissistic.' Annabelle flung the last words carelessly.

'Do you want to work, Annabelle?' Andreas voice betrayed his lacerated feelings.

Annabelle could see how deeply she hurt him and was moved for a moment by his willingness to help her.

'I do,' she said. There was a pleading look in her eyes.

'Good, Annabelle.'

'I lied about the young man. I didn't enjoy having sex with him. It was a wretched compromise, an act of desperation to punish you. It was like a bad dream. I had to get drunk. All I can remember was the longing and the pain. I'm a hopeless case really, I should go into a convent, that's what I really wanted to be when I was young, a nun. I would probably have been happier, except convents aren't as interesting now as they were in Héloise's time ...'

'Yes, well, you could have seduced the monks then.'

Annabelle looked at Andreas with disgust.

'I don't want to fuck monks!' she shouted in consternation. 'God, you've got a pathetic, disgusting one-track mind. You see me as the great seductress, the spider lady who devours her mate after copulation, a bewitcher, that's what you called me, *casting spells over us.* You would have had me burnt at the stake. You would have been in your element as a member of the Inquisition. I can just see you, sitting behind a big oak table in your heavy robes, heartless, vengeful, cold, devoid of any compassion. Do you still do that party trick you told me about, where you stick a needle in your flesh? I would stop it if I were you because it says a lot about you that's not very flattering. It says, 'Look no feelings.' Psychopaths have no feelings.'

Annabelle shut up, waiting for Andreas to speak.

'Why don't you say something?' she was begging him to defend himself.

'This is your session, not mine. You're the one who's paying me to listen.'

'It's all a waste of time, really. All I feel for you now is contempt and mistrust. You lied to me even when you said we could be friends if we couldn't be lovers. You know what hurt most? Knowing you were in pain and you didn't call me. You went to someone else. I would have comforted you.'

'You need to be needed.' Andreas's voice was dull, devoid of expression.

It was disconcerting for her.

'I missed you, Andreas.'

'To miss someone is to treat them as an object. All those stories in women's magazines where boy meets girl, fall in love, quarrel then part—the realization they can't live without one another, isn't love. True love is different. The person's love is felt very strongly whether they're there or not.'

'Why do we have to be apart? Why can't we be together?' Annabelle almost entreated Andreas .

'I told you, it's not doing you any good.'

Annabelle noticed the sharp edge of impatience in his voice.

'You treat me like a child instead of a woman.'

'I think we'll have to find you another therapist if you can't work with me seriously.'

'We? Who is we?' Annabelle confronted Andreas. Then she added:

'So that slag is getting the better of you. Soon she'll have it all her way and you won't see me at all.'

'You regard everything around you with a curious detachment or indifference, Annabelle. *La belle indifference,* they call it. A major symptom of the hysteric. The hysteric uses strong passionate words but she remains detached from her feelings.'

'It's not true. I do have feelings. I just don't want to show them. I feel so bad inside, I just want to die,' she cried, and with all her strength she swung and crashed against the window.

To her astonishment, the glass still refused to break. Annabelle beat on it furiously, afraid of failing again. She slammed her arms and body against the window as hard as she could. She wanted Andreas to watch her bleed, to see her severed head with blood spurting in every direction. She would give him what he wished for after all, a bloody mess he would never forget. With each blow the glass buckled while Andreas sat calmly watching her. It felt dreamlike, staged.

Suddenly the door flew open and one of the doctors who had rooms down the corridor came running in. The doctor froze, expecting the window to come crashing down, then during a momentary pause when Annabelle swung away to regain momentum, he lunged towards her.

It was then that Andreas reacted. It would have looked bad to let his patient kill herself while he sat and watched. He reached Annabelle before his colleague and, grabbing her by the wrists, threw her on the settee. Then he stood back and nodded to the doctor, communicating that he had the situation under control and no longer needed any assistance.

'You failed again,' Andreas said, when they were alone.

Annabelle held her bruised and throbbing arms close to her. On the floor lay her gold bracelet, smashed and twisted. She bent down and picked up the pieces, vainly trying to put them together again.

* * *

Next time Annabelle saw Andreas, he gave her a few broken pieces of her bracelet that he had found on the floor. He was looking at her differently to the last time she was in the room. It made her uneasy.

Annabelle did not trust him.

'I thought of you when I played golf with Leonard yesterday,' Andreas said. 'I couldn't get you out of my mind.'

'Why didn't you call me, then?'

'Because, if I am to help you …'

'Help me?' Annabelle cut in.

'Yes, help you. I accept your anger, Annabelle.'

'*Unconditional positive regard*?' she mocked.

'Yes,' he said.

'More clichés. Jargon and psychobabble for the shrink to hide behind. Meaningless, when you don't even know the meaning of love. You remind me of that redneck American general in Vietnam, who said: 'To save the city we had to destroy the city'. He destroyed the city of Hue, and *lost* it. There was nothing left when he finished.'

'Sometimes we have to appear cruel. Don't you think this is hard for me?'

Annabelle glanced up at Andreas, mystified to see tears welling up in his eyes. She could not understand what was happening. If he still loved her, then why did he make her suffer? There were times when she wanted to trust him. But Annabelle felt he was mad, playing a dreadful and cruel game with her. He may have been truthful when he kept telling her that he wanted to help her, but something unforseen was happening. Andreas no longer knew what he was doing. It was uncharted territory he had stumbled into—and lost his way.

'If I am to help you,' his voice came to her as if from far away.

'Why did you hurt me? How can you hurt me if you still love me?'

'You held back on me. You wouldn't let yourself go. You didn't trust me enough. When we made love you froze. You've changed. You were not like you once were.'

'It's not true, Andreas. I adored making love with you. You made me feel incredible. You only needed to look at me, touch me and I felt myself melt completely. It was the sweetest, most sensuous feeling I've ever experienced. Wasn't it enough reassurance for you? Yes, there were times when I felt frightened, tense, making love in this room. After all we were almost caught on a few occasions. I could hear people moving about, heard their voices. I guess I acquired some bad habits, anxiety, and then I was also tense when you insisted on me having orgasms. You'd ask me: 'Did you come?' As if orgasms were everything. I hate that word. *Orgasm*. It has an ugly, coarse, rasping, sound. It angered me that you were so concerned about performance, as if it were a contest. And sometimes I felt your hostility, which affected your erection. You'd lose it, and I felt responsible because I didn't come fast enough for you. Or made you angry, or was not good enough.'

'You've attacked my sexuality. You want to castrate me,' Andreas said.

'You attacked mine.'

'Yes, we're into game-playing again,' he said. After a while, he looked up and said with a certain tenderness she found bewildering: 'I was concerned about your pleasure, Annabelle.'

'You were concerned about your *power*.' Annabelle's voice rose angrily. 'Your power to control me through sex.'

'You were determined not to relinquish control to me,'

'Because I didn't trust you,' Annabelle said.

'You've never trusted anybody.'

'With good reason,' she replied.

'Don't give them what they want, eh?'

'Yes!' There was daring and determination in her voice.

'You're a proud, stubborn woman. But can you see how you lose by winning?'

Annabelle ignored him.

'I suppose your landlady has plenty of orgasms—*multiple vaginal orgasms?* Only immature women like me have clitoral orgasms Freud said, right? Wrong! You really should read *The Hite Report*. It's been out for two years now. But are you going to thank me for awakening your comatose sexuality now that you're with a liberated *real* woman? Are you taking those vitamin pills I bought you to help you keep it up, as you seemed to have such great difficulty, right from the very first time when I had to console you. Poor Andreas. Poor *Andy*.'

Annabelle looked around, pretending to be bored. The angry silence between them was unbearable and she was desperate to escape it. At the same time, she longed to rush over to Andreas, put her arms around his neck, ask him to forgive her and tell him how much she loved him still.

Slowly, she lifted her eyes to his. Andreas was watching her. 'Did I ever tell you about my baby sister, Isabelle?'

Andreas did not move. Annabelle wondered whether he was ever going to speak to her again after all the terrible things she had said to him. But he slowly responded, shaking his head.

'No.'

'She was killed by a doctor. He botched her operation.'

'Go on, Annabelle,' Andreas said. He was suddenly his old caring, gentle self, totally concentrating on her, praying she would reveal something important.

'It turned out he killed several people, through incompetence and hubris. Children especially. Nobody stopped him because he was the great professor, a man commanding respect.'

'You're married to one,' Andreas said, making his point which he immediately regretted.

'Yes.'

'Is that why you want to destroy us? To avenge Isabelle's death?'

Their conversation was suddenly interrupted by a knock on the door. It was Shirley and she looked as though she wanted to spit out something distasteful from her mouth.

'Frida wants you to drive her and the children home. I told her you were in session but she insisted.'

'I'll have to take a few minutes off. Shirley will make you a cup of tea till I get back,' Andreas said to Annabelle, hurrying out of the room.

Shirley rolled her eye balls and shrugged her shoulders. 'He's crazy,' she said turning to leave. 'It's the male menopause,' she added.

Twenty minutes later, Andreas returned. He was breathing hard, and seemed stressed.

'Sorry about that but it had to be done.'

'Had to be done,' Annabelle echoed.

'Yes.'

'Why didn't she call a taxi?'

Andreas shrugged, wanting to dismiss the subject.

'This place depresses me,' Annabelle said, looking around the room. It suddenly appeared to her in poor taste, with its inelegant furnishings and ugly objects that his patients had given him. How could she have ever seen it differently? Could the room have changed so much in three years?

'Why?' Andreas asked.

'I don't care to have my sessions interrupted while you perform some chore for your girlfriend,' Annabelle added. 'Nor do I like having her lurking about giving me hate stares when I arrive. I don't think your other patients like it either. Frankly, I find it all rather nauseating, your squabbles, your messes.'

'Okay, Annabelle. Enough with the sarcasm and the stinging dialogue. I don't think you can hear how cruel you sound sometimes. I'm sure if you understood the effect your words have, you wouldn't say such things. You really like giving me hell, don't you?'

'I just tell the truth and you call it hell. Anyway, I could say the same for you. The only difference is that your aggression is more subtle, but just as deadly.' She pointed to the inscription by Hippocrates on the wall: *And I will keep pure and holy both my life and my art*. 'You certainly live by your *hypocritical* oath.'

'I've made a mess of things, I know. But it's not true that I'm full of aggression as you say.'

'You really hate people because you hate yourself. When I was tripping and you were witnessing my pain, I asked you: 'You do this for a living?' I forgot what you said but you sounded as though you really despised your patients. I thought then, he's a misogynist, and I was glad because I didn't want you to love any other women except me. But now I know that if you hated them, it's because you hate yourself, and if you hate yourself, then you cannot love anyone, and that includes me.'

'I don't hate you, Annabelle. What I'm trying to do is for *you*. It's an unselfish act on my part. It may be the *only* thing that will make you grow up. You'll never change otherwise. You'll destroy yourself and those around you. Perhaps one day you'll see it. Then maybe you won't hate me so much.'

26 The Physician's Love

The waiting room was empty and the office was locked. For a moment Annabelle was gripped by a feeling of dread. Where was everybody? Where was Andreas? She would even have welcomed the waspish sight of Frida.

Andreas's door was closed. Annabelle pressed her ear against it and was relieved to hear voices, so she returned to the waiting room. From where she sat, Annabelle could see into the recreation area. A patient was talking on the wall phone, and her voice seemed to ricochet along the walls of the empty room until it reached Annabelle.

'I played two games of scrabble with the male nurse,' the woman was saying. 'I made a couple of ashtrays out of clay, but there's still so much time to fill in, and I wish, Ted would come. Why doesn't he come? Oh, why doesn't he come?' The woman's voice quivered with pain.

Annabelle was suffocating. She leapt up and opened the small window, hoping the noise of the outside world might drown out the sound of misery inside. She pressed her face against the window frame and closed her eyes.

'There you are Annabelle. I've been waiting for you. What were you doing?'

Andreas was standing in the room behind her.

'Just getting some fresh air. I didn't like the smell in here. I thought you had a patient.'

'I was listening to some Chinese language tapes. Everybody is away with the new flu. What would you like to talk about today?'

Annabelle shrugged.

'How about anger?' Andreas asked.

'All right.'

'Tell me, Annabelle, what makes you angry?'

'Everything, Andreas. Cruelty, greed, politicians, war, poverty, waiting—even the Queen of England makes me angry. I think she should give her money to the poor, do something useful. But most of all I'm angry with myself, for how I've behaved with you. I feel so ambivalent, like a pendulum swinging wildly. Sometimes I feel as if there are two of me, and one is trying to kill the other. There's a constant war going on inside. Does it mean I'm schizophrenic?'

'No, you're a hysteric …'

'Oh …'

'Hysterical women never grow out of a desire to possess their fathers. Freud said that such women are capable of inflicting enormous suffering in their sexual and marital lives.'

'Poor David. Poor Andreas.'

'You've used your hysteria to get out of responsibilities and difficulties which, as a mature woman, you would have had to face. What you are really seeking is the security and comfort of dependent childhood that you never had as an infant. You need the attention and protection which you were deprived of …'

'*The physician's love heals the patient,*' Annabelle reminded him.

Andreas stared at Annabelle. He seemed to want to tell her something—open up to her—reveal why it was necessary for him to be so harsh. Let her know how difficult it all was, how much he loved her and hated himself. And how he hoped for a miracle.

'I want to help you, Annabelle.'

'So you say.'

'You must keep seeing me, and we must work.'

'It's unbearable to see you here under these circumstances,' Annabelle fought back tears.

'Don't you think it's hard for me, too?'

Annabelle looked at him. She could see his anguish, felt it deeply within her being. But it only added to her confusion. The turmoil she was in left her tense and fearful.

'Will we be together again when this is over?' she asked. Her voice was small, almost inaudible.

Andreas nodded.

'I don't believe you. You'd rather be without me. You want me because you think that ultimately you can't have me, because you're convinced you don't deserve me.' Her voice rose sharply. 'You think you only deserve that tub of margarine you're living with …'

'Annabelle, stop it!'

She stared at him in awe. He had never shouted at her before.

'Don't talk to me like that!' Annabelle retaliated.

Andreas despaired. His eyes were moist. He could weep.

'You're wasting your time talking about Frida. We're not getting anywhere.'

Annabelle rose and went and stood in front of the window with her back to him. She did not want him to see her crying. In the time they had known each other, it had happened rarely, once, under LSD. She felt very vulnerable now and wanted to hide from him.

'You're crying, Annabelle,' Andreas said. His voice was so tender it made her break into sobs.

Annabelle tried to reply, to minimise the sorrow she was feeling. Instead she sobbed harder, grieving for what was lost.

'Damn!' she said, turning around. 'I can't stand it. You must see so many weeping women.'

'I do. But watching you cry, feels extraordinary—and strange. I feel a tremendous sense of satisfaction, like your father must have felt when you cried for him.'

'That's why I didn't want you to see me like this!'

'Now, will you work, Annabelle?' Andreas had regained his authority, appearing confident, stern even, which distressed Annabelle further. She felt defeated. If only he would put his arms around her, the way he had done when he loved her.

'If you don't work with me, we can't continue. You'll have to see another therapist.'

Annabelle looked up at him. Her eyes brimming with tears again. She tried very hard to stop them falling on her cheeks, brushing them away.

But Andreas remained unmoved.

'I had a dream,' she whispered.

'Speak up, Annabelle, please.'

'I was in the bedroom with my mother ...'

'Go on.'

'I'm in the room with my mother and there was an accident outside.'

'The present, Annabelle,' Andreas insisted.

'There's an accident, a terrible sound, a crunch of flesh—I mean metal—and broken glass. I look out to the street below and I see the road covered in blood. There are cars all smashed up and at the end of the street is a bottle, a big *Coca Cola* bottle. Inside it, there's me. I hate the product.'

'You hate yourself. You kill people's love.' Andreas stopped. He looked at Annabelle and tried to be reassuring. 'Put your mother in that chair, Annabelle, and talk to her.'

'I call to my mother from inside the bottle but she can't hear me.'

'Talk to her,' Andreas insisted.

'You're never there, Mother. You're in the room but you never hear me or see me.'

'Now Annabelle. Change seats with her. Sit in her chair and answer as your mother.'

'I never loved you, Annabelle, because I didn't want you. You were born nine months after my wedding night, and you were a girl. A mistake. I tried to abort you, but it didn't work. I would have liked to have given your father, and grandfather, a son because that's what they wanted. Instead, you came along. Your grandfather wouldn't talk to me, and your father was very disappointed. You tried to separate us, did everything to steal his love.'

'Now change seats,' Andreas directed her.

'I can't help it if he didn't love you, Mamma.'

Andreas stopped her.

'How do you feel towards your mother now?'

'I feel sorry for her.'

'Tell her then.'

'I'm sorry, Mamma.'

'Why do you have your arms around you like that, Annabelle?'

'I'm holding myself,' Annabelle replied, dropping her hands down in her lap again.

'No. Put them back where they were. See? Your arms are like the sides of the bottle. You withdraw into that bottle but others collide with you and then there's blood. Their blood.'

'What about my blood, my suffering? Freud said that every component of a dream belongs to the person who is having the dream. It's my blood splattered on the road, my collisions, my unhappiness. That other dream I had when I first came to see you—the one about the horrible naked-hermaphrodite-albino creature in the gutter, was *me* not *you*. You're so concerned about wanting to be loved and accepted, that you can't see my pain. You're so sure that the repulsive creature was you, that the spilt blood was *yours*— I think your thoughts are a re-juggling of your own personal problems, which you project onto me. How can you help me when you're *so wrong?'*

* * *

When next Annabelle walked into the consulting room for her weekly appointment, she noticed that Andreas had moved his leather chair, in order to increase the distance from where she usually sat on the settee. He was ensconced in his armchair, hands clasped as if in prayer. Waiting.

Annabelle stared at him, her eyes moving to his mouth—those lips she had known and felt so intimately on her body. She sighed and looked around the room.

'This is a whole lot of emotional masturbation. It's not even mind fucking. It's a drag.'

'I agree. We've arrived at the same conclusion,' Andreas said.

'Well, cut the deception, then.'

'I don't lie to you.'

'How can you say that? You're sick, Andreas.'

'I know I have a lot of work to do, too,' he said.

'Physician heal thyself.'

'I'm trying. I'm changing every day. There's a lot of work we must do. We mustn't stop, Annabelle.'

'Frida doesn't want you to go on seeing me. I can tell by the way she sneaks looks at me. Hasn't she got anything better to do? Like look after her children? She's spying on you the way Jean did.'

'Let's talk about you. How've you been?'

'Awful,' Annabelle resumed. 'I'm being swept by a tide of melancholy. Everything makes me cry now. Crying hurts. I found myself crying when David and I were walking in the park. Tears were streaming down my face, behind my sunglasses. I told David it was pollen but it was the trees, their silky, silvery trunks reaching bravely to the sky made me cry. I cried when I saw the horses riding by because they're not free. I cried in a restaurant when we were having dinner with friends, and a girl walked in, a cripple. I felt foolish. I think I'm fracturing.'

'Perhaps you need to.'

'And end up like that woman I heard talking on the telephone, making ashtrays out of clay, waiting for her Ted to arrive? No. I won't be that! My defences are useless now, I know. I feel naked and vulnerable, but I won't let you, or anyone else destroy me!'

'Feeling naked and vulnerable is part of changing,' Andreas said.

'Changing to what? I don't have anyone to model myself on. I've been surrounded by frightened children all my life. My parents, you, David. I can't fathom him, he's a closed book. Secretive. We inhabit different planets.' Annabelle looked up at him with tears in her eyes. 'Oh, Andreas, you were a god to me. Where did you disappear to? Perhaps you didn't exist. Did I imagine you?'

'There aren't any gods, Annabelle, only human beings.'

'A lot of desperate, lonely children.'

'Full of longings and desires which cannot ever be fulfilled. These longings lie deep in childhood.'

There was much sorrow between them, yet when their eyes met they found they could still smile.

'Sometimes I like you,' Annabelle said.

'And sometimes I like you too,' Andreas responded.

'I'll write about you, one day.'

'What will you write?'

'About how horrible you are.'

An expression of hurt swept across his face.

'Just kidding. I will write about your Russian melancholy, how we were destined to meet, and how we loved… I'll call it: *The Man With The Sad Eyes.*'

Andreas remained silent. Annabelle wondered if her words were affecting him.

'I've been making notes in the car after every session, about everything which is said here, everything we've done,' she continued.

'Everything?' Andreas asked. There was now a note of alarm in his voice.

'That's why I came to you in the first place—I was in search of a subject for a book—and I wanted to experience LSD.'

'I see.'

'Tell me more about hysteria and hysterical women. I love listening to you,' she said.

'I've noticed. You're a good listener. It's very seductive.' Andreas paused. He was still thinking about what she had revealed, her notes. He tried to push it out of his mind. 'Freud wrote of the agony and the dark passion of the suffering hysterical woman. He found them demanding, seductive, irrational, emotionally charged. He was frightened of them because he was also attracted to them. A lot of his patients were young middle-class women. The reason for this hysteria, was the emotional disturbance stemming from early trauma, sexual abuse, in childhood, that had been suppressed. Freud said so in a paper he gave in Vienna in 1896 called *Aetiology of Hysteria*. As a young doctor, he had gone to Paris to study with Charcot. While he was in Paris, he spent time in the courts and at the morgue, examining autopsies of battered bodies of children who'd died of injuries from rape and sexual abuse. But all this caused an uproar because he was exposing the hypocrisy of Victorian middle-class Vienna. He recanted. Had to, otherwise psychoanalysis wouldn't have survived. So he had to say he had been wrong—that parents, grandfathers or uncles didn't rape, seduce or sexually abuse their children. Rather, it was the children who wanted to seduce their parents. Their hysteria was a result of their sexual fantasies. Freud felt conflicted about abandoning his *seduction theory*. I think the years he spent in agony with his mouth cancer had a lot to do with having had to keep his mouth shut.'

'So the whole of Freudian analysis is built upon a lie!'

Freud lied. Andreas lied. They all lied.

Andreas nodded in agreement.

'The problem with our society,' he went on, 'is that we believe we own our children. We don't see them as individuals. That same twisted perception carries on into marriage where the woman is the child without rights, for men to abuse verbally, emotionally or physically. And sometimes kill. We have the same attitude towards animals. But back to Freud and the hysterical woman. I think he was threatened because of the sexual feelings they aroused in him. He devised the analytical couch so that he could sit behind them, listening and taking notes, instead of looking at them. He was protecting himself. Freud also invented the process of free association. He asked the patient to say anything that came into his or her mind. If you listen to people, you will find that no matter how innocent or trivial something sounds, it really is quite significant. There is always a reason, a demand, a revelation.' Andreas paused. 'But these social discussion aren't going to help you very much. Have you decided what you want to do today, Annabelle?'

'I don't know,' she said. She was still affected by what he had told her about Freud and the seduction theory.

'I feel desperate, Annabelle, when you act so helpless.'

'Why?'

'Because I have an investment in you getting somewhere.'

'How noble of you.'

'I find your sarcasm deeply upsetting. Something's happening. I don't know what it is but I know it's destructive,' he said.

'I don't know what's going on, either,' Annabelle said, feeling despondent.

'Of course,' Andreas said.

'Of course,' Annabelle echoed.

'I'm going to stop here,' he said, rising from his arm-chair. 'Will you see Shirley about an appointment for next week?'

Andreas walked across to his desk and sat down to read a report.

He was deliberately turning his back on Annabelle.

On her way out Annabelle hoped Andreas would be deeply concerned about what she had revealed. If she had written down their conversations, described their lovemaking when she was supposed to be in treatment and David found her notes, Andreas could be ruined. Were she to bring a lawsuit against him, she could win. She wondered if he would enjoy the excitement, the theatre of a court of law and the attention of the media. Their passion, secrets and sexual involvement would all be highlighted.

She sauntered down the path to where she had parked her car.

'How thrilling!' she told a man in a white suit, tanned face and long hair badly dyed, mahogany brown.

'An inmate of the asylum,' she laughed.

27 The Greatest Fear

The elation Annabelle had felt when she walked out of the clinic did not last. The damage and cost of a court case against Andreas would be devastating for him. So many would be hurt. His daughter, such a sensitive age, had endured so much already. His wife, too. And David, of course.

Instead, Annabelle decided to retreat from Andreas and her sessions. She sought distractions. Work was one of them. Drawing on her resources, her knowledge of languages, she became an interpreter. Most days, the agency would send her to orthopaedic surgeons in Macquarie Street. The patients were emigrants—from Italy, Greece, Spain and the Lebanon.

There was someone else who involved and moved her deeply, Andrew St John. He had been one of the young, bright and beautiful people who had deserted Australia for the excitement of Swinging London in the 1960s. He returned home ten years later because of chronic ill-health.

One day, Andrew called Annabelle from the hospital where he had been recently admitted.

Annabelle was distraught when she found out what happened to her friend. She could not talk to David about him because her husband had disliked her friendship with the young man. David regarded Andrew as a miscreant.

She needed to tell Andreas.

'I went to the hospital this morning to visit a very dear friend. Andrew had been such a beautiful young man. Girls and boys were always falling in love with him. He was clever too, made millions managing a business for the Beatles in London. Then he lost it all—looks, money, friends—just blew it on drugs, alcohol, casinos. It happened after an accident in which someone close to him was killed in his sports car.

Andrew had let his friend drive his car, while he sat in the passenger seat, high on drugs, drinking *Southern Comfort*. His friend was decapitated by a truck. Andrew hit the drugs hard, after that. He's spent a long time in hospitals.

'Last Saturday night, a terrible thing happened. He went to a party and afterwards decided to score some heroin in Kings Cross. He was attacked and beaten savagely—left for dead in an alley. When Andreas was eventually found by the police, they said it was the worst beating they'd seen. It's a miracle he's still alive.'

Annabelle looked up at Andreas. The blood had drained from his face. For a moment she thought he might have had a stroke.

They were *both* speechless.

'You said, *Andreas,* instead of Andrew,' he said, when he recovered. His tone was accusatory.

'What?' she cried out alarmed, as the realisation of her slip of the tongue and its consequences struck her.

Annabelle was badly shaken. She felt a desperate urge to run away and hide. Instead, she buried her head in her hands and hoped for mercy.

'I'm so ashamed, Andreas. I'm so ashamed,' she said.

'This is the first time you have faced your aggression, Annabelle. You really want to destroy me.'

It was not a mere slip of the tongue. Annabelle's subconscious had revealed her compulsion to destroy Andreas.

'Oh, god, I don't like it, I don't like *me,*' she wailed, holding her arms around her body, and rocking to and fro.

'No, that's why you over-compensate with your softness, your femininity, your seductiveness. But you have a lot of destructive tendencies and aggression towards men.'

'No! It was my father who gave me all the love. I love men.'

'Precisely. You hate the bind. It takes away your freedom.'

'I feel like dying. I'm scared of botching it up, though. I've heard some horror stories from a friend who works in a hospital about people waking up after a failed suicide. They're worse off, brain damaged, paralysed—and then they have to live with that. I could slash my throat like Madame Butterfly. My mother's favourite opera, she sang it all the time and drove me crazy.'

'That's not such a good way. You need to know what you're doing,' Andreas said.

'What about a combination of alcohol and drugs? Nembutal and some scotch? Valium and vodka?'

'Not too much scotch. You end up vomiting the pills.'

'A pistol to the temple is more romantic. My father had a small revolver with a mother of pearl handle.'

'I've got my suicide planned,' Andreas said.

'We could die together. When you decide to kill yourself, call me please?' Annabelle said it all with a smile, trying to sound light-hearted.

'Perhaps we should have tried *living* together,' Andreas said with a certain sadness. 'How tragic. We're not afraid of dying, but we're afraid of living. Of loving. Of being together.'

'Yes,' Annabelle said. She looked sorrowful, her head was lowered, her face hidden by her long dishevelled hair.

'The greatest fear of all has nothing to do with hatred and aggressive acts. The greatest fear is of loving and being loved,' Andreas said.

* * *

Annabelle visited Andrew in hospital every day. He did not have long to live. She tried to tell Andreas how difficult it was to watch her friend dying.

'It must be very distressing for you,' Andreas said.

There were other things Annabelle wanted to talk to Andreas about, things she had found out from her friend.

'Andrew told me that Timothy Leary said: 'Tripping with another man is the greatest act of infidelity. In the future, it would be grounds for divorce.'

'It sounds as if he's jealous of me,' Andreas said.

'All the jealous men,' Annabelle murmured.

'What does that mean, Annabelle?'

'It's not Andrew who's jealous. He doesn't love me that way. We're more like brother and sister. I care about him. And he cares about me. He thinks I'm brave. But what he had to say about LSD is that you can programme people, and the CIA have used it to manipulate individuals and reach inside them. They could programme one to self-destruct or commit acts they would never do under normal circumstances. He said that LSD was a magnificent drug, but a dangerous one. It could cause people to become psychotic and undergo personality changes.'

'Your friend seems to consider himself quite an authority on LSD.'

'He is. Andrew grew up part of the drug culture of the sixties. He's tried everything. Now he's paying the price. He's only thirty-five, yet his life is already over. His lungs are calcified with emphysema, his kidneys are packing up, and his liver is badly damaged. He's had hepatitis, as well. The doctors told him he won't see his fortieth birthday. Still, better than to have lived a moribund existence,' she added. Annabelle could not restrain herself from punishing Andreas.

'He appears to have a death wish. Or he's trying to gain your sympathy and use you.'

'No, no, no,' Annabelle shook her head with frustration. 'Andrew told me to stop taking the Valium you've been giving me for my depression. He read an article in *Time* magazine on drugs and psychiatry. It reported that if a doctor ignores the patient is really depressed and gives him Valium, he may make the patient more depressed and even suicidal.'

The silence that followed was full of recriminations. Annabelle looked at Andreas. His face was like a death mask. Her heart went out to him for a moment, and she wanted to tell him that she understood how he felt. But there was so much that still perplexed her.

'It was like the magic potion in the fairy tale, wasn't it? That's why you wanted to keep me at the clinic. You didn't want me to go home because you wanted to be *the one* I'd see first when I awoke and fall deeply and irresistibly in love with you. Well, it worked. But look. I'm not the beautiful princess who is going to live happily ever after. I'm really quite wretched.'

'I tried to help you. I wanted very much to help you. LSD is the most powerful mind-expanding drug there is. I wanted to break through your defences. I wanted you to reach those memories and early experiences and help you release them from your severely repressed unconscious. I was hoping you would find yourself and achieve the peace of mind you're so desperate to find. I was hoping you would look realistically at your relationships.'

'You thought I might break up with my husband?'

'Yes! If it were necessary,' Andreas said.

'You forget my husband gives me security.'

'I wouldn't have given it to you if I hadn't experienced it myself,' Andreas said, ignoring Annabelle's comment.

'It didn't seem to help you. Andrew said that the effects are superficial and short lived,' Annabelle persisted with her accusations.

'Perhaps he's right.'

'A pity,' she said.

Annabelle gathered her scarf and her bag and left.

* * *

One day, the agency she worked for called. They wanted Annabelle to accompany a barrister to a maximum security prison outside Sydney. She had never been to a prison before. It was a chilling experience. So much iron, concrete and noise. The sound of clashing steel as door after door shut behind them was unnerving.

The man the lawyer had come to see was a young Italian migrant. He had been caught in a raid on a farm growing marijuana. He had been brought out from Italy by his uncle to work on the farm. He had never seen marijuana before, but was working the day the police swooped from the sky in their helicopters.

The police were disappointed to find only the worker on the farm. It made their raid look ridiculous. So they beat up the young man, venting their frustrations on him.

'They broke a shotgun on my back. It broke in two parts after they hit me with it,' he told Annabelle in his hard to understand Sicilian accent.

The young man had languished in gaol for over a year. Even though he was allowed bail no one had come to help him. His uncle had disappeared. The police thought he might have been murdered by his associates. It was only because a reporter had drawn attention to the young Italian's plight that something was being done about the case.

When David found out that Annabelle had been to the gaol, he over-reacted. 'You could have been killed! They're hardened criminals. I forbid you to ever go there again.'

He rang the lawyer and abused him for taking Annabelle to the prison. He in turn complained to the agency, who dismissed her.

Annabelle resented David's intrusion in her work, but in a way she felt protected. There was also her disappointment at how *she* had reacted to her job. In the beginning she had felt excited, wanting to help the emigrants. But slowly she became disillusioned. Some of them were almost as dishonest as the physicians, taking thousands of dollars from tax payers by faking their disabilities. Sitting for hours in stuffy rooms, hearing lies and watching manipulative behaviour, was boring as well as disheartening. There had to be something else, something she loved, somewhere she could make a difference.

In the meantime, Annabelle would continue with the sessions. She was not ready to stop seeing Andreas. Life would be desolate and deathly without him.

* * *

When Annabelle arrived at the Bollingen Clinic and sat down in her usual place, she noticed a parcel on the coffee table. It was wrapped in brown paper and held together with string. For a moment she thought it might be something from Andreas, a gift, some old family photos.

'It's for you,' Andreas said, when he saw her looking at it. 'Jess left it here, before leaving. She's gone home. To Ireland.'

'Why?' she asked.

'She's very ill,' Andreas told her.

'How could it be?' Annabelle asked, feeling flat and dispirited.

Another person she had liked, who seemed to have been an ally, had vanished from her life. Jess had been warm and friendly to her from the beginning, unlike Andreas's other secretary, Shirley.

'She's never been the same since she was banned from practising.'

'Practising what?' Annabelle was confused and wished Andreas would be more forthcoming about what had happened to Jess.

'Psychiatry. She fell in love with a patient, another woman, who had an erotic transference on her. They had a tumultuous affair. When Jess tried to end it, the woman committed suicide. Her family found some cassettes—her lover had been recording their sessions, their lovemaking—and their quarrels. The family took Jess to court. She was never able to practise again. I gave her the job to help her.'

'I wondered why you had two secretaries,' Annabelle said.

'Aren't you going to see what's in the parcel?' Andreas seemed curious to see what Jess had given Annabelle.

'I suppose so,' she said, still stunned from what she had learned.

Annabelle took the parcel and undid the string. An expression of surprise, followed by one of delight, came from her lips. There were several pieces of exquisite old lace. Then she covered her face and sobbed.

* * *

'You're looking well, Annabelle. Alive,' Andreas said.

'The more I learn about myself, the more I learn about you,' Annabelle told Andreas. 'I understand you now that the black cloud's lifting. I can see you. I know you, really know you. 'You want most what you fear most,' you told me once.'

'Yes, you've discovered me.' It was an accurate assessment, he could not deny it.

'What do you fear about me, Andreas?' Annabelle said, with great tenderness.

'What everybody fears. *Rejection.* You told me once you could destroy me if you wanted to. My father was afraid of rejection.'

'I can't destroy you. And even if I could, I wouldn't want to. I love you too much. We hurt ourselves, people don't hurt us unless we let them!'

'Why are you sitting like that?' he asked.

'How am I sitting? What's wrong with how I'm sitting?'

'You're sitting like a little girl, on the edge of the seat. Look at your hands, it's as if they're holding something.'

Annabelle glanced down at her lap. The white silk scarf hanging from her neck fell over her hands when she moved her head, covering them. She held the position carefully and bending her head, picked up the edge of the scarf between her teeth.

'I'm holding something precious,' she said.

'What are you holding?'

'I'm not sure.'

'What's the first thought that comes into your head?'

'I'm holding … I'm holding, *you*,' Annabelle said.

'Why?'

'Because you need holding …'

'What about your father? Did you want to mother him too?'

'Why must you drag my father into our conversation?'

'Do you feel ashamed to want to mother your father?'

'I think it's natural to want to comfort someone you love. But why drag him in? He's just a red herring you drag in every time we get close. Why do you hide behind him?'

'*Touché.*' Andreas said, giving her a weak smile. 'I use the counter-transference to escape, I guess. I feel like patting you on the head like your father did and say, *Clever,* instead of just letting it be.'

'Tell me about *your* father Andreas,' Annabelle tried to coax him.

'He told me before he died that he had been rejected by someone he loved, and so he married on the rebound.'

'How sad,' Annabelle said.

'Your father was afraid of rejection too.'

'How do you know? You never met him.'

'Because he had mistresses. Men and women who go from one person to the other are frightened of rejection. They're trying to prove to themselves that they're lovable.'

'You identify with him, and you're also very alike. How strange, how complicated,' Annabelle said.

'How complex. But through him, through becoming him in the countertransference, I have learned a lot about myself,' Andreas responded. 'You've made me discover myself and see things about me I had never seen before. Sometimes, I wonder who is getting more benefit out of this, you or me. I should be paying you.' Andreas's eyes briefly communicated his love, gratitude and vulnerability. He reminded her of a wounded dog, wanting to trust but ready to flee at the slightest approach. But he was swift to replace his professional mask. He had revealed too much.

'What other personal insights have you had?' Andreas said, trying to shift the attention away from himself.

'When I'm unhappy, I conceal it. I don't want anyone to see how I feel. When I was little, I developed a terrible rash. The doctor said he had never seen anything like it. It was all over my throat, from my chin to my chest, a crust of weeping sores. The puss seeping from the sores stung and itched. I nearly went mad. Eventually it came off, like a snake skin, leaving my throat pink and raw. This happened during a time when my parents fought a lot. They always fought, as your parents did. If I tried to show my feelings, that I was frightened by their shouting and threats, they would use me to escalate their quarrels and blame one another.'

'So you decided it was not safe to show your feelings.'

'Yes.'

'I don't think you ever had permission to be yourself. It's inconceivable to think that all of a person's goodness and heroism, and all of his or her wickedness and cowardice, is shaped in a child before the age of five. Usually much earlier. When you're cruel, you're trying to identify with your assailants, because of how unbearable it is to you to be a victim.'

'I refuse to be a victim,' Annabelle replied. 'I want to take charge of my destiny. I want to help others do the same.'

'I believe you do. You will change. You will grow. You have the courage. I have great faith in you,' Andreas said.

Annabelle smiled. 'Thank you doctor.' She felt grateful that Andreas believed in her. It was rare to hear such wonderful, inspiring words.

Her attention shifted to another parcel lying at her feet. It was time to give it to him.

'There's something for you,' she said. 'I wasn't here for your birthday.'

Andreas's face lightened and she suddenly had a rare glimpse of the small boy in the man. He took it almost hungrily from her.

'Thank you, Annabelle, you're very sweet.'

'See you next week, Andreas,' Annabelle said, looking shyly away from him and disappearing before he could open his parcel.

* * *

A lot can happen in a week and Annabelle was not prepared for what was waiting for her when she walked into his consulting room at the Bollingen Clinic. Andreas was standing by the window. He seemed troubled.

'I can't accept your gift,' Andreas said, pointing to the parcel. 'It's too personal. If you're going to play seductive games, I think it's best we find you another doctor. I'm sorry. The truth is I've failed you, and now the best thing I can do is let you go. You're emotionally blocked. You've built up a resistance. I've searched through the books to try and find a solution. Freud said that if the patient's relationship to the physician is disturbed, analysis cannot proceed to its proper goal. I can't help you anymore. Believe me when I tell you that I'm doing this for your own good.'

'That's not true!' Annabelle cried, full of anguish and the fear of abandonment. 'You've helped me more than you can imagine. Your love has helped me, despite yourself. I've changed. Can't you see?'

'We mustn't delude ourselves,' Andreas said.

'Please believe me!'

'This gift is proof,' Andreas was pointing to the parcel which had unravelled on the coffee table, spilling the black silk. 'It's too personal. You're playing seduction games again.'

'What do you mean *personal*?' she cried. 'After all we've been through, all we've done? You're telling me not to be personal? What did you think was in that parcel when you took it? A nice calendar desk set? A cuckoo clock? Slippers for an old man?'

Annabelle pulled the heavy black silk kimono from between the layers of tissue paper clinging to it. 'This was a gift of love, for you. It's an antique Japanese kimono and inside the lining there are golden lions, a symbol of longevity. Did Frida demand that you return it? Did she threaten to leave you? Tell you you'd be a lonely old man, stuck with having to look after your crippled son?'

'That's the reality of things as they are, Annabelle. I'm stuck with my son.'

'I'd help you. I need to make a commitment for the first time in my life.'

'He's not a child, Annabelle. He's a fully grown man. He could live for another thirty years in a wheelchair. No, I could never impose that on you. You're a butterfly, remember? It's cruel to pin a butterfly down.'

'You're afraid I'd leave you, so you're prepared to spend the rest of your life with some domineering woman you don't love.'

'I do, and she loves me. And her children are very fond of me and…'

'What about your own children? Why don't you love them? You've abandoned them. You're dependent on Frida because you're in a desperate frame of mind. You have lost your home, your wife, your daughter's love, your son is handicapped, and there's me. You could lose your work if I wanted to make trouble for you and take legal action against you—and you could lose your mind. You're vulnerable and frightened, so you cling to Frida. And Frida is taking advantage of the situation to use you and control you. That's not love, Andreas. You'd even go so far as to emulate your father and marry someone on the rebound. 'If you love someone, you have to let them go,' you told me. So now you are with Frida, as you were with Jean, as you were with your first wife. All women you didn't love. Do you realise Andreas, you have spent most of your life with women you don't love?'

Andreas's face was flushed. Annabelle's analysis of him was acute.

'I wasn't being seductive. I gave you the gift to cheer you up because

I heard you've been very unhappy lately,' Annabelle continued.

'Who told you?'

'It doesn't matter,' Annabelle said, shrugging it away.

They sat in silence, shrouded in bitterness and despair. Eventually, Annabelle spoke.

'If I go to another psychiatrist, does it mean we won't be seeing each other again?'

Andreas nodded.

'I don't understand,' Annabelle said, in a small voice, as if she was talking to herself. She shook her head to clear the confusion. 'I don't understand anything. I really didn't expect this. I really thought I was getting somewhere at last. I thought I understood the books I've been reading on psychology. Suddenly, it doesn't make sense anymore. I have taken a giant step backwards. No, I've been given an almighty shove. Do you, honestly, never want to see me again, Andreas?'

'Yes,' he said.

Annabelle looked around helplessly, hoping something would happen to change the situation. But Andreas remained unmoved, wooden.

'What went wrong, Andreas?'

'You didn't love me. You loved a fantasy. The real me is unacceptable to you.'

Annabelle shook her head. 'You've got it all wrong. I do love you. It's you who doesn't believe you are worthy of my love.'

'It came out when we made love, and you wouldn't let yourself go with me. You didn't accept me. You told me so once, under acid. You wanted to destroy me.'

'I was very destructive, what I said about your sexuality. I know how obsessed men are about their penises. But I wasn't talking about penises when I was tripping. I was talking about *love*. I was angry, because you hadn't come to see me when I was sick with pneumonia. I wanted to hurt you, to make you feel how I felt. I think you're trying to punish me about something that probably belongs in your past. I can't bear this. It's an icy death. My mouth is dry, I need some water. It's all those anti-depressant pills.'

'I'll get it for you.'

'I'll get it myself.'

Behind the screen by the sink was a knife with a pointy blade. Annabelle stared at it, seeing herself plunging it into his heart. Instead, in a last attempt to revive him, she emptied the glass of water over his head.

'That's a silly thing to do,' Andreas said, brushing the water off himself. 'You'd better leave, if you won't behave.'

'I'm sorry.'

'I've arranged for you to see Dr Leonard Kew as from next week,' Andreas announced, after regaining his composure. 'You'll find him in this clinic in the other wing.'

Andreas had wanted to believe that Leonard could help Annabelle—but also report on her progress to him on a regular basis. He had intended to keep Annabelle close and made it clear to his friend that she was his protégé. But he also knew that Annabelle would not be attracted to Leonard, he was an ugly looking man who used fake tan and dyed his hair a terrible colour, and although he had success with some women many others rejected him. Besides, Leonard had just had a prostate operation and had become impotent. He was no longer the crowing cock he had imagined himself to be.

But Annabelle saw it differently. Andreas was passing her to his friend, the one who could not keep his hands off his patients. A wave of nausea swept over her. It was imperative to get away as quickly as possible from these deeply disturbed men who fed like rats on the attentions of their female patients. It suddenly occurred to Annabelle that if you divide the word therapist in two, it becomes *the rapist.*

Annabelle shook her head. 'No, I won't see him. I won't give you that kind of control over me. I will not be a pawn in anyone's sick script any longer,' she said, rising to leave.

'Will you see another psychiatrist then? A woman?'

'Goodbye, Andreas.'

Andreas moved quickly from his armchair, grasping Annabelle's arm, trying to stop her leaving. But she twisted herself free and kept on walking, until she walked right out of the Bollingen Clinic, forever.

* * *

In the days that followed Annabelle's departure from the Bollingen Clinic, Andreas sank into deep despair. There had been two suicides in one generation on his mother's side of the family. His mother had said that her brother had died of disappointment, and her other brother had killed himself because he had failed his duty. She never told Andreas what that was, but she did say that he had been a near-degenerate. In fact, the reason he shot himself, was because of a broken heart.

Death was not a choice for Andreas. He had no choices whatsoever. It was inconceivable the he would abandon his son. There was no one who would take care of him.

28 The Bind

The last link is broken
That bound me to thee
And the words thou has spoken
Have rendered me free.

Like Ophelia in her madness Annabelle sang a song from a play, except the freedom she felt when she had walked out of Andreas's life, would prove to be illusory.

Alone in the big house, Annabelle's sense of loss was catastrophic. Each day her grief and desolation overwhelmed her. She was like a brittle autumn leaf, disintegrating in the wind. Sometimes her legs would buckle and she would end up on the floor, howling in anguish. All the pain she had ever experienced under LSD, she lived through again with greater poignancy. She lay spent on the ground, to be licked back to life by the only creature who cared, her dog Byron. He had been abandoned by the neighbours when they moved and she reluctantly embraced him as her own. Reluctantly, because she knew how painful it would be to lose him.

Annabelle's great fear was that she might be taken to the Bollingen Clinic, or to a hospital. She had made a decision to disguise her symptoms and see her breakdown through alone, as a sick animal copes with its pain. Annabelle avoided leaving the house, fearing she would lose control, and when she had no choice, she marvelled at how easily she could recognise the walking wounded. It was as if a big *W* had been branded on their foreheads and she imagined a signal, a secret language, a faint smile as they passed each other in the street.

Once, when she ventured into a department store and came across a rude salesgirl, Annabelle immediately understood the girl was in pain. She disarmed the young woman with her acceptance, signalling she was not offended by her behaviour. The girl was so taken aback by the unexpected kindness of the stranger that she shed a few tears. They parted with small gestures—hand waves and goodbye smiles.

But Annabelle needed comfort too, especially when she was stricken with grief in front of the perfume counter. People hurried past, glancing briefly over their shoulders at the weeping woman in black. Crossing the street became a major feat. Cars came and went and Annabelle stood lost, unable to make it to the other side.

Other times, Annabelle would become obsessed with a man in the street who looked remotely like Andreas. She would follow that person, staring at the back of his head, hoping it was Andreas. The same thing would happen if Annabelle and David were at the Opera House for a concert. Sitting in her seat, hardly aware of the music, Annabelle would imagine Andreas a few rows in front of her.

This nightmarish existence continued for a year. Annabelle's appearance began to mirror her distress. Her skin was dull and spotty, her hair lost its shine and hung in a straggly fall. Her eyes constantly scanned her surroundings as though she was being tormented by an invisible foe. Night after night she lay awake, reaching a point of exhaustion, feeling her heart would stop beating. A blessing, she imagined.

It was a relief when David was away. There were always his trips abroad, tennis camps, involvement with his partner and mentor—and the pursuit of riches and rewards. When he was home, Annabelle would use the shower to disguise her falling tears. Not that David would have noticed the anguish his wife was in. He had always been spectacularly self-absorbed.

Annabelle never thought of calling Andreas, although she did receive several silent phone calls and wondered if they were from him.

In the end, she believed the dog saved her. He had sat beside her, day after day, quietly watching her, licking her face and hands, curling up on the floor with her. He was the best mother she ever had.

Annabelle visited her doomed friend Andrew in hospital and sat by his bed holding his hand. He was no longer communicating but she hoped he liked her being there. The whiff of alcohol and disinfectant reminded her of the Bollingen Clinic—and added to her distress.

At times, she felt strange vibrations coursing through her body. Andrew had warned her about re-experiencing some of her previous LSD trips. 'He never should have given it to you,' Andrew had said, his thin pale face pinched with worry. 'It's too dangerous, Annabelle. Psychiatrists stopped using it years ago. There were too many suicides.'

Death, strangely enough was not something she feared. Like Psyche, Annabelle had experienced Death at the top of the mountain—the dark side of love. No matter. Let Death become her companion in her grief.

* * *

One evening Annabelle wandered into the garden. The stone pavers were cold beneath her feet and the pale moon cast an eerie light on her surroundings. When she caught sight of herself in a windowpane, she uttered a little cry and ran inside to escape the frightful creature she had become. She hid in the library, having never felt sheltered in the large, cold Victorian house David had bought. The high ceilings intensified the loneliness she felt. Annabelle had painted the library blood red, because everywhere else was surgical white and she needed warmth, a red womb where she felt safe. The library was her refuge. Annabelle fingered the dusty covers of the books, removing one book from a shelf, then another, losing herself in distant voices.

A volume, bound in black leather with gold lettering, caught her eye. The book had come to David after his mother's death, together with antiques and other objects, all the way from Vienna. Annabelle pulled a chair and climbed up to retrieve it.

It was a book of *Satanism and Witchcraft*. Annabelle opened it but after reading a few pages could read no further. The gruesome inventions for inflicting pain and suffering on women and girls accused of witchcraft were beyond imagination. There were drawings of instruments of torture used to pierce, tear, burn, impale and immure fragile human bodies. For three centuries millions of women were tormented and burned alive at the stake, their only sin that they aroused desire, hatred and fear in men. How could human beings behave so abominably? And why did women let their men commit such atrocities? All the mothers, wives, daughters, sisters—how could they let their men do such things?

She remembered something a Jewish doctor, Gisela Perl, survivor of Auschwitz, had said about Mengele, who performed horrific medical experiments on the prisoners. 'He was so seductive, so satanic, that some girls would forget that he had killed their mothers, their fathers, their sisters, their husbands. Many times young girls would come to me crying: 'Gisi doctor, I want just to be with him for one night.'

Annabelle flung the book on the floor and cried caustic tears. When she had stopped crying, her attention was once again drawn to the book at her feet. It had fallen open on a chapter: *Charms and Love Potions*. If she could sell her soul to the devil to have Andreas love her again, and erase all the hurt they had done to each other, she would do it.

* * *

Annabelle looked all over the house for a red heart. She would also need seven pearl-tipped pins, a red candle, a photograph of her lover and something belonging to him.

There was an urgency to perform the ritual. Annabelle believed she would die otherwise. She cut a red heart from her dress and searched for a red candle, but there were only white ones on silver candlesticks on the dining table. Then she remembered the Christmas decorations and found the candles in a box with the angels and the glass balls. The only photograph she had of Andreas was the one of him as a schoolboy, at Bedales. She had asked for it because she thought he looked angelic. She did not have anything else of his, except the gold chain with the little heart, which she still wore around her neck.

Annabelle set up an altar with her props and threw open the French doors to allow the night spirits to assist her. Then she removed her nightdress and stood naked in front of the altar. She took the candle and anointed it with her perfume before lighting it. The flame spluttered and flickered and threw dancing shadows on the walls of her bedroom. Annabelle concentrated on the photograph, her eyes burned with a feverish glow, as she intoned three times:

I call to thee Beloved One
To need me more than anyone
Seven times I pierce thy heart
With Cupid's sacred magic dart
I bind thy heart and soul to me
Until I choose to set thee free
I send my call to torment thee
And as my will
So mote be

The candle became a glowing red phallus. She took it in her hand where it vibrated with a devilish force and put the flame out against her cold body. She let out a scream from deep within before falling down in a faint.

When she woke up some time later, the moon had disappeared. Annabelle was shivering uncontrollably. Slowly she raised herself on her hands and knees and crawled back to bed to bury herself beneath the doona. She lost consciousness again but was woken by something which caused her heart to beat wildly and erratically. She knew immediately what it was. Andreas was close by—and in grave danger. He was being stalked through the dark alleys of Kings Cross.

Andreas had come to seek the same fate as Annabelle's friend. She remembered Andreas's reaction at her distress when Andrew was beaten up and left for dead. She had made daily visits to the hospital. There was Annabelle's Freudian slip during her session as she described what happened to Andrew. The unforgivable slip, when she mixed up their names.

Now Andreas was wandering and weaving unsteadily through the back streets of Kings Cross, stopping for shots of vodka in bars, unaware of the men in the shadows watching him. Perhaps his impressive stature would protect him because bullies liked to beat up people who did not look capable of fighting back. Or they could mistake him for a cop in a suit. They retreated into their dark holes to wait for a more likely victim.

Andreas needed to get drunk. There was a small bar with pulsating orange lights beckoning him. He asked for vodka. The proprietor, an exile, sick for home, recognised a fellow compatriot and offered Andreas his best vodka. After a while, the two men embraced their Russian melancholy, and the conversation soon turned to the women they had loved. And lost.

His new friend, Nikolai, wanted to help. He made a brief telephone call.

Andreas was slumped over the small round metal table when the girl arrived. She had a drink with the two men, and then took Andreas to a room above the nightspot where there was a bed, a towel and a washbasin. And more pulsating coloured lights.

The girl sat Andreas on the bed and began to undress. She stood naked in front of him waiting for instruction. He looked at her with interest, trying to adjust his eyes to the semi-darkness.

'You're beautiful. My god, you're beautiful,' he slurred his words.

The girl was surprised but not convinced. Had the light not been so dim, he would have seen her ribs protruding, her skin uneven in colour with red and purple blotches, and the pus-filled eruptions on her back. There were also needle marks on the inside of her arms and thighs. She pushed Andreas gently onto the pillows and removed his shoes and his trousers. Then she took his organ in her hands. She rubbed and sucked, working hard to bring the necessary blood flow to make it erect. To no avail.

The sound of his snoring brought her some relief and she covered Andreas with a blanket and left. She had other business to attend to.

* * *

This was not the only time Andreas had wandered from the North Shore to the Eastern Suburbs, Annabelle's territory. He had come on many occasions, hoping to catch a glimpse of her.

One hot summer afternoon when she was in Double Bay, Annabelle saw Andreas. She had just finished shopping at the greengrocer and was about to cross the street, when she caught sight of his reflection in a shop window on the opposite side.

Andreas was standing on the sunless side of the street, in front of an antique shop. He had his back to her, but Annabelle could see not only his image mirrored on the dark glass, but also hers, spotlighted by the afternoon sun. He was watching her.

Andreas had a pram and an older child holding on to him.

Annabelle fled.

* * *

For a year, Annabelle had mourned Andreas and had just begun to live a normal life again, but that encounter with Andreas and the children unsettled her completely. Did he really still hate her? Enough to come with his newborn and one of Frida's children to where he might find her—to cause her more pain?

A week later she booked a flight to India—to Kashmir and the Himalayas. She wanted to climb a mountain. Or perhaps to die.

The mountain Annabelle climbed made her ill when she was caught in a blizzard. First she experienced the excruciating pain of snow-blindness. Then she contracted another bout of pneumonia and spent the rest of the journey lying semi-conscious in a shepherd's hut, before being taken to a house boat in Kashmir and in due time, flown out of India.

While in her feverish state, Annabelle was convinced Andreas kept her alive—he was at her side reminding her of his love.

'To suffer one's death and be reborn is not easy,' he had whispered.

The most bitter lesson for Annabelle was that she had had so little insight into what she put Andreas through. Andreas had longed to tell her what it had cost him, the sacrifice made. He had tried to aid her development, after almost stunting it, true, but he had hated himself for having succumbed, for the mess he had made of things, nearly destroying her. Annabelle was the only woman he had ever loved, could *ever* love who, for a brief moment brought him the intense happiness that had eluded him all his life. He had had the fantastic notion of living with her. But he knew it could never be. Annabelle remembered the time when he decided he must let her go, how he seemed to shiver, even his bowels had reacted with fear, and he had left the room to rush to the bathroom.

Annabelle struggled with remorse and self-hatred. She had been heartless. Her youth, self-absorption and lack of awareness were cruel. It was only with age that her understanding and compassion would expand. In time, she would try to live by the words of Philo of Alexandria. *Be kind, for everyone you meet is fighting a great battle.*

* * *

When Annabelle recovered from her illness, she enrolled at university to study for her degree in psychology. She had taken the course before, in her youth, but had refused to sit for the final exam even though she had always received distinctions for her essays. Annabelle hated any system that separated human beings into winners and losers.

Part of her training to become a psychotherapist required Annabelle to continue seeing an analyst for at least two years. It had to be someone in the Eastern Suburbs—she could not bear having to cross the Harbour Bridge again, even though she had heard Andreas was no longer practising at the Bollingen Clinic. He had moved to a country town.

Annabelle searched for a female therapist and found a Jewish one from South Africa. She liked the woman immediately but, after listening to her story, the therapist explained why she could not help her. Her case was hopeless—the damage that had been done by Andreas would last forever. Annabelle was devastated—and felt rejected once again.

It took Annabelle several more searches before she was accepted by a seemingly sane, emotionally stable and ethical therapist. He was a Hungarian, who had fled with his parents from Vienna, the war and Hitler. He had grown up in Quetta, near the Khyber Pass in Afghanistan. It seemed the world was full of exiles.

'We're all like Ulysses,' Annabelle said, 'trying to find our way home. Some of us, never make it. Like Andreas.'

Her therapist was not interested in Andreas. He insisted she attend his rooms three times a week and only take holidays when he took his. At first Annabelle baulked at the restrictions, but in time, she complied and grew in strength. So much so, that after two years, she announced she no longer needed to see him. At the end of her final session, after she had offered to shake hands with him, he held on to her hand and would not let her leave.

After graduating, and completing her therapy with the man from Quetta, Annabelle began to practice as a psychotherapist under the supervision of another highly respected psychiatrist. Annabelle wanted to be a caring therapist, guiding her patients on their journeys, opening doors and helping them look at what they had uncovered. Above all, she wished to do no harm. Annabelle regarded her job to be a witness.

One day, Annabelle read in the newspaper that her supervisor, the highly regarded and respected doyen of the psychiatric profession, had been deregistered. Charges of professional misconduct had been brought against him.

A patient of this revered man had been the victim of childhood sexual abuse. This did not deter the psychiatrist from seducing the woman and having intercourse during his patient's sessions. On someone's advice, the woman had taken a recorder with her and taped one of the sessions. The therapist was heard to ask the patient after they had sex whether he could sit on her lap in all his nakedness.

* * *

After a time, however, Annabelle discovered that psychotherapy was a very difficult profession indeed, and that perhaps she was not suited to it. The therapist was constantly tested, harassed and having to respond to the endless clamour of those in need. There was the longing too. The world was full of unfulfilled longings. Some longed for fame and recognition. Others for riches. Or freedom. For acts of kindness, warmth or sex. Someone to witness their existence. All longed for love and acceptance. Everyone was steeped in longing. Longing, was their cursed heritage.

Patients made demands on her time, leaving messages on the telephone, wanting to talk to her, stalking her. And they set all kinds of traps. One of these was asking for a hug. It was a difficult task for Annabelle, who had never enjoyed physical contact except with Andreas. In the end, she had to refuse, much as it grieved her, as the male patients turned it into a sexual embrace. It inevitably ended with them pressing their erections against her body.

Annabelle felt disheartened at her inability to find satisfaction in any aspect of her life. In truth, her depression had never left her. She had stopped taking the dangerous drugs Andreas had prescribed the day she walked out of his clinic. Her health improved, and she no longer suffered from migraine. Two years later, she fell pregnant. Annabelle worried that her child would be born to a sad mother. Her own mother had felt abandoned when her husband went to work in Libya for an oil company and left her with child. The news of Annabelle's pregnancy seemed to distance David further from her. His trips away became more frequent. Personal letters arrived for him from Paris, New York and Hawaii. He made secretive long phone calls in the middle of the night, and bought beautiful cards meant for someone else. She had seen one on his desk, before he posted it. It was *The Kiss* by Gustav Klimt and had mistakenly thought it was for her as her birthday was not far away. It dawned on Annabelle that David had always had his secret affairs, his other life, but she had never noticed. She had needed the distance it created between them.

Annabelle developed a murmur of the heart. The heart needs warmth—a lack of love, heartbreak or heartache can harm the heart. The loneliness and isolation in her marriage could kill her.

One night, eight weeks into her pregnancy, Annabelle woke up. Something strange was happening. She ran her fingers along the bedclothes and found them wet and sticky. She was bleeding—alone and terrified.

The next time she opened her eyes, she was in a hospital room with tubes attached to her arms. She tried to free herself by shaking them off. A nurse came and injected her with a drug, sedating her.

Shocking as the experience had been of losing her baby, Annabelle was relieved. She had saved her unborn child from suffering.

29 The Unexpected

The tragic resurrection of her lover occurred a year after her miscarriage.

Annabelle had conveniently forgotten about the ritual she had performed—her shameful and desperate need to enslave Andreas with incantations and magic spells. As far as she was aware, Andreas had disappeared to Siberia, or some other hell. Until that day, when Annabelle was driving to the airport to meet her husband's flight from New York.

While waiting for the aeroplane to land, Annabelle felt a tap on her shoulder and turned around to see a man grinning at her. Annabelle felt annoyed at the liberty the stranger had taken, invading her space, particularly as she found his appearance repugnant. She would have turned away brusquely, were it not for the fact that he seemed to know her.

He was a man in his late fifties with hair undulating to his shoulders and dyed mahogany brown. His skin looked as if it had been rubbed with tan boot polish. He was wearing a cream safari suit with short sleeves unbuttoned to his chest where a copper medallion dangled in the centre of grey curling hairs—and white moccasins on his sockless feet. Annabelle's eyes fixed for a moment on his jewellery—a naked man encircled by equally naked cavorting women.

'You probably don't remember me. I'm Leonard Kew. I'd watch you come to the Bollingen Clinic to see Doctor Zill. I was a friend of Andy's. He confided in me. I've been watching you and trying to decide whether I should tell you. I know how much you meant to each other and would want to know that he's very ill. He's only got a short time to live.'

Of course Annabelle remembered. She had bumped into him outside the clinic one afternoon when she had danced along the path on the way out—and mistaken him for an inmate of the asylum.

Andreas had been Leonard Kew's anaesthetist during his operation.

Andreas had specialised in anaesthesia before switching to psychiatry. But she also remembered the afternoon when Andreas had announced that he could no longer see her, and wanted to pass her on to his friend who had erotic transferences on his patients.

'I'm sorry to hear that,' Annabelle said.

'I saw him in Paddington, at St Vincent Hospital a week ago. He's got inoperable colorectal cancer. Had it for a long time but he wouldn't do anything about it. You might like to visit him.'

'I'm sorry to hear that,' she repeated, turning away, discouraging any further communication.

Although Kew found Annabelle's manner unnerving, he persisted.

'You know he married Frida soon after you left us at Bollingen? Andy and Frida had two children.' He continued to talk fast because Annabelle kept looking over her shoulder for David. 'Andy left the Bollingen and moved west. He was working at Mortalloc. So sorry to bring you such bad tidings. But you, my dear, look wonderful. He always believed you'd be fine. Had lots of faith in you, more than you'll ever know. Let me buy you a drink, catch up on lost time,' he said, taking possession of Annabelle's arm.

'Please, let me go!' Annabelle said, holding her ground. 'David!' she called and waved to him.

'Too bad,' Leonard Kew said. 'Some other time, perhaps?'

* * *

Mortalloc. Annabelle silently repeated the name. It had a strange, sickening effect on her. Of course, it could have been the first half of the name, *mort,* he was already dead to her. How fitting that Andreas had chosen that place when he left the city.

'Where is Mortalloc ?' Annabelle asked David, as they were driving home from the airport.

'It's a town south-west, known for the gaol and asylum for the criminally insane.'

David turned and looked at her while they were stopped at the red lights.

'Why?' he asked, giving Annabelle an affectionate pat on the thigh. She instinctively withdrew her leg.

'I just overheard someone talking about it, at the airport,' Annabelle said, turning her face away to look at the driver of another car.

The monotony of the journey along the expressway lulled her into a stupor. Her head was resting against the window, watching but not seeing the advertising billboards as they sped past. Andreas had left the Bollingen Clinic to live and work in a country town with a gaol and an asylum for the criminally insane. Was that where he felt he really belonged? Did he hope that by listening to the dark rantings of the deranged he would learn something? Or was it to punish himself, the way sinners have been known to do throughout the centuries, choosing to exile themselves into communities of lepers, the poor or the lost?

The moment they were home, David checked his messages and went straight to bed, as he usually did after a long flight, nursing his jet lag and his two weeks at the conference. He complained to Annabelle how tiring it was, even though he was staying in luxury hotels, being entertained and dining in the best restaurants as a guest of a large pharmaceutical corporation.

Amongst the many telephone messages left on the answering machine for Doctor Eichler, was one for Annabelle, from Frida Zill. She had left her telephone number and a short message to ring her. But David forgot to tell her.

* * *

Annabelle was disturbed to have been accosted by Leonard Kew. This was the man Andreas had wanted to send her to when she was in such a fragile state. She was glad she had rebelled against Andreas, walking out on him, leaving him standing there, stunned.

Andreas dying? It was troubling, no, shocking Annabelle suddenly realised. She had never given up hope they would be reunited one day, never stopped loving him, even though she had succeeded in pushing him out of her mind—but not her heart. It was all too, too sad, she lamented, cradling her head in her arms and resting them on her lap.

Annabelle had tried to leave her husband after her miscarriage, secretly hoping and wishing Andreas would hear about it and contact her. But David had talked her out of it, telling her she was in a fragile state of mind and would find it difficult to survive on her own.

Now Andreas was dying, close by, at St Vincent Hospital. No, she did not want to see him. It was too late. He would not want to see her, either. That was the sad and bleak reality.

Whenever Annabelle was angry, or lost, she ran to the park. Or the sea. Nature had always been a consolation, harbouring and nourishing her and she sought it now like a young animal seeks its mother. She found the abandoned section of the grounds where the homeless and the deviant went. 'Andreas is dying,' she said, over and over. But it did not make any sense to her. Yet.

Annabelle kept on running until she came to that wild unkempt part of the park, and there among the ailing she-oaks, she sat down and wept.

* * *

Two days later, Frida telephoned again. At first Annabelle could not understand her, she seemed to be calling from far away.

'I rang to tell you that Andy is dying. He's been asking for you. You must come.' Frida made it sound like an order.

'Why?' Annabelle said, feeling dazed and shaken, and rejecting what she was hearing. The re-appearance of Andreas in her life was something she had secretly craved. The desire, the dreams and the yearning had never ceased but she had not been prepared for Andreas dying and *calling* for her.

'I don't know,' Frida replied. 'Probably to allay old ghosts.' There was a pause while she waited for Annabelle to speak. 'He's dying,' she stated again, sounding very matter of fact, but leaving Annabelle no escape.

Shock gave way to panic and confusion. All the feelings Annabelle tried to suppress were resurfacing. Now Andreas was dying and he was asking for her. What was she to do? How was she to behave? A scene from a film about Chopin and George Sand appeared in her mind—the actress turning her back on the ailing composer. Annabelle had played the scene with her grandfather when she had stood outside his room and he had beckoned to her to come to him.

Andreas wanted her. How extraordinary.

'I'll come and see him,' she said, at last.

Annabelle heard Frida give a sigh of relief.

'Andy was at St Vincent in Paddington, but we moved him back here, to Mortalloc. There's nothing more they can do for him.'

'Is he at home?' Annabelle asked.

'No, I can't look after him. I've been ill, too, had an operation. He's at Mortalloc Hospital. It'll take you four or five hours to drive here. You can stay the night at our house.'

'I'll see if there's a flight,' Annabelle said. 'I'll have to check.' Then she added, 'I won't be staying the night, thank you.'

'As you like,' Frida said. There was a note of disappointment in her voice.

The thought of staying in Andreas's home, of being exposed to his life with Frida and his children, listening to intimate details about their cohabitation horrified Annabelle. What if Frida wanted to vent her anger at Annabelle, blaming her for his physical if not mental disintegration? Where could she escape in the middle of the night in a town lurking with crazies and murderers? A town with no taxis as soon as darkness fell.

'Another thing. Could you bring some food? You know, French pastries. And something to drink, wine or spirits. We're broke and he really would love something nice to eat.'

Annabelle was at first bewildered then deeply troubled by what Frida told her. How could someone who had bowel cancer cope with food? But she accepted how comforting that simple, natural function would be. Andreas had enjoyed the meals she cooked that summer when they were meeting at his house. For love in the afternoon.

How had it come to this? Andreas starving? It was suddenly all too shocking, too distressing. She had tried to protect herself by pulling away but now she could so easily unravel again.

'There's one more thing,' Frida was telling her. 'Please do me a favour and don't call him Andreas. Everybody calls him *Andy.*'

* * *

Soon after Frida's telephone call, Leonard Kew rung, surprising and annoying Annabelle.

'I thought you might have been thinking about going to visit him after what I told you at the airport.'

'I was.'

'You really mustn't,' Kew said. He sounded agitated.

'Why not? I've had a call from Frida. Andreas has asked to see me.'

'That's why you mustn't. Come and talk to me instead. Give me a call at the clinic.'

'Why shouldn't I go?' Annabelle was curious. It was odd behaviour, even for someone as bizarre as Leonard Kew.

'Because it'll be distressing for you. There'll be changes in his appearance. He won't recognise you. He was hallucinating when I was there last, something about the nuns at St Vincent being after him, punishing him.'

'Oh, really?'

'I think it's dangerous for you to go,' Kew said.

'What do you mean?'

'Just that! I think it's dangerous for you to see him.'

His warning sounded ominous.

But Annabelle would not let him scare her, although she was wildly irritated by him. 'Could you be more specific?' she said.

'When I left him, I stood outside his room chatting with the nursing sister. I heard Andy talking to himself. It was very odd. I heard him say: 'If he were only a fornicator, he could be forgiven, but…' He didn't finish his sentence. I think if he had, he would have said: 'If he were only a fornicator he could be forgiven, but he's a murderer.'' There was a moment of silence while Kew waited for Annabelle's reaction. Finally, he resumed his monologue. 'It is my belief Annabelle, that Andy thinks he's a murderer. I think he feels guilty about a lot of things—you, his children, especially his son who died in the nursing home where they'd sent him because he and Frida could not look after him. There are the two patients who died while having ECT. And other deaths, suicides. If he believes he's a murderer, he could behave like one.'

'What's that got to do with me seeing him?' Annabelle said.

'Well, he harbours a lot of anger and resentment towards you. It's natural after what you did to him. He could easily have something—a weapon—concealed under his pillow when you see him.'

'Where would he get a weapon from? He's a very ill man. You told me he's at death's door, Doctor Kew. It seems a bit incredible.' Annabelle was tempted to hang up on him.

'He could have got one from the gaol as self-protection. He was working with some pretty dangerous types. Or he could have bought it from a criminal. These things are easy to get if you know the right people.'

'You mean, a gun?'

'Or a knife,' he said, and again waited for his words to take effect.

'That's your opinion,' Annabelle said.

There was a pause, she suspected she had offended him.

'By the way, Doctor Kew …'

'Call me Lenny,' he offered.

'Len … Lenny?'

He forgave her.

'Yes, Annabelle, my sweet …?'

'Don't hold your breath expecting my visit. You're a lunatic!'

30 The Memory of Scent

There was a morning flight to Mortalloc, returning late afternoon which suited Annabelle. She would make the journey in one day. David need not know.

The aircraft seated eight. The other passengers were all men, a mix of public servants, farmers and graziers. The men of the land wore cowboy hats, boots and moleskin trousers. It was a perfect morning with a clear cold sky, the light was sharp and a freshness in the air lingered after recent rain.

Andreas was dying, she repeated many times because it was incomprehensible to her. What did it mean? It felt strange, very strange indeed.

The aeroplane landed near a paddock of dandelions where a flock of sheep were grazing. Annabelle waited in a shed at the airport for the taxi to arrive.

On the drive to the hospital, Annabelle tried to imagine the world Andreas had inhabited during the last years of his life. The town had the usual blight of ugly garish yellow-on-red arches she hated so much—as well as a Pizza Hut, a KFC, several second-hand car sales yards, a pub, and the ubiquitous supermarket.

Andreas had left behind the beautiful lakes and valleys of Switzerland; the excitement of living in London and Sydney; the lavender fields of Provence; and the enchantment of childhood holidays by the sea in the South of France; for an Australian town called Mortalloc.

Once, Annabelle had revelled in his arms, listening to him whispering the names of the French towns he wanted to take her to, delighting her with each appellation: *Saint Raphael-Valescure, Cap Ferrat, Juan-les-Pins, Cap d'Antibes, Nice, Villefranche, Beaulieu.* They invoked images of sun-filled days at the beach, romantic engagements and sensuous afternoons of love-making. The Fitzgeralds, Hemingways and Murphys, had all loved and played there.

Andreas, had exiled himself to a country at the other end of the world—to die in a godforsaken town. Why?

* * *

The hospital consisted of a series of liver-red brick buildings strung together in a line like barracks, built after the war. Inside, the walls were green and the floors covered in dark brown linoleum. Annabelle waited while the nurse went ahead to announce her arrival, and beckoned to her from a doorway at the far end.

As Annabelle walked the length of the corridor to where Andreas was waiting, she felt suspended in time. Thoughts she had suppressed came tumbling and dancing wildly around her. What would he look like? Would he be emaciated? Would she be able to recognise him? Would he recognise her? Would she *see* the disease? Would the toxins have poisoned his brain, causing him to rave beyond reach, mad, irrational?

Annabelle had been warned by the lunatic.

* * *

With a start, Annabelle realised she had reached Andreas's ward. She braced herself before entering and was almost blinded by the light pouring in from a large open window overlooking a grey concrete yard. A couple of wilting pot plants languished on the window sill.

'Annabelle,' Andreas tried to raise himself from the bed.

Annabelle looked at him for a moment, spellbound. She was surprised and thankful to see how little he had changed. He was still as handsome as she remembered him. His hair was perhaps greyer and a little thinner, his skin pale and smooth like wax, stretched tightly over his sculpted features, and his eyes were a great deal sadder. She had once thought of him as a beautiful blue-eyed Buddha. He was still beautiful, except now he looked like Buddha at the end of a long fast. She put her parcels down on a chair and lent over to kiss him.

For an instant, Annabelle recalled the lunatic's warning. She was aware of the underside of her body, unprotected and vulnerable, when she leaned over Andreas to kiss his cheek. So it was with a small sigh of relief that she retreated from him unharmed, and sat down on a chair beside the bed. She listened attentively as he recounted his misfortunes.

Sometimes Andreas appeared lucid as he talked. At other times, he was confused, and Annabelle could not follow what he was saying. He may have been hallucinating. Painkillers did that. She wondered whether he was in pain. There was a large bottle of white tablets on the bedside table. Morphine.

There were interruptions from a nurse; then a colleague with a plate of Jatz biscuits, cubed cheddar and pineapple on toothpicks; an ex-patient, a young woman, clearly in love with him, arrived carrying another pot plant she had hastily put together. The plants were suffering from shock having been roughly transplanted in the middle of the day. The woman filled the air with noise, talking incessantly and treating Andreas as though this was another therapy session.

Annabelle sat calmly collected, a reluctant observer.

Eventually his patient left and Annabelle hoped there would be no other visitors for a while. There was so little time left. She looked at her watch, her flight was leaving in two hours.

When they were alone, Andreas spoke to Annabelle about his son, Nicolas, who had died in an institution for the handicapped. He talked until his voice became weak and difficult to hear. He spoke about regrets, though he never brought up what happened between them. There was something very tragic about a dying man with so much remorse.

It was lunch time and Andreas would be hungry. Annabelle unpacked the food she had brought him: smoked salmon, cream cheese, rye, French pastries, Swiss chocolates and a bottle of Champagne.

Annabelle was aware of Andreas keenly watching her as she spread the cream cheese on the bread and added a slice of salmon on top. When she handed it to him, their eyes met for a moment in that unique familiar connection they had. It brought a smile to their lips. Andreas ate in silence, seeming to savour every mouthful. The champagne made him forget for a while that he was ill.

'You seem calm, Annabelle, as though you have found some inner peace. There seems to be a new strength in you. But you're dressed like a nun,' he said, with a smile.

Annabelle regretted for a moment wearing her blue dress with the small white collar and cuffs. Perhaps it would have been more cheering for Andreas if she had dressed in her old beguiling, eclectic style but Annabelle had no wish to be seductive—she had cloistered her heart away. She would never love again.

'I meditate,' she said.

Andreas gave a broken, fearful sigh. 'I tried meditation. It doesn't work for me. I'm afraid, because I don't feel at peace. I haven't been able to come to terms with my illness. Everybody tells me I'm dying but I don't feel as if I am. It's very puzzling. They say I've only got a few weeks. It's very puzzling indeed, Annabelle.'

Annabelle was overcome with pity and went to his side, taking him in her arms and holding him—like a mother does when a child is afraid of the dark. She stroked his head and kissed his cheek and felt him surrender briefly to a sweet memory.

'You are so good, Annabelle, so good. I don't deserve your kindness, after all I did to you. I am so sorry, if only you knew how sorry I am, how much I hate and despise myself.'

'Hush, darling' Annabelle whispered. 'We didn't know any better. We were brave to have loved at all, considering how damaged we are. You tried to protect me. But it was not possible. Our love was stronger than any rules, because that's what love is like, lawless. And there is always a price to pay. I wouldn't have missed our encounter for anything in the world. I have felt your love in spite of everything, Andreas.' Annabelle stroked his cheek, desperate to reassure him.

Andreas kissed her hand and closed his eyes. For a moment he looked peaceful. When he opened them again, he was surprised to see tears running down Annabelle's face. He sighed. It was true, she cared. 'How did it begin?' he asked.

'How could you forget?' Annabelle smiled, knowing what had been indelibly set in memory.

They wanted to relive the spell. Andreas was lost in wonderment, gratitude and regret.

'The most important moment of my life—when I first saw you. A beautiful apparition, all in white,' Andreas said.

'It was an antique wedding dress.'

'I'd never seen such a beautiful woman. I feared that you were going to disappear out of my life before the night was over.'

'It was how I felt about you, too. But I was also afraid of you,' Annabelle said.

'We were both fearful. When later, I told you: 'You want most what you fear most,' I was also speaking for myself,' Andreas sighed, kissing the palm of her hand. 'We talked about your passion for all things Russian—especially Pushkin and Tolstoy. You mentioned a great love and affinity with Russia, but didn't know why.'

'You were the link. I had been waiting for you. When I looked into your eyes and saw the Russian melancholy, I felt the pain of centuries. It was as if an arrow of sorrow shot straight to my heart. I was enraptured, beguiled, lost! Especially lost,' Annabelle said, looking up at Andreas with all the naked love she had been too frightened to express in the past.

'Lost,' Andreas echoed. 'Enchantment.'

'I was lost in your gaze. I never wanted to return to my life. But that was not possible.'

They remained in silence for a while, while their and mistakes and regrets flowed past. There were sweet, as well as harrowing memories.

'You said I reminded you of a princess, one of the Czar's daughters. Such terrible deaths.'

'Did I ever tell you what Tolstoy said? 'The moment a man loves a beautiful woman, he becomes the most wretched.' I loved you so much, I thought you would destroy me.'

'I died for you a thousand deaths,' Annabelle said. 'I hated you.'

'I know. I suffered, too.'

The winter afternoon sun was beginning to dim. It was time to leave.

Annabelle kissed Andreas's head. But when she saw the longing in his eyes, she kissed his lips.

'Goodbye, Andreas.'

Annabelle pressed Andreas close to her heart, where he belonged. Then she let him fall gently back on the pillows.

Andreas followed her with his eyes until she was gone.

Annabelle found herself in the gloomy corridor again. She quickened her step, afraid the taxi would not wait for her.

* * *

The whole experience had been deeply distressing for Annabelle—to see the state Andreas was in—humbled, suffering, alone. She wished she could rescue him, take him to the sea, feed him good food, make him well again. But it was not permitted.

Annabelle cursed and burst into loud sobs. She was angry with herself most of all, for having been childish and playing destructive games; for her cruelty and ignorance; for not realising how great their love was; for lost time; and for the end of everything as she now saw it.

The taxi driver glanced in the mirror.

'A relative of yours?' he said, looking over his shoulder.

* * *

Aboard the aeroplane, Annabelle sat close to the window with her cheek pressed against the cold glass, watching the blue slowly fading from the sky, giving in to impending darkness.

I bind thy heart and soul to me, Until I choose to set thee free. She had only pretended that he no longer existed, while all the time she had held him a prisoner, sending her call to torment him. She needed to release him.

* * *

In the months that followed, Annabelle thought about him night and day.

Andreas, lying in his bed of pain.

Pain, the unwelcome visitor.

It was worse at night. In the dark, Andreas could not see it coming. It ensnared, stabbed, crushed, hammered, burned and nauseated him. He could not escape it. Blackness concentrated his agony, there was nothing to distract him, to focus upon.

When the pain became too bad, Andreas would conjure Annabelle in her white dress, waiting for him to take her in his arms. He would offer her his hand and she would place hers into his, then he would waltz her to her favourite music, the *Russian Waltz* by Shostakovich. They would spin and spin until the dance became a succession of love-making interludes. Andreas would sigh and smile and forget about the dying. The past was a distraction, and comfort, from the unbearable present.

Andreas watched and waited for the stealthy fingers of dawn to creep into his room. At night no one could help him. It would be different during the day, he hoped. Nurses, colleagues, patients would drop by and distract him. His wife was still away, on vacation, with children and friends.

He had made the decision to cease taking the painkillers. He would keep it a secret for as long as he could bear it, although now, he was experiencing withdrawals to the morphine. His eyes and nose were watering. He was sweating, his muscles ached, and a disturbing restlessness had taken over. The nausea was pretty awful, too.

Andreas had stopped taking morphine because it reduced his levels of consciousness, especially his emotional reactions and his awareness of his surroundings. It also made him dizzy and drowsy. And he was waiting for Annabelle.

Andreas was certain she was going to surprise him with another visit and he wanted to be fully conscious, not stupefied. He had regrets from the first time she had come to see him—he had not told her all the things he had wanted to say. In fact, he had felt tongue-tied at times, had become a child again through illness. What had held him back? Seeing Annabelle had been overwhelming.

How he longed for her now. He hoped this time he would find the right words. And so Andreas waited.

* * *

Four months after Annabelle's visit to Mortalloc, she received another call from Frida.

'Andy died this morning,' Frida said, weeping and choking.

Annabelle felt a burst of compassion for Frida but did not know what to say.

'I'm sorry.'

'The last few months have been absolute hell. Even his doctor was despairing. The doctor said he had never seen so much pain. What he suffered was horrible.' Frida's voice broke off and she faded away on the line.

* * *

Annabelle took the letter Andreas had sent her soon after she visited him in hospital, and went into the garden to read it once more. She had looked at it when she received it, and remembered how shocked she was at how much his handwriting had altered. It had become small, and slanted backwards. A chiromancer had once pointed out the similarities between their handwriting. One of the things they had in common was the straightness and boldness of the way they formed the letters, which placed them as being compatible. No more.

Dear Annabelle,

Thank you for making the journey and coming to see me, and for all the good things you brought me, how kind and generous you are. I also want to say how much I enjoyed the novel about Jung you sent me. I can't help feeling you chose it because you wanted to help me with the burden of my guilt.

Your intuition was right about my guilt. For a long time, I had wanted to tell you something I have kept a secret all my life, because I could not bear to face it. Yet it's been there all along, metastasising, spreading injuriously in my psyche—and now in my body. I don't want to excuse all the awful things I've done—that's one of the reasons why I hesitated from telling you. I have been defective as a doctor and a failure many times over as a husband. And as a father. I believe I almost destroyed you, Annabelle, when I betrayed your trust. I know I've been manipulative, cowardly and a hypocrite. I've lied about many things. I became an impostor, impersonating your father, and taking advantage of your love.

So now I can tell you what happened when I was five years old. It concerns the death of my Nanny, Anna. We were living in Geneva. Anna was a lovely young woman who looked after me and showed me a lot of kindness, unlike my mother, who was never there for me, and only ever took an interest in my sister and me, when she had something to criticise.

I had been bad, demanding—Anna had felt ill for some time—every day, every morning. I felt she no longer cared for me. She seemed distracted. I panicked, played up, screamed—even bit her when she tried to give me a bath one morning. One day, she locked herself in the bathroom. I banged on the glass door but she wouldn't let me in. My father heard the noise I was making, and rushed in. Anna had locked herself in the bathroom and turned on the gas. My father became frantic, struggling to unlock the door and yelling like a mad person.

I watched in horror as my father bled when he cut himself on the glass after he smashed the bathroom door. There was blood everywhere. I thought he was going to die. But he and I failed to save Anna.

What I didn't know then, was that Anna had been in love with my father. She was pregnant by him. Mother would have thrown her out when she would have found out. Poor Anna.

I also know that we stumble through life trying to recreate painful situations when we felt helpless or unloved. By replaying them, we hope to change the script, find a solution, bring about a happy ending. Some of us never make it, no matter how many times we've replayed the scene of our demise.

But let me tell you about something extraordinary that happened a few days ago. On more than one occasion, I could smell your perfume in the room, and I knew it was you because I have never smelt it on anyone else. You were there, invisible, but with me.

I hope the visit wasn't too disturbing for you. I am very grateful you came. I cannot tell you how much it has meant to me.

I have sent you this poem from an anonymous 14th century Chinese poet. I hope you like it.

Live your full life, Annabelle. I have faith in you.

Always,

Andreas

On a separate sheet of paper, he had copied out the poem:

She left a short while ago
yet remains near to me
her perfume alive
still warm from her body
so intoxicating

Annabelle doubled over, wailing, sobbing, trying to hold back the pain she felt. After a while she straightened up, walked around in endless circles holding herself, weeping and shaking. He was gone. Andreas was dead. And she wanted him back.

Annabelle was certain her grief would last a lifetime. What purpose did it serve? Why do we grieve? Why do we mourn? Why did she feel her loss so poignantly? *Grief.* What is it? Dogs grieve and cats grieve, and cows when their young are taken away for slaughter. Chimps grieve and bonobos grieve and gorillas, birds and rats. And elephants weep.

* * *

In time, Annabelle came to realise the gift Andreas had given her. Theirs had been a great love. A love that would not leave her. There would never be a day or a night, when Annabelle would not feel Andreas beside her. And so, she opened her heart and her memories to him. Finally, she could allow herself to reach out to him, to call his name in the dark, like the mermaids of his childhood. And he would enter into her bed, her dreams, her soul and whisper *Annabelle,* before he left her to the next wave of sleep.

Author's note

The Assault On Truth: Freud's Suppression Of The Seduction Theory by Jeffrey Moussaieff Masson, written when he was a psychoanalyst, helped me understand some painful and perplexing situations when I was writing *The Secret Seduction and the Enigma of Attraction.* Jeffrey has been an inspiration in many ways. He is acutely perceptive, truthful and courageous. His courage came to the fore when he revealed the contents of Freud's letters when he was put in charge of the archives by Anna Freud. His book is 'a devastating and highly controversial expose´ of the origins of psychoanalysis.'

Jeffrey continues to inspire me with his many books on animal suffering. I will follow his path with my next book, for the love of animals. There is a line at the end of *The Secret Seduction*: 'And elephants weep,' which comes from the title of his seminal work on the consciousness of animals: *When Elephants Weep*

Acknowledgements

I am deeply grateful to Nick Walker for publishing my book. Michael Wilding too, for bringing my work to the attention of Nick and Arcadia/Australian Scholarly Publishing.

I also wish to express my gratitude to James Cowen for his endless generosity of spirit and masterful teachings. Anouska Jones, for her wonderful guidance and encouragement. The writings and friendship of the inimitable Jeffrey Moussaieff Masson inspired me and continue to do so.

If it weren't for John Mitchell, psychoanalyst/psychotherapist, owner of Mary Ryan's Bookshop, and supreme lover of books, *The Secret Seduction* would have remained buried. When I told him about the novel I'd written many years before, but had never published, he said: 'There is a need for the story to be told—more people are seeing psychotherapists now than ever before. And besides, it is such a damn good story!'

So many friends have contributed and offered help—Frank Moorhouse, Susan Chenery, Margaret Gee, Philippa Drynan, Lee Kofman, Julie Clarke-Neville, Joanne Rees, Paula Garrod, Irina Dunn, Deb Adamson and Rosemary Dan (who knew me then and now).

And of course, Marlene Donovan, who has always been there—listening, advising, comforting. My sis.

Thank you to Dr Robert Gordon, and Dr Thomas F. Wilmot—each person I have mentioned have helped in their own way. Some, perhaps are not even aware of how they helped me. I am grateful just the same.

The writings and ideas of Nikki Gemmell and Ruth Ostrow often inform me. Nikki and Ruth, too, have written about a new direction for sex. I like to call it, a return to tenderness. It is something I had often thought about because of a revulsion of sex without tenderness, which seems to be common in our society.

Alain de Botton, writes about 'a new pornography' that doesn't 'ask us to leave behind our ethics, our aesthetic sense and our intelligence.' There is nothing new about this—it is to be found in the teachings of the Tao of Sex. Including women directing sex. It is heartening to see writers such as Nikki, Ruth and Alain bringing forth these ideas again.

This story was first written many years ago, for one person, then buried in a drawer. I did not take much notice of my sources when I used a quote—most of the time I wrote something down because I had read it, was said, or loved it. I read so many books over the years, always in search of answers.

Reading Goethe's *Elective Affinities* was electrifying because it was an idea I had reflected upon most of my life.

I have quoted near the beginning of the book from Eugene Onegin by Pushkin, (Penguin Books, 1965). Also from David Cooper's The Grammar of Living (Pantheon Books, 1974).

I came across a website called: *Compassionate Dragon Healing*. I have quoted from the website for the chapter *The Tao of Sex*. I think the quote is from *The Tao Of Sexology: The Book of Infinite Wisdom* by Dr Stephen Thomas Chang (Tao Publishing Jan 1986). Or possibly *The Tao Te Ching.* I'm not certain. Wherever I could, I have acknowledged my sources, and even tried to contact others for permission but have not always succeeded. Many books have been lost over the years, which hasn't helped.

Deirdre Bair's *Jung. A Biography* (Little, Brown, 2004) and *Man and His Symbols* Carl Jung (Aldus Books, 1964) were important too, although I reached a point where I could not tell whether something had come from a book or whether it had been said to me. I read too many books by Freud, and about Freud to even begin to mention them.

The poem: 'Come to the edge he said', is by Guillaume Apollinaire.

And finally my endless gratitude to the unmentionable one.

About the Author

VICTORIA THOMPSON was born in Alexandria, Egypt, of French, Italian, Spanish and English parentage. She grew up speaking five languages and was educated at The Sacred Heart British Girl's Convent. Her parents left Egypt after King Farouk was exiled. Victoria trained as an actress and worked in film, television and theatre. She left acting to study psychology and became a psychotherapist. She eventually gave it up to return to her love of books and writing. Her memoir, *Losing Alexandria* (Picador, Sydney), was a literary success, appearing for several weeks on the Melbourne Age best-seller list and has been compared to Durrell's *The Alexandria Quartet. City of Longing,* (Australian Scholarly Publishing/Arcadia) was launched at the Melbourne Writer's Festival in 2011. Victoria has also worked as an interpreter in the medical profession and has travelled to Japan, China, Russia, India and the Himalayas, England, Europe and America. She is an animal rights advocate and her next book is for them—to stop their suffering, to make the world a better place.

Author's web:

http://www.victoriathompson.com.au

www.ingramcontent.com/pod-product-compliance
Lightning Source LLC
LaVergne TN
LVHW101917220826
846093LV00009B/280

* 9 7 8 1 9 2 5 0 0 3 9 9 4 *